In *The Teachings of Don Juan: A Yaqui Way of Knowledge,* Carlos Castaneda published the account of his five-year apprenticeship to don Juan, a 70-year-old Yaqui Indian known to be a brujo—"a medicine man, curer, sorcerer." In it he told of the uses of peyote, jimson weed and other hallucinogenic plants in opening the doors of perception to a world of "non-ordinary reality" completely beyond the concepts of Western civilization. And, at the end of that book, he told how in fear and exhaustion he had stopped his search.

The Teachings of Don Juan has since become an acknowledged classic, discovered by hundreds of thousands of readers and hailed by *The New York Times* as "an extraordinary spiritual and psychological document...destined for fame."

Now, in *A Separate Reality,* Carlos Castaneda tells how he returned to don Juan and resumed the dangerous initiation necessary to become "a man of knowledge." [continued on next page]

Determined to go deeper still into don Juan's world of mystical sensation and perception, Castaneda recounts how he learned to see beyond the surface realities of life—partly with the aid of drugs, but finally and essentially through a supremely difficult and demanding effort of intelligence and will.

"One can't exaggerate the significance of what Castaneda has done. He is describing a shamanistic tradition, a prelogical cultural form that is no-one-knows how old. It has been described often....But it seems that no other outsider, and certainly not a 'Westerner,' has ever participated in its mysteries from within; nor has anyone described them so well.

"A SEPARATE REALITY is extraordinary in every sense of the word, and much more than a sequel. While it has the same intelligent modesty, graceful modulation and narrative skill as the first book, Castaneda here abandons his frustrating reticence. As he comes closer to don Juan in his struggle through his mystical obstacle course, their relationship takes on another dimension. The book ceases to be simply phenomenological reportage. The anthropologist's rescue of an alien language from oblivion becomes a moving personal quest, an autobiography." —Roger Jellinek, *The New York Times*

A SEPARATE REALITY
was originally published by Simon and Schuster.

Books by Carlos Castaneda

Journey to Ixtlan: The Lessons of Don Juan
A Separate Reality: Further Conversations with Don Juan
The Teachings of Don Juan: A Yaqui Way of Knowledge

Published by POCKET BOOKS

A Separate Reality

Further Conversations
With Don Juan

CARLOS CASTANEDA

PUBLISHED BY POCKET BOOKS NEW YORK

A SEPARATE REALITY
Further Conversations with Don Juan

Simon and Schuster edition published 1971

POCKET BOOK edition published October, 1972
9th printing......................August, 1974

L

This POCKET BOOK edition includes every word contained
in the original, higher-priced edition. It is printed from
brand-new plates made from completely reset, clear, easy-to-
read type. POCKET BOOK editions are published by POCKET
BOOKS, a division of Simon & Schuster, Inc., 630 Fifth
Avenue, New York, N.Y. 10020. Trademarks registered
in the United States and other countries.

Contents

Introduction

Ten years ago I had the fortune of meeting a Yaqui Indian from northwestern Mexico. I call him "don Juan." In Spanish, *don* is an appellative used to denote respect. I made don Juan's acquaintance under the most fortuitous circumstances. I was sitting with Bill, a friend of mine, in a bus depot in a border town in Arizona. We were very quiet. In the late afternoon the summer heat seemed unbearable. Suddenly he leaned over and tapped me on the shoulder.

"There's the man I told you about," he said in a low voice.

He nodded casually toward the entrance. An old man had just walked in.

"What did you tell me about him?" I asked.

"He's the Indian that knows about peyote. Remember?"

I remembered that Bill and I had once driven all day looking for the house of an "eccentric" Mexican Indian who lived in the area. We did not find the man's house and I had the feeling that the Indians whom we had asked for directions had deliberately misled us. Bill had told me that the man was a "yerbero," a person who gathers and sells medicinal herbs, and that he knew a great deal about the hallucinogenic cactus, peyote. He had also said that it would be worth my while to meet him. Bill was my guide in the Southwest while I was collecting information and specimens of medicinal plants used by the Indians of the area.

Bill got up and went to greet the man. The Indian was of medium height. His hair was white and short, and grew a bit over his ears, accentuating the roundness of his head.

1

He was very dark; the deep wrinkles on his face gave him the appearance of age, yet his body seemed to be strong and fit. I watched him for a moment. He moved around with a nimbleness that I would have thought impossible for an old man.

Bill signaled me to join them.

"He's a nice guy," Bill said to me. "But I can't understand him. His Spanish is weird, full of rural colloquialisms, I suppose."

The old man looked at Bill and smiled. And Bill, who speaks only a few words of Spanish, made up an absurd phrase in that language. He looked at me as if asking whether he was making sense, but I did not know what he had had in mind; he then smiled shyly and walked away. The old man looked at me and began laughing. I explained to him that my friend sometimes forgot that he did not speak Spanish.

"I think he also forgot to introduce us," I said, and I told him my name.

"And I am Juan Matus at your service," he said.

We shook hands and remained quiet for some time. I broke the silence and told him about my enterprise. I told him that I was looking for any kind of information on plants, especially peyote. I talked compulsively for a long time, and although I was almost totally ignorant on the subject, I said I knew a great deal about peyote. I thought that if I boasted about my knowledge he would become interested in talking to me. But he did not say anything. He listened patiently. Then he nodded slowly and peered at me. His eyes seemed to shine with a light of their own. I avoided his gaze. I felt embarrassed. I had the certainty that at that moment he knew I was talking nonsense.

"Come to my house some time," he finally said, taking his eyes away from me. "Perhaps we could talk there with more ease."

I did not know what else to say. I felt uneasy. After a while Bill came back into the room. He recognized my discomfort and did not say a word. We sat in tight silence for some time. Then the old man got up. His bus had come. He said goodbye.

"It didn't go too well, did it?" Bill asked.

"No."

"Did you ask him about plants?"

"I did. But I think I goofed."

"I told you, he's very eccentric. The Indians around here know him, yet they never mention him. And that's something."

"He said I could come to his house, though."

"He was bullshitting you. Sure, you can go to his house, but what does it mean? He'll never tell you anything. If you ever ask him anything he'll clam up as if you were an idiot talking nonsense."

Bill said convincingly that he had encountered people like him before, people who gave the impression of knowing a great deal. In his judgment, he said, such people were not worth the trouble, because sooner or later one could obtain the same information from someone else who did not play hard to get. He said that he had neither patience nor time for old fogies, and that it was possible that the old man was only presenting himself as being knowledgeable about herbs, when in reality he knew as little as the next man.

Bill went on talking but I was not listening. My mind kept on wondering about the old Indian. He knew I had been bluffing. I remembered his eyes. They had actually shone.

I went back to see him a couple of months later, not so much as a student of anthropology interested in medicinal plants but as a person with an inexplicable curiosity. The way he had looked at me was an unprecedented event in my life. I wanted to know what was involved in that look. It became almost an obsession with me. I pondered it and the more I thought about it the more unusual it seemed to be.

Don Juan and I became friends, and for a year I paid him innumerable visits. I found his manner very reassuring and his sense of humor superb; but above all I felt there was a silent consistency about his acts, a consistency which was thoroughly baffling to me. I felt a strange delight in his presence and at the same time I experienced a strange discomfort. His mere company forced me to make a tremendous reevaluation of my models of behavior. I had been reared, perhaps like everyone else, to have a readiness to accept man as an essentially weak and fallible creature. What impressed me about don Juan was the fact that he did not make a point of being weak and helpless, and just being around him insured an unfavorable comparison between his way of behaving and mine. Perhaps one of the most impressive statements he made to me at that time was concerned with our inherent difference. Prior to one of my visits I had been feeling quite unhappy about the total course of my life and about a number of pressing personal conflicts that I had. When I arrived at his house I felt moody and nervous.

We were talking about my interest in knowledge; but, as usual, we were on two different tracks. I was referring to academic knowledge that transcends experience, while he was talking about direct knowledge of the world.

"Do you know anything about the world around you?" he asked.

"I know all kinds of things," I said.

"I mean do you ever feel the world around you?"

"I feel as much of the world around me as I can."

"That's not enough. You must feel everything, otherwise the world loses its sense."

I voiced the classical argument that I did not have to taste the soup in order to know the recipe, nor did I have to get an electric shock in order to know about electricity.

"You make it sound stupid," he said. "The way I see it, you want to cling to your arguments, despite the fact that they bring nothing to you; you want to remain the same even at the cost of your well-being."

"I don't know what you're talking about."

"I am talking about the fact that you're not complete. You have no peace."

That statement annoyed me. I felt offended. I thought he was certainly not qualified to pass judgment on my acts or my personality.

"You're plagued with problems," he said. "Why?"

"I am only a man, don Juan," I said peevishly.

I made that statement in the same vein my father used to make it. Whenever he said he was only a man he implicitly meant he was weak and helpless and his statement, like mine, was filled with an ultimate sense of despair.

Don Juan peered at me as he had done the first day we met.

"You think about yourself too much," he said and smiled. "And that gives you a strange fatigue that makes you shut off the world around you and cling to your arguments. Therefore, all you have is problems. I'm only a man too, but I don't mean that the way you do."

"How do you mean it?"

"I've vanquished my problems. Too bad my life is so short that I can't grab onto all the things I would like to. But that is not an issue; it's only a pity."

I liked the tone of his statement. There was no despair or self-pity in it.

In 1961, a year after our first meeting, don Juan disclosed to me that he had a secret knowledge of medicinal plants. He told me he was a "brujo." The Spanish word *brujo* can be rendered in English as sorcerer, medicine man, curer. From that point on the relation between us changed; I became his apprentice and for the next four years he endeavored to teach me the mysteries of sorcery. I have written about that apprenticeship in *The Teachings of Don Juan: A Yaqui Way of Knowledge.*

Our conversations were conducted in Spanish, and thanks to don Juan's superb command of that language I obtained detailed explanations of the intricate meanings of his system of beliefs. I have referred to that complex and well-systematized body of knowledge as sorcery and I have referred to him as a sorcerer because those were categories he himself used in informal conversations. In the context of more serious elucidations, however, he would use the terms "knowledge" to categorize sorcery and "man of knowledge" or "one who knows" to categorize a sorcerer.

In order to teach and corroborate his knowledge don Juan used three well-known psychotropic plants: peyote, *Lophophora williamasii;* jimson weed, *Datura inoxia;* and a species of mushroom which belongs to the genus *Psylo-cebe*. Through the separate ingestion of each of these hallucinogens he produced in me, as his apprentice, some peculiar states of distorted perception, or altered consciousness, which I have called "states of nonordinary reality." I have used the word "reality" because it was a major premise in don Juan's system of beliefs that the states of consciousness produced by the ingestion of any of those three plants were not hallucinations, but concrete, although unordinary, aspects of the reality of everyday life. Don Juan behaved toward these states of nonordinary reality not "as if" they were real but "as" real.

To classify these plants as hallucinogens and the states they produced as nonordinary reality is, of course, my own device. Don Juan understood and explained the plants as being vehicles that would conduct or lead a man to certain impersonal forces or "powers" and the states they produced as being the "meetings" that a sorcerer had to have with those "powers" in order to gain control over them.

He called peyote "Mescalito" and he explained it as being a benevolent teacher and protector of men. Mescalito taught the "right way to live." Peyote was usually ingested at gatherings of sorcerers called "mitotes," where the participants would gather specifically to seek a lesson on the right way to live.

Don Juan considered the jimson weed and the mushrooms to be powers of a different sort. He called them "allies" and said that they were capable of being manipulated; a sorcerer, in fact, drew his strength from manipulating an ally. Of the two, don Juan preferred the mushroom. He maintained that the power contained in the mushroom was his personal ally and he called it "smoke" or "little smoke."

Don Juan's procedure to utilize the mushrooms was to let them dry into a fine powder inside a small gourd. He kept the gourd sealed for a year and then mixed the fine powder with five other dry plants and produced a mixture for smoking in a pipe.

In order to become a man of knowledge one had to

"meet" with the ally as many times as possible; one had to become familiar with it. This premise implied, of course, that one had to smoke the hallucinogenic mixture quite often. The process of "smoking" consisted of ingesting the fine mushroom powder, which did not incinerate, and inhaling the smoke of the other five plants that made up the mixture. Don Juan explained the profound effects that the mushrooms had on one's perceptual capacities as the "ally removing one's body."

Don Juan's method of teaching required an extraordinary effort on the part of the apprentice. In fact, the degree of participation and involvement needed was so strenuous that by the end of 1965 I had to withdraw from the apprenticeship. I can say now, with the perspective of the five years that have elapsed, that at that time don Juan's teachings had begun to pose a serious threat to my "idea of the world." I had begun to lose the certainty, which all of us have, that the reality of everyday life is something we can take for granted.

At the time of my withdrawal I was convinced that my decision was final; I did not want to see don Juan ever again. However, in April of 1968 an early copy of my book was made available to me and I felt compelled to show it to him. I paid him a visit. Our link of teacher-apprentice was mysteriously reestablished, and I can say that on that occasion I began a second cycle of apprenticeship, very different from the first. My fear was not as acute as it had been in the past. The total mood of don Juan's teachings was more relaxed. He laughed and also made me laugh a great deal. There seemed to be a deliberate intent on his part to minimize seriousness in general. He clowned during the truly crucial moments of this second cycle, and thus helped me to overcome experiences which could easily have become obsessive. His premise was that a light and amenable disposition was needed in order to withstand the impact and the strangeness of the knowledge he was teaching me.

"The reason you got scared and quit is because you felt too damn important," he said, explaining my previous withdrawal. "Feeling important makes one heavy, clumsy, and vain. To be a man of knowledge one needs to be light and fluid."

Don Juan's particular interest in his second cycle of apprenticeship was to teach me to "see." Apparently in his system of knowledge there was the possibility of making a semantic difference between "seeing" and "looking" as two distinct manners of perceiving. "Looking" referred to the ordinary way in which we are accustomed to perceive the world, while "seeing" entailed a very complex process by virtue of which a man of knowledge allegedly perceives the "essence" of the things of the world.

In order to present the intricacies of this learning process in a readable form I have condensed long passages of questions and answers, and thus I have edited my original field notes. It is my belief, however, that at this point my presentation cannot possibly detract from the meaning of don Juan's teachings. The editing was aimed at making my notes flow, as conversation flows, so they would have the impact I desired; that is to say, I wanted by means of a reportage to communicate to the reader the drama and directness of the field situation. Each section I have set as a chapter was a session with don Juan. As a rule, he always concluded each of our sessions on an abrupt note; thus the dramatic tone of the ending of each chapter is not a literary device of my own, it was a device proper of don Juan's oral tradition. It seemed to be a mnemonic device that helped me to retain the dramatic quality and importance of the lessons.

Certain explanations are needed, however, to make my reportage cogent, since its clarity depends on the elucidation of a number of key concepts or key units that I want to emphasize. This choice of emphasis is congruous with my interest in social science. It is perfectly possible that another person with a different set of goals and expectations would single out concepts entirely different from those I have chosen myself.

During the second cycle of apprenticeship don Juan made a point of assuring me that the use of the smoking mixture was the indispensable prerequisite to "seeing." Therefore I had to use it as often as possible.

"Only the smoke can give you the necessary speed to catch a glimpse of that fleeting world," he said.

With the aid of the psychotropic mixture, he produced in me a series of states of nonordinary reality. The main feature of such states, in relation to what don Juan seemed to be doing, was a condition of "inapplicability." What I perceived in those states of altered consciousness was incomprehensible and impossible to interpret by means of our everyday mode of understanding the world. In other words, the condition of inapplicability entailed the cessation of the pertinence of my world view.

Don Juan used this condition of inapplicability of the states of nonordinary reality in order to introduce a series of preconceived, new "units of meaning." Units of meaning were all the single elements pertinent to the knowledge don Juan was striving to teach me. I have called them units of meaning because they were the basic conglomerate of sensory data and their interpretations on which more complex meaning was constructed. One example of such a unit is the way in which the physiological effect of the psychotropic mixture was understood. It produced a numbness and loss of motor control that was interpreted in don Juan's system as an act performed by the smoke, which in this case was the ally, in order "to remove the body of the practitioner."

Units of meaning were grouped together in a specific way, and each block thus created formed what I have called a "sensible interpretation." Obviously there has to be an endless number of possible sensible interpretations that are pertinent to sorcery that a sorcerer must learn to make. In our day-to-day life we are confronted with an endless number of sensible interpretations pertinent to it. A simple example could be the no longer deliberate interpretation, which we make scores of times every day, of the structure we call "room." It is obvious that we have learned to interpret the structure we call room in terms of room; thus room is a sensible interpretation because it requires that at the time we make it we are cognizant, in one way or another, of all the elements that enter into its composition. A system of sensible interpretation is, in other words, the process by virtue of which a practitioner is cognizant of all the units of meaning necessary to make assumptions, deductions, predictions, etc., about all the situations pertinent to his activity.

By "practitioner" I mean a participant who has an adequate knowledge of all, or nearly all, the units of meaning involved in his particular system of sensible interpretation. Don Juan was a practitioner; that is, he was a sorcerer who knew all the steps of his sorcery.

As a practitioner he attempted to make his system of sensible interpretation accessible to me. Such an accessibility, in this case, was equivalent to a process of re-socialization in which new ways of interpreting perceptual data were learned.

I was the "stranger," the one who lacked the capacity to make intelligent and congruous interpretations of the units of meaning proper to sorcery.

Don Juan's task, as a practitioner making his system accessible to me, was to disarrange a particular certainty which I share with everyone else, the certainty that our "common-sense" views of the world are final. Through the use of psychotropic plants, and through well-directed contacts between the alien system and myself, he succeeded in pointing out to me that my view of the world cannot be final because it is only an interpretation.

For the American Indian, perhaps for thousands of years, the vague phenomenon we call sorcery has been a serious bona fide practice, comparable to that of our science. Our difficulty in understanding it stems, no doubt, from the alien units of meaning with which it deals.

Don Juan had once told me that a man of knowledge had predilections. I asked him to explain his statement.

"My predilection is to *see*," he said.

"What do you mean by that?"

"I like to *see*," he said, "because only by *seeing* can a man of knowledge know."

"What kind of things do you *see*?"

"Everything."

"But I also see everything and I'm not a man of knowledge."

"No. You don't *see*."

"I think I do."

"I tell you, you don't."

"What makes you say that, don Juan?"

"You only look at the surface of things."

"Do you mean that every man of knowledge actually sees through everything he looks at?"

"No. That's not what I mean. I said that a man of knowledge has his own predilections; mine is just to *see* and to know; others do other things."

"What other things, for example?"

"Take Sacateca, he's a man of knowledge and his predilection is dancing. So he dances and knows."

"Is the predilection of a man of knowledge something he does in order to know?"

"Yes, that is correct."

"But how could dancing help Sacateca to know?"

"One can say that Sacateca dances with all he has."

"Does he dance like I dance? I mean like dancing?"

"Let's say that he dances like I *see* and not like you may dance."

"Does he also *see* the way you *see*?"

"Yes, but he also dances."

"How does Sacateca dance?"

"It's hard to explain that. It is a peculiar way of dancing he does when he wants to know. But all I can say about it is that, unless you understand the ways of a man who knows, it is impossible to talk about dancing or *seeing*."

"Have you *seen* him doing his dancing?"

"Yes. However, it is not possible for everyone who looks at his dancing to *see* that it is his peculiar way of knowing."

I knew Sacateca, or at least I knew who he was. We had met and once I had bought him a beer. He was very polite and told me I should feel free to stop at his house anytime I wanted to. I toyed for a long time with the idea of visiting him but I did not tell don Juan.

On the afternoon of May 14, 1962, I drove up to

Sacateca's house; he had given me directions how to get there and I had no trouble finding it. It was on a corner and had a fence all around it. The gate was closed. I walked around it to see if I could peek inside the house. It appeared to be deserted.

"Don Elias," I called out loud. The chickens got frightened and scattered about cackling furiously. A small dog came to the fence. I expected it to bark at me; instead, it just sat there looking at me. I called out once again and the chickens had another burst of cackling.

An old woman came out of the house. I asked her to call don Elias.

"He's not here," she said.

"Where can I find him?"

"He's in the fields."

"Where in the fields?"

"I don't know. Come back in the late afternoon. He'll be here around five."

"Are you don Elias' wife?"

"Yes, I'm his wife," she said and smiled.

I tried to ask her about Sacateca but she excused herself and said that she did not speak Spanish well. I got into my car and drove away.

I returned to the house around six o'clock. I drove to the door and yelled Sacateca's name. This time he came out of the house. I turned on my tape recorder, which in its brown leather case looked like a camera hanging from my shoulder. He seemed to recognize me.

"Oh, it's you," he said, smiling. "How's Juan?"

"He's fine. But how are you, don Elias?"

He did not answer. He seemed to be nervous. Overtly he was very composed, but I felt that he was ill at ease.

"Has Juan sent you here on some sort of errand?"

"No. I came here by myself."

"What in the world for?"

His question seemed to betray very bona fide surprise.

"I just wanted to talk to you," I said, hoping to sound as casual as possible. "Don Juan has told me marvelous things about you and I got curious and wanted to ask you a few questions."

Sacateca was standing in front of me. His body was lean and wiry. He was wearing khaki pants and shirt. His eyes were half-closed; he seemed to be sleepy or perhaps drunk. His mouth was open a bit and his lower lip hung. I noticed that he was breathing deeply and seemed to be almost snoring. The thought came to me that Sacateca was undoubtedly plastered out of his mind. But that thought seemed to be very incongruous because only a few minutes before, when he came out of his house, he had been very alert and aware of my presence.

"What do you want to talk about?" he finally said.

His voice was tired; it was as though his words dragged after each other. I felt very uneasy. It was as if his tiredness was contagious and pulling me.

"Nothing in particular," I answered. "I just came to chat with you in a friendly way. You once asked me to come to your house."

"Yes, I did, but it's not the same now."

"Why isn't it the same?"

"Don't you talk with Juan?"

"Yes, I do."

"Then what do you want with me?"

"I thought maybe I could ask you some questions?"

"Ask Juan. Isn't he teaching you?"

"He is, but just the same I would like to ask you about what he is teaching me, and have your opinion. This way I'll be able to know what to do."

"Why do you want to do that? Don't you trust Juan?"

"I do."

"Then why don't you ask him to tell you what you want to know?"

"I do. And he tells me. But if you could also tell me about what don Juan is teaching me, perhaps I will understand better."

"Juan can tell you everything. He alone can do that. Don't you understand that?"

"I do, but then I'd like to talk with people like you don Elias. One does not find a man of knowledge every day."

"Juan is a man of knowledge."

"I know that."

"Then why are you talking to me?"

"I said I came to be friends."

"No, you didn't. There is something else about you this time."

I wanted to explain myself and all I could do was mumble incoherently. Sacateca did not say anything. He seemed to listen attentively. His eyes were half-closed again but I felt he was peering at me. He nodded almost imperceptibly. Then his lids opened and I saw his eyes. He seemed to be looking past me. He casually tapped the floor with the tip of his right foot, just behind his left heel. His legs were slightly arched; his arms were limp against his sides. Then he lifted his right arm; his hand was open with the palm turned perpendicular to the ground; his fingers were extended and pointing toward me. He let his hand wobble a couple of times before he brought it to my face level. He held it in that position for an instant and then he said a few words to me. His voice was very clear, yet the words dragged.

After a moment he dropped his hand to his side and remained motionless, taking a strange position. He was standing, resting on the ball of his left foot. His right foot was crossed behind the heel of the left foot and he was tapping the floor rhythmically and gently with the tip of his right foot.

I felt an unwarranted apprehension, a form of restlessness. My thoughts seemed to be dissociated. I was thinking unrelated nonsensical thoughts that had nothing to do with what was going on. I noticed my discomfort and tried to steer my thoughts back to the situation at hand, but I couldn't in spite of a great struggle. It was as if some force was keeping me from concentrating or thinking relevant thoughts.

Sacateca had not said a word, and I didn't know what else to say or do. Quite automatically, I turned around and left.

Later on I felt compelled to tell don Juan about my encounter with Sacateca. Don Juan roared with laughter.

"What really took place there?" I asked.

"Sacateca danced!" don Juan said. "He *saw* you, then he danced."

"What did he do to me? I felt very cold and dizzy."

"He apparently didn't like you and stopped you by tossing a word at you."

"How could he possibly do that?" I exclaimed incredulously.

"Very simple; he stopped you with his will."

"What did you say?"

"He stopped you with his will!"

The explanation did not suffice. His statements sounded like gibberish to me. I tried to probe him further, but he could not explain the event to my satisfaction.

Obviously that event or any event that occurred within this alien system of sensible interpretation could be explained or understood only in terms of the units of meaning proper to that system. This work is, therefore, a reportage and should be read as a reportage. The system I recorded was incomprehensible to me, thus the pretense to anything other than reporting about it would be misleading and impertinent. In this respect I have adopted the phenomenological method and have striven to deal with sorcery solely as phenomena that were presented to me. I, as the perceiver, recorded what I perceived, and at the moment of recording I endeavored to suspend judgment.

PART ONE

The Preliminaries of "Seeing"

1

April 2, 1968

Don Juan looked at me for a moment and did not seem at all surprised to see me, even though it had been more than two years since I last visited him. He put his hand on my shoulder and smiled gently and said that I looked different, that I was getting fat and soft.

I had brought him a copy of my book. Without any preliminaries I took it out of my brief case and handed it to him.

"It's a book about you, don Juan," I said.

He took it and flipped through the pages as if they were a deck of cards. He liked the green color on the dust jacket and the height of the book. He felt the cover with his palms, turned it around a couple of times, and then handed it back to me. I felt a great surge of pride.

"I want you to keep it," I said.

He shook his head with a silent laugh.

"I better not," he said, and then added with a broad smile: "You know what we do with paper in Mexico."

I laughed. I thought his touch of irony was beautiful.

We were sitting on a bench in the park of a small town in the mountainous area of central Mexico. I had absolutely no way of letting him know about my intention of paying him a visit, but I was certain I was going to find him, and I did. I waited only a short while in that town before don Juan came down from the mountains and I found him at the market, at the stand of one of his friends.

Don Juan told me, matter-of-factly, that I was there

19

just in time to take him back to Sonora, and we sat in the park to wait for a friend of his, a Mazatec Indian with whom he lived.

We waited about three hours. We talked about different unimportant things, and toward the end of the day, right before his friend came, I related to him some events I had witnessed a few days before.

During my trip to see him my car broke down in the outskirts of a city and I had to stay in town for three days while it was being repaired. There was a motel across the street from the auto shop, but the outskirts of towns are always depressing for me, so I took lodgings in a modern eight-story hotel in the center of town.

The bellboy told me that the hotel had a restaurant, and when I came down to eat I found that there were tables out on the sidewalk. It was a rather handsome arrangement set on the street corner under some low brick arches of modern lines. It was cool outside and there were empty tables, yet I preferred to sit in the stuffy indoors. I had noticed upon entering that a group of shoeshine boys were sitting on the curb in front of the restaurant, and I was certain they would have hounded me had I taken one of the outside tables.

From where I was seated I could see the group of boys through the glass window. A couple of young men took a table and the boys flocked around them, asking to shine their shoes. The young men refused and I was amazed to see that the boys did not insist and went back to sit on the curb. After a while three men in business suits got up and left and the boys ran to their table and began eating the leftovers; in a matter of seconds the plates were clean. The same thing happened with leftovers on all the other tables.

I noticed that the children were quite orderly; if they spilled water they sponged it up with their own shoeshine cloths. I also noticed the thoroughness of their scavenging procedures. They even ate the ice cubes left in the glasses of water and the lemon slices from the tea, peel and all. There was absolutely nothing that they wasted.

In the course of the time I stayed in the hotel I found

out that there was an agreement between the children and the manager of the restaurant; the boys were allowed to hang around the premises to make some money from the customers and were also allowed to eat the leftovers, provided that they did not harass anybody and did not break anything. There were eleven in all, ranging in age from five to twelve; the oldest, however, was kept a distance from the rest of the group. They deliberately ostracized him, taunting him with a singsong that he already had pubic hair and was too old to be among them.

After three days of watching them go like vultures after the most meager of leftovers I became despondent, and I left that city feeling that there was no hope for those children whose world was already molded by their day-after-day struggle for crumbs.

"Do you feel sorry for them?" don Juan exclaimed in a questioning tone.

"I certainly do," I said.

"Why?"

"Because I'm concerned with the well-being of my fellow men. Those are children and their world is ugly and cheap."

"Wait! Wait! How can you say that their world is *ugly* and *cheap?*" don Juan said, mocking my statement. "You think that you're better off, don't you?"

I said I did; and he asked me why; and I told him that in comparison to those children's world mine was infinitely more varied and rich in experiences and in opportunities for personal satisfaction and development. Don Juan's laughter was friendly and genuine. He said that I was not careful with what I was saying, that I had no way of knowing about the richness and the opportunities in the world of those children.

I thought don Juan was being stubborn. I really thought he was taking the opposite view just to annoy me. I sincerely believed that those children did not have the slightest chance for any intellectual growth.

I argued my point for a while longer and then don Juan asked me bluntly, "Didn't you once tell me that in your opinion man's greatest accomplishment was to become a man of knowledge?"

I had said that, and I repeated again that in my opinion to become a man of knowledge was one of the greatest intellectual accomplishments.

"Do you think that your very rich world would ever help you to become a man of knowledge?" don Juan asked with slight sarcasm.

I did not answer and he then worded the same question in a different manner, a thing I always do to him when I think he does not understand.

"In other words," he said, smiling broadly, obviously aware that I was cognizant of his ploy, "can your freedom and opportunities help you to become a man of knowledge?"

"No!" I said emphatically.

"Then how could you feel sorry for those children?" he said seriously. "Any of them could become a man of knowledge. All the men of knowledge I know were kids like those you saw eating leftovers and licking the tables."

Don Juan's argument gave me an uncomfortable sensation. I had not felt sorry for those underprivileged children because they did not have enough to eat, but because in my terms their world had already condemned them to be intellectually inadequate. And yet in don Juan's terms any of them could achieve what I believed to be the epitome of man's intellectual accomplishment, the goal of becoming a man of knowledge. My reason for pitying them was incongruous. Don Juan had nailed me neatly.

"Perhaps you're right," I said. "But how can one avoid the desire, the genuine desire, to help our fellow men?"

"How do you think one can help them?"

"By alleviating their burden. The least one can do for our fellow men is to try to change them. You yourself are involved in doing that. Aren't you?"

"No. I'm not. I don't know what to change or why to change anything in my fellow men."

"What about me, don Juan? Weren't you teaching me so I could change?"

"No. I'm not trying to change you. It may happen that

one day you may become a man of knowledge—there's no way to know that—but that will not change you. Some day perhaps you'll be able to *see* men in another mode and then you'll realize that there's no way to change anything about them."

"What's this other mode of seeing men, don Juan?"

"Men look different when you *see*. The little smoke will help you to *see* men as fibers of light."

"Fibers of light?"

"Yes. Fibers, like white cobwebs. Very fine threads that circulate from the head to the navel. Thus a man looks like an egg of circulating fibers. And his arms and legs are like luminous bristles, bursting out in all directions."

"Is that the way everyone looks?"

"Everyone. Besides, every man is in touch with everything else, not through his hands, though, but through a bunch of long fibers that shoot out from the center of his abdomen. Those fibers join a man to his surroundings; they keep his balance; they give him stability. So, as you may *see* some day, a man is a luminous egg whether he's a beggar or a king and there's no way to change anything; or rather, what could be changed in that luminous egg? What?"

2

My visit to don Juan started a new cycle. I had no trouble falling back again into my old pattern of enjoying his sense of drama and his humor and his patience with me. I definitely felt that I had to visit him more often. Not to see don Juan was indeed a great loss for me; besides, I had something of particular interest that I wanted to discuss with him.

After I had finished the book about his teachings I began to reexamine the field notes I had not used. I had discarded a great deal of data because my emphasis had been on the states of nonordinary reality. Rehashing my old notes I had come to the conclusion that a skillful sorcerer could bring forth the most specialized range of perception in his apprentice by simply "manipulating social cues." My whole argument about the nature of these manipulatory procedures rested on the assumption that a leader was needed to bring forth the necessary range of perception. I took as a specific test case the sorcerer's peyote meetings. I contended that in those meetings sorcerers reached an agreement about the nature of reality without any overt exchange of words or signs, and my conclusion was that a very sophisticated code was employed by the participants to arrive at such an agreement. I had constructed a complex system to explain the code and procedures, so I went back to see don Juan to ask his personal opinion and advice about my work.

May 21, 1968

Nothing out of the ordinary happened during my trip to see don Juan. The temperature in the desert was over a hundred degrees and was quite uncomfortable. The heat subsided in the late afternoon and by the time I arrived at his house, in the early evening, there was a cool breeze. I was not very tired, so we sat in his room and talked. I felt comfortable and relaxed, and we talked for hours. It was not a conversation that i would have liked to record; I was not really trying to make great sense or trying to draw great meaning; we talked about the weather, the crops, his grandson, the Yaqui Indians, the Mexican government. I told don Juan how much I enjoyed the exquisite sensation of talking in the dark. He said that my statement was consistent with my talkative nature; that it was easy for me to like chattering in the darkness because talking was the only thing I could do at that time, while sitting around. I argued that it was more than the mere act of talking that I enjoyed. I said that I relished the soothing warmth of the darkness around us. He asked me what I did at home when it was dark. I said that invariably I would turn on the lights or I would go out into the lighted streets until it was time to go to sleep.

"Oh!" he said incredulously. "I thought you had learned to use the darkness."

"What can you use it for?" I asked.

He said the darkness—and he called it "the darkness of the day"—was the best time to "see." He stressed the word "see" with a peculiar inflection. I wanted to know what he meant by that, but he said it was too late to go into it then.

May 22, 1968

As soon as I woke up in the morning, and without any preliminaries, I told don Juan that I had constructed a system to explain what took place at a peyote meeting, a mitote. I took my notes and read to him what I had done. He listened patiently while I struggled to elucidate my schemata.

I said that I believed a covert leader was necessary in order to cue the participants so they could arrive at any pertinent agreement. I pointed out that people attend a mitote to seek the presence of Mescalito and his lessons about the right way to live; and that those persons never exchange a word or a gesture among them, yet they agree about the presence of Mescalito and his specific lesson. At least that was what they purportedly did in the mitotes I had attended; they agreed that Mescalito had appeared to them individually and had given them a lesson. In my personal experience I had found that the form of the individual visit of Mescalito and his consequent lesson were strikingly homogeneous, although varying in content from person to person. I could not explain this homogeneity except as a result of a subtle and complex system of cueing.

It took me close to two hours to read and explain to

don Juan the scheme I had constructed. I ended my talk by begging him to tell me in his own words what were the exact procedures for reaching agreement.

When I had finished he frowned. I thought he must have found my explanation challenging; he appeared to be involved in deep deliberation. After a reasonable silence I asked him what he thought about my idea.

My question made him suddenly turn his frown into a smile and then into roaring laughter. I tried to laugh too and asked nervously what was so funny.

"You're deranged!" he exclaimed. "Why should anyone be bothered with cueing at such an important time as a mitote? Do you think one ever fools around with Mescalito?"

I thought for a moment that he was being evasive; he was not really answering my question.

"Why should anyone cue?" don Juan asked stubbornly. "You have been in mitotes. You should know that no one told you how to feel, or what to do, no one except Mescalito himself."

I insisted that such an explanation was not possible and begged him again to tell me how the agreement was reached.

"I know why you have come," don Juan said in a mysterious tone. "I can't help you in your endeavor because there is no system of cueing."

"But how can all those persons agree about Mescalito's presence?"

"They agree because they *see*," don Juan said dramatically, and then added casually, "Why don't you attend another mitote and *see* for yourself?"

I felt that was a trap. I did not say anything, but put my notes away. He did not insist.

A while later he asked me to drive him to the house of one of his friends. We spent most of the day there. During the course of a conversation his friend John asked me what had become of my interest in peyote. John had provided the peyote buttons for my first experience nearly eight years before. I did not know what to say to him. Don Juan came to my aid and told John I was doing fine.

On our way back to don Juan's house I felt obliged to make a comment about John's question and I said, among other things, that I had no intention of learning any more about peyote, because it required a kind of courage I did not have; and that I had really meant it when I said I had quit. Don Juan smiled and did not say anything. I kept on talking until we got to the house.

We sat on the clean area in front of the door. It was a warm, clear day, but there was enough of a breeze in the late afternoon to make it pleasant.

"Why do you have to push so hard?" don Juan said suddenly. "How many years now have you been saying that you don't want to learn any more?"

"Three."

"Why are you so vehement about it?"

"I feel that I'm betraying you, don Juan. I think that's why I'm always talking about it."

"You're not betraying me."

"I have failed you. I have run away. I feel I am defeated."

"You do what you can. Besides, you haven't been defeated yet. What I have to teach you is very hard. I, for instance, found it perhaps even harder than you."

"But you kept at it, don Juan. My case is different. I gave up and I have come to see you not because I want to learn, but only because I wanted to ask you to clarify a point in my work."

Don Juan looked at me for a moment and then he looked away.

"You ought to let the smoke guide you again," he said forcefully.

"No, don Juan, I can't use your smoke any more. I think I have exhausted myself."

"You haven't begun."

"I am too afraid."

"So you're afraid. There is nothing new about being afraid. Don't think about your fear. Think about the wonders of *seeing!*"

"I sincerely wish I could think about those wonders, but I can't. When I think of your smoke I feel a sort of darkness coming upon me. It is as if there were no more people on the earth, no one to turn to. Your smoke has shown me the ultimate of loneliness, don Juan."

"That's not true. Take me, for example. The smoke is my ally and I don't feel such a loneliness."

"But you're different; you've conquered your fear."

Don Juan patted me gently on the shoulder.

"You're not afraid," he said softly. His voice carried a strange accusation.

"Am I lying about my fear, don Juan?"

"I'm not concerned with lies," he said severely. "I'm concerned with something else. The reason you don't want to learn is not because you're afraid. It's something else."

I vehemently urged him to tell me what it was. I pleaded with him, but he did not say anything; he just shook his head as if he could not believe I did not know it.

I told him that perhaps it was inertia which kept me from learning. He wanted to know the meaning of the word "inertia." I read to him from my dictionary: "The tendency of matter to remain at rest if at rest, or, if moving, to keep moving in the same direction, unless affected by some outside force."

" 'Unless affected by some outside force,' " he repeated. "That's about the best word you've found. I've told you already, only a crackpot would undertake the task of becoming a man of knowledge of his own accord. A sober-headed man has to be tricked into doing it."

"I'm sure there must be scores of people who would gladly undertake the task," I said.

"Yes, but those don't count. They are usually cracked. They are like gourds that look fine from the outside and yet they would leak the minute you put pressure on them, the minute you filled them with water.

"I had to trick you into learning once, the same way my benefactor tricked me. Otherwise you wouldn't have learned as much as you did. Perhaps it's time to trick you again."

The tricking to which he was referring was one of the most crucial points of my apprenticeship. It had taken place years before, yet in my mind it was as vivid as if it had just happened. Through very artful manipulations don Juan had once forced me into a direct and terrifying confrontation with a woman reputed to be a sorceress. The clash resulted in a profound animosity on her part. Don Juan exploited my fear of the woman as motivation to continue with the apprenticeship, claiming that I had to learn more about sorcery in order to protect myself against her magical onslaughts. The end results of his "tricking" were so convincing that I sincerely felt I had no other recourse than to learn as much as possible if I wanted to stay alive.

"If you're planning to scare me again with that woman I simply won't come back any more," I said.

Don Juan's laughter was very joyous.

"Don't worry," he said reassuringly. "Tricks with fear won't work with you any more. You're no longer afraid. But if it is needed, you can be tricked wherever you are; you don't have to be around here for that."

He put his arms behind his head and lay down to sleep. I worked on my notes until he woke up a couple of hours later; it was almost dark then. Noticing that I was writing, he sat up straight and, smiling, asked me if I had written myself out of my problem.

May 23, 1968

We were talking about Oaxaca. I told don Juan that once I had arrived in the city on a day when the market was open, a day when scores of Indians from all over the area flock to town to sell food and all kinds of trinkets. I mentioned that I was particularly interested in a man who was selling medicinal plants. He carried a wooden kit in which he kept a number of small jars with dry, shredded plants, and he stood in the middle of the street holding one jar, yelling a very peculiar singsong.

"I bring here," he would say, "for fleas, flies, mosquitoes, and lice.

"Also for pigs, horses, goats, and cows.

"I have here for all the maladies of man.

"The mumps, the measles, rheumatism, and gout.

"I bring here for the heart, the liver, the stomach, and the loin.

"Come near, ladies and gentlemen.

"I bring here for fleas, flies, mosquitoes, and lice."

I had listened to him for a long time. His format consisted of enumerating a long list of man's diseases for which he claimed to have a cure; the device he used to give rhythm to his singsong was to pause after naming a set of four.

Don Juan said that he also used to sell herbs in the market in Oaxaca when he was young. He said he still remembered his selling pitch and he yelled it for me. He said that he and his friend Vicente used to make concoctions.

"Those concoctions were really good," don Juan said. "My friend Vicente used to make great extracts of plants."

I told don Juan that once during one of my trips to Mexico I had met his friend Vicente. Don Juan seemed to be surprised and wanted to know more about it.

I was driving through Durango at that time and remembered that don Juan had once told me I should pay a visit to his friend, who lived there. I looked for him and found him, and talked to him for a while. Before I left he gave me a sack with some plants and a series of instructions for replanting one of them.

I stopped on my way to the town of Aguas Calientes. I made sure there were no people around. For at least ten minutes I had been watching the road and surrounding areas. There had not been any houses in sight, nor cattle grazing alongside the road. I stopped on the top of a small hill; from there I could see the road ahead and behind me. It was deserted in both directions as far into the distance as I could see. I waited for a few minutes to orient myself and to remember don Vicente's instructions. I took one of the plants, walked into a field of cacti on the east side of the road, and planted it as don Vicente had instructed me. I had with me a bottle of mineral water with which I intended to sprinkle the plant. I tried to open it by hitting the cap with the small iron bar I had used as a digging stick, but the bottle exploded and a glass sliver nicked my upper lip and made it bleed.

I walked back to my car to get another bottle of mineral water. As I was getting it out of my trunk a man driving a VW station wagon stopped and asked me if I needed help. I said that everything was all right and he drove away. I returned to water the plant and then I started back toward my car. When I was perhaps a hundred feet away I heard some voices. I hurried down a slope onto the highway and found three Mexicans at the car, two men and one woman. One of the men was sitting on the front bumper. He was perhaps in his late thirties, of medium height, with black curly hair. He was carrying a bundle on his back and was wearing old slacks and a worn-out pinkish shirt. His shoes were untied and perhaps too big for his feet; they seemed to be loose and uncomfortable. He was sweating profusely.

The other man was standing about twenty feet away from the car. He was small-boned and shorter than the other man, and his hair was straight and combed backwards. He carried a smaller bundle and was older, perhaps in his late forties. His clothes were in better condition. He had on a dark blue jacket, light blue slacks, and black shoes. He was not perspiring at all and seemed aloof, uninterested.

The woman appeared to be also in her forties. She was fat and had a very dark complexion. She wore black Capris, a white sweater, and black, pointed shoes. She did not carry a bundle, but was holding a portable transistor radio. She seemed to be very tired and her face was covered with beads of perspiration.

When I approached them the younger man and the woman accosted me. They wanted a ride. I told them I did not have any space in my car. I showed them that the back seat was loaded to capacity and there was really no room left. The man suggested that if I drove slow they could go perched on the back bumper, or lying across the front fender. I thought the idea was preposterous. Yet there was such an urgency in their plea that I felt very sad and ill at ease. I gave them some money for their bus fare.

The younger man took the bills and thanked me, but the older man turned his back disdainfully.

"I want transportation," he said. "I'm not interested in money."

Then he turned to me. "Can't you give us some food or water?" he asked.

I really had nothing to give them. They stood there looking at me for a moment and then they began to walk away.

I got into my car and tried to start the motor. The heat was very intense and the motor seemed to be flooded. The younger man stopped when he heard the starter grinding and came back and stood behind my car ready to push it. I felt a tremendous apprehension. I was actually panting desperately. The motor finally ignited and I zoomed away.

After I had finished relating this, don Juan remained pensive for a long while.

"Why haven't you told me this before?" he said without looking at me.

I did not know what to say. I shrugged my shoulders and told him that I never thought it was important.

"It's damn important!" he said. "Vicente is a first-rate sorcerer. He gave you something to plant because he had his reasons; and if you encountered three people who seemed to have popped out of nowhere right after you had planted it, there was a reason for that too; but only a fool like you would disregard the incident and think it wasn't important."

He wanted to know exactly what had taken place when I paid don Vicente the visit.

I told him that I was driving across town and passed by the market; I got the idea then of looking for don Vicente. I walked into the market and went to the section for medicinal herbs. There were three stands in a row but they were run by three fat women. I walked to the end of the aisle and found another stand around the corner. There I saw a thin, small-boned, white-haired man. He was at that moment selling a birdcage to a woman.

I waited around until he was by himself and then I asked him if he knew Vicente Medrano. He looked at me without answering.

"What do you want with that Vicente Medrano?" he finally said.

I told him I had come to pay him a visit on behalf of his friend, and gave him don Juan's name. The old man looked at me for an instant and then he said he was Vicente Medrano and was at my service. He asked me to sit down. He seemed to be pleased, very relaxed, and genuinely friendly. I told him about my friendship with don Juan. I felt that there was an immediate bond of sympathy between us. He told me he had known don Juan since they were in their twenties. Don Vicente had only words of praise for don Juan. Toward the end of our conversation he said in a vibrant tone: "Juan is a true man of knowledge. I myself have dwelled only briefly with plant powers. I was always interested in their curative properties; I have even collected botany books, which I sold only recently."

He remained silent for a moment; he rubbed his chin a couple of times. He seemed to be searching for a proper word.

"You may say that I am only a man of lyric knowledge," he said. "I'm not like Juan, my Indian brother."

Don Vicente was silent again for another moment. His eyes were glassy and were staring at the floor by my left side.

Then he turned to me and said almost in a whisper, "Oh, how high soars my Indian brother!"

Don Vicente got up. It seemed that our conversation was finished.

If anyone else had made a statement about an Indian brother I would have taken it for a cheap cliché. Don Vicente's tone, however, was so sincere and his eyes were so clear that he enraptured me with the image of his Indian brother soaring so high. And I believed he meant what he had said.

"Lyric knowledge, my eye!" don Juan exclaimed after

I had recounted the whole story. "Vicente is a brujo. Why did you go to see him?"

I reminded him that he himself had asked me to visit don Vicente.

"That's absurd!" he exclaimed dramatically. "I said to you, some day, when you know how to *see,* you should pay a visit to my friend Vicente; that's what I said. Apparently you were not listening."

I argued that I could find no harm in having met don Vicente, that I was charmed by his manners and his kindness.

Don Juan shook his head from side to side and in a half-kidding tone expressed his bewilderment at what he called my "baffling good luck." He said that my visiting don Vicente was like walking into a lion's den armed with a twig. Don Juan seemed to be agitated, yet I could not see any reason for his concern. Don Vicente was a beautiful man. He seemed so frail; his strangely haunting eyes made him look almost ethereal. I asked don Juan how a beautiful person like that could be dangerous.

"You're a damn fool," he said and looked stern for a moment. "He won't cause you any harm by himself. But knowledge is power, and once a man embarks on the road of knowledge he's no longer liable for what may happen to those who come in contact with him. You should have paid him a visit when you knew enough to defend yourself; not from him, but from the power he has harnessed, which, by the way, is not his or anybody else's. Upon hearing that you were my friend, Vicente assumed that you knew how to protect yourself and then made you a gift. He apparently liked you and must have made you a great gift, and you chucked it. What a pity!"

May 24, 1968

I had been pestering don Juan all day to tell me about don Vicente's gift. I had pointed out to him in various ways that he had to consider our differences; I said that what was self-explanatory for him might be totally incomprehensible for me.

"How many plants did he give you?" he finally asked.

I said four, but I actually could not remember. Then don Juan wanted to know exactly what had taken place after I left don Vicente and before I stopped on the side of the road. But I could not remember either.

"The number of plants is important and so is the order of events," he said. "How can I tell you what his gift was if you don't remember what happened?"

I struggled unsuccessfully to visualize the sequence of events.

"If you would remember everything that happened," he said, "I could at least tell you how you chucked your gift."

Don Juan seemed to be very disturbed. He urged me impatiently to recollect, but my memory was almost a total blank.

"What do you think I did wrong, don Juan?" I said, just to continue the conversation.

"Everything."

"But I followed don Vicente's instructions to the letter."

"So what? Don't you understand that to follow his instructions was meaningless?"

"Why?"

"Because those instructions were designed for someone who could *see*, not for an idiot who got out with his life just by sheer luck. You went to see Vicente without preparation. He liked you and gave you a gift. And that gift could easily have cost you your life."

"But why did he give me something so serious? If he's a sorcerer he should've known that I don't know anything."

"No, he couldn't have *seen* that. You look as though you know, but you don't know much really."

I said I was sincerely convinced that I had never misrepresented myself, at least not deliberately.

"I didn't mean that," he said. "If you were putting on airs Vicente could've seen through you. This is something worse than putting on airs. When I *see* you, you look to me as if you know a great deal, and yet I myself know that you don't."

"What do I seem to know, don Juan?"

"Secrets of power, of course; a brujo's knowledge. So when Vicente *saw* you he made you a gift and you acted toward it the way a dog acts toward food when his belly is full. A dog pisses on food when he doesn't want to eat any more, so other dogs won't eat it. You did that on the gift. Now we'll never know what really took place. You have lost a great deal. What a waste!"

He was quiet for some time; then he shrugged his shoulders and smiled.

"It's useless to complain," he said, "and yet it's so difficult not to. Gifts of power happen so rarely in one's life; they are unique and precious. Take me, for instance; nobody has ever made me such a gift. There are few people, to my knowledge, who ever had one. To waste something so unique is a shame."

"I see what you mean, don Juan," I said. "Is there anything I can do now to salvage the gift?"

He laughed and repeated several times, "To salvage the gift."

"That sounds nice," he said. "I like that. Yet there isn't anything one can do to salvage your gift."

May 25, 1968

Don Juan spent nearly all his time today showing me how to assemble trapping devices for small animals. We had been cutting and cleaning branches nearly all morning. There were many questions in my mind. I had to talk to him while we worked, but he had made a joke and said that of the two of us only I could move my hands and my mouth at the same time. We finally sat down to rest and I blurted out a question.

"What's it like to *see*, don Juan?"

"You have to learn to *see* in order to know that. I can't tell you."

"Is it a secret I shouldn't know?"

"No. It's just that I can't describe it."

"Why?"

"It wouldn't make sense to you."

"Try me, don Juan. Maybe it'll make sense to me."

"No. You must do it yourself. Once you learn, you can *see* every single thing in the world in a different way."

"Then, don Juan, you don't see the world in the usual way any more."

"I see both ways. When I want to *look* at the world I see it the way you do. Then when I want to *see* it I look at it the way I know and I perceive it in a different way."

"Do things look consistently the same every time you *see* them?"

"Things don't change. You change your way of looking, that's all."

"I mean, don Juan, that if you *see,* for instance, the same tree, does it remain the same every time you *see* it?"

"No. It changes and yet it's the same."

"But if the same tree changes every time you *see* it, your *seeing* may be a mere illusion."

He laughed and did not answer for some time, but seemed to be thinking. Finally he said, "Whenever you look at things you don't *see* them. You just look at them, I suppose, to make sure that something is there. Since you're not concerned with *seeing,* things look very much the same every time you look at them. When you learn to *see,* on the other hand, a thing is never the same every time you *see* it, and yet it is the same. I told you, for instance, that a man is like an egg. Every time I *see* the same man I *see* an egg, yet it is not the same egg."

"But you won't be able to recognize anything, since nothing is the same; so what's the advantage of learning to *see?*"

"You can tell things apart. You can see them for what they really are."

"Don't I see things as they really are?"

"No. Your eyes have learned only to look. Take, for example, the three people you encountered, the three Mexicans. You have described them in detail, and even told me what clothes they wore. And that only proved to me that you didn't *see* them at all. If you were capable of *seeing* you would have known on the spot that they were not people."

"They were not people? What were they?"

"They were not people, that's all."

"But that's impossible. They were just like you and me."

"No, they were not. I'm sure of it."

I asked him if they were ghosts, spirits, or the souls of dead people. His reply was that he did not know what ghosts, spirits, and souls were.

I translated for him the Webster's New World Dictionary definition of the word ghosts: "The supposed disembodied spirit of a dead person, conceived of as appearing to the living as a pale, shadowy apparition." And then the definition of spirit: "A supernatural being, especially one thought of . . . as a ghost, or as inhabiting a certain region, being of a certain (good or evil) character."

He said they could perhaps be called spirits, although the definition I had read was not quite adequate to describe them.

"Are they guardians of some sort?" I asked.

"No. They don't guard anything."

"Are they overseers? Are they watching over us?"

"They are forces, neither good nor bad, just forces that a brujo learns to harness."

"Are they the allies, don Juan?"

"Yes, they are the allies of a man of knowledge."

This was the first time in eight years of our association that don Juan had come close to defining an "ally." I must have asked him to do so dozens of times. He usually disregarded my question, saying that I knew what an ally was and that it was stupid to voice what I already knew. Don Juan's direct statement about the nature of an ally was a novelty and I was compelled to probe him.

"You told me the allies were in the plants," I said, "in the jimson weed and in the mushrooms."

"I've never told you that," he said with great conviction. "You always jump to your own conclusions."

"But I wrote it down in my notes, don Juan."

"You may write whatever you want, but don't tell me I said that."

I reminded him that he had at first told me his benefactor's ally was the jimson weed and his own ally was the little smoke; and that he had later clarified it by saying that the ally was contained in each plant.

"No. That's not correct," he said, frowning. "My ally is the little smoke, but that doesn't mean that my ally is in the smoking mixture, or in the mushrooms, or in my pipe. They all have to be put together to get me to the ally, and that ally I call little smoke for reasons of my own."

Don Juan said that the three people I had seen, whom he called "those who are not people"—*los qué no son gente*—were in reality don Vicente's allies.

I reminded him that he had established that the difference between an ally and Mescalito was that an ally could not be seen, while one could easily see Mescalito.

We involved ourselves in a long discussion then. He said that he had established the idea that an ally could not be seen because an ally adopted any form. When I pointed out that he had once also said that Mescalito adopted any form, don Juan dropped the whole conversation, saying that the "seeing" to which he was referring was not the ordinary "looking at things" and that my confusion stemmed from my insistence on talking.

Hours later don Juan himself started back again on the topic of the allies. I had felt he was somehow annoyed by my questions so I had not pressed him any further. He was showing me then how to make a trap for rabbits; I had to hold a long stick and bend it as far as possible so he could tie a string around the ends. The stick was fairly thin but still demanded considerable strength to bend. My head and arms were shivering with the exertion and I was nearly exhausted when he finally tied the string.

We sat down and began to talk. He said it was obvious to him that I could not comprehend anything unless I talked about it, and that he did not mind my questions and was going to tell me about the allies.

"The ally is not in the smoke," he said. "The smoke takes you to where the ally is, and when you become one with the ally you don't ever have to smoke again. From then on you can summon your ally at will and make him do anything you want.

"The allies are neither good nor evil, but are put to use by the sorcerers for whatever purpose they see fit. I like the little smoke as an ally because it doesn't demand much of me. It's constant and fair."

"How does an ally look to you, don Juan? Those three people I saw, for instance, who looked like ordinary people to me; how would they look to you?"

"They would look like ordinary people."

"Then how can you tell them apart from real people?"

"Real people look like luminous eggs when you *see* them. Nonpeople always look like people. That's what I meant when I said you cannot *see* an ally. The allies take different forms. They look like dogs, coyotes, birds, even tumbleweeds, or anything else. The only difference is that when you *see* them they look just like what they're pretending to be. Everything has its own way of being when you *see*. Just like men look like eggs, other things look like something else, but the allies can be seen only in the form they are portraying. That form is good enough to fool the eyes, our eyes, that is. A dog is never fooled, neither is a crow."

"Why would they want to fool us?"

"I think we are all clowns. We fool ourselves. The allies just take the outward appearance of whatever is around and then we take them for what they are not. It is not their fault that we have taught our eyes only to look at things."

"I'm not clear about their function, don Juan. What do allies do in the world?"

"This is like asking me what we men do in the world. I really don't know. We are here, that's all. And the allies are here like us; and maybe they have been here before us."

"What do you mean before us, don Juan?"

"We men have not always been here."

"Do you mean here in this country or here in the world?"

We involved ourselves in another long argument at this point. Don Juan said that for him there was only the world, the place where he put his feet. I asked him how he knew that we had not always been in the world.

"Very simple," he said. "We men know very little about the world. A coyote knows much more than we do. A coyote is hardly ever fooled by the world's appearance."

"How come we can catch them and kill them?" I asked. "If they are not fooled by appearances how come they die so easily?"

Don Juan stared at me until I became embarrassed.

"We may trap or poison or shoot a coyote," he said. "Any way we do it a coyote is an easy prey for us because he is not familiar with man's machinations. If the coyote survived, however, you could rest assured that we'd never catch up with him again. A good hunter knows that and never sets his trap twice on the same spot, because if a coyote dies in a trap, every coyote can *see* his death, which lingers on, and thus they will avoid the trap or even the general area where it was set. We, on the other hand, never *see* death, which lingers on the spot where one of our fellow men has died; we may suspect it, but we never *see* it."

"Can a coyote *see* an ally?"

"Certainly."

"How does an ally look to a coyote?"

"I would have to be a coyote to know that. I can tell you, however, that to a crow it looks like a pointed hat. Round and wide at the bottom, ending in a long point. Some of them shine, but the majority are dull and appear to be very heavy. They resemble a dripping piece of cloth. They are foreboding shapes."

"How do they look to you when you *see* them, don Juan?"

"I've told you already; they look like whatever they're pretending to be. They take any shape or size that suits them. They could be shaped like a pebble or a mountain."

"Do they talk, or laugh, or make any noise?"

"In the company of men they behave like men. In the company of animals they behave like animals. Animals are usually afraid of them; however, if they are accustomed to seeing the allies, they leave them alone. We ourselves do something similar. We have scores of allies among us, but we don't bother them. Since our eyes can only look at things, we don't notice them."

"Do you mean that some of the people I see in the street are not really people?" I asked, truly bewildered by his statement.

"Some of them are not," he said emphatically.

His statement seemed preposterous to me, yet I could not seriously conceive of don Juan's making such a remark purely for effect. I told him it sounded like a science-fiction tale about beings from another planet. He said he did not care how it sounded, but some people in the streets were not people. "Why must you think that every person in a moving crowd is a human being?" he asked with an air of utmost seriousness.

I really could not explain why, except that I was habituated to believe that as an act of sheer faith on my part.

He went on to say how much he liked to watch busy places with a lot of people, and how he would sometimes *see* a crowd of men who looked like eggs, and among the mass of egg-like creatures he would spot one who looked just like a person.

"It's very enjoyable to do that," he said, laughing, "or at least it's enjoyable for me. I like to sit in parks and bus depots and watch. Sometimes I can spot an ally right away; at other times I can *see* only real people. Once I saw two allies sitting in a bus, side by side. That's the only time in my life I have seen two together."

"Did it have a special significance for you to see two of them?"

"Certainly. Anything they do is significant. From their actions a brujo can sometimes draw his power. Even if a brujo does not have an ally of his own, as long as he knows how to *see*, he can handle power by watching the acts of the allies. My benefactor taught me to do that, and for years before I had my own ally I watched for allies among crowds of people and every time I *saw* one it taught me something. You found three together. What a magnificent lesson you wasted."

He did not say anything else until we finished assembling the rabbit trap. Then he turned to me and said suddenly, as if he had just remembered it, that another important thing about the allies was that if one found two of them they were always two of the same kind. The two allies he saw were two men, he said; and since I had seen two men and one woman he concluded that my experience was even more unusual.

I asked if the allies portray children; if the children could be of the same or of different sex; if the allies portrayed people of different races; if they could portray a family composed of a man, a woman, and a child; and finally I asked him if he had ever seen an ally driving a car or a bus.

Don Juan did not answer at all. He smiled and let me do the talking. When he heard my last question he burst out laughing and said that I was being careless with my questions, that it would have been more appropriate to ask if he had ever *seen* an ally driving a motor vehicle.

"You don't want to forget the motorcycles, do you?" he said with a mischievous glint in his eye.

I thought his making fun of my question was funny and lighthearted and I laughed with him.

Then he explained that the allies could not take the lead or act upon anything directly; they could, however, act upon man in an indirect way. Don Juan said that coming in contact with an ally was dangerous because the ally was capable of bringing out the worst in a person. The apprenticeship was long and arduous, he said, because one had to reduce to a minimum all that was unnecessary in one's life, in order to withstand the impact of such an encounter. Don Juan said that his benefactor, when he first came in contact with an ally, was driven to burn himself and was scarred as if a mountain lion had

mauled him. In his own case, he said, an ally pushed
him into a pile of burning wood, and he burned himself a
little on the knee and shoulder blade, but the scars disappeared in time, when he became one with the ally.

3

On June 10, 1968, I started on a long journey with don
Juan to participate in a mitote. I had been waiting for this
opportunity for months, yet I was not really sure I wanted
to go. I thought my hesitation was due to my fear that at
a peyote meeting I would have to ingest peyote, and I had
no intention whatsoever of doing that. I had repeatedly
expressed those feelings to don Juan. He laughed patiently
at first, but finally he firmly stated that he did not want to
hear one more thing about my fear.

As far as I was concerned, a mitote was ideal ground
for me to verify the schemata I had constructed. For one
thing, I had never completely abandoned the idea that a
covert leader was necessary at such a meeting in order to
insure agreement among the participants. Somehow I had
the feeling that don Juan had discarded my idea for reasons
of his own, since he deemed it more efficacious to explain
everything that took place at a mitote in terms of "seeing."
I thought that my interest in finding a suitable explanation in my own terms was not in accordance with what
he himself wanted me to do; therefore he had to discard
my rationale, as he was accustomed to doing with whatever did not conform to his system.

Right before we started on the journey don Juan eased
my apprehension about having to ingest peyote by telling
me that I was attending the meeting only to watch. I felt
elated. At that time I was almost certain I was going to

discover the covert procedure by which the participants arrive at an agreement.

It was late afternoon when we left; the sun was almost on the horizon; I felt it on my neck and wished I had a venetian blind in the rear window of my car. From the top of a hill I could see down into a huge valley; the road was like a black ribbon laid flat over the ground, up and down innumerable hills. I followed it with my eyes for a moment before we began descending; it ran due south until it disappeared over a range of low mountains in the distance.

Don Juan sat quietly, looking straight ahead. We had not said a word for a long time. It was uncomfortably warm inside the car. I had opened all the windows, but that did not help because it was an extremely hot day. I felt very annoyed and restless. I began to complain about the heat.

Don Juan frowned and looked at me quizzically.

"It's hot all over Mexico this time of the year," he said. "There is nothing one can do about it."

I did not look at him, but I knew he was gazing at me. The car picked up speed going down the slope. I vaguely saw a highway sign, *Vado*—dip. When I actually saw the dip I was going quite fast, and although I did slow down, we still felt the impact and bobbed up and down on the seats. I reduced the speed considerably; we were going through an area where livestock grazed freely on the sides of the road, an area where the carcass of a horse or a cow run down by a car was a common sight. At a certain point I had to stop completely and let some horses cross the highway. I was getting more restless and annoyed. I told don Juan that it was the heat; I said that I had always disliked the heat since my childhood, because every summer I used to feel suffocated and I could hardly breathe.

"You're not a child now," he said.

"The heat still suffocates me."

"Well, hunger used to suffocate me when I was a child," he said softly. "To be very hungry was the only thing I knew as a child, and I used to swell up until I could not breathe either. But that was when I was a child. I cannot suffocate now, neither can I swell like a toad when I am hungry."

I didn't know what to say. I felt I was getting myself into an untenable position and soon I would have to defend a point I really didn't care to defend. The heat was not that bad. What disturbed me was the prospect of driving for over a thousand miles to our destination. I felt annoyed at the thought of having to exert myself.

"Let's stop and get something to eat," I said. "Maybe it won't be so hot once the sun goes down."

Don Juan looked at me, smiling, and said that there were not any clean towns for a long stretch and that he had understood my policy was not to eat from the stands on the roadside.

"Don't you fear diarrhea any more?" he asked.

I knew he was being sarcastic, yet he kept an inquisitive and at the same time serious look on his face.

"The way you act," he said, "one would think that diarrhea is lurking out there, waiting for you to step out of the car to jump you. You're in a terrible fix; if you escape the heat, diarrhea will eventually get you."

Don Juan's tone was so serious that I began to laugh. Then we drove in silence for a long time. When we arrived at a highway stop for trucks called Los Vidrios— Glass—it was already quite dark.

Don Juan shouted from the car, "What do you have to eat today?"

"Pork meat," a woman shouted back from inside.

"I hope for your sake that the pig was run down on the road today," don Juan said to me, laughing.

We got out of the car. The road was flanked on both sides by ranges of low mountains that seemed to be the solidified lava of some gigantic volcanic eruption. In the darkness the black, jagged peaks were silhouetted against the sky like huge menacing walls of glass slivers.

While we ate I told don Juan that I could see the reason why the place was called Glass. I said that to me the name was obviously due to the glass-sliver shape of the mountains.

Don Juan said in a convincing tone that the place was called Los Vidrios because a truck loaded with glass had overturned on that spot and the glass shreds were left lying around the road for years.

I felt he was being facetious and asked him to tell me if that was the real reason.

"Why don't you ask someone here?" he said.

I asked a man who was sitting at a table next to ours; he said apologetically that he didn't know. I went into the kitchen and asked the women there if they knew, but they all said they didn't; that the place was just called Glass.

"I believe I'm right," don Juan said in a low voice. "Mexicans are not given to noticing things around them. I'm sure they can't see the glass mountains, but they surely can leave a mountain of glass shreds lying around for years."

We both found the image funny and laughed.

When we had finished eating don Juan asked me how I felt. I told him fine, but I really felt somewhat queasy. Don Juan gave me a steadfast look and seemed to detect my feeling of discomfort.

"Once you decided to come to Mexico you should have put all your petty fears away," he said very sternly. "Your decision to come should have vanquished them. You came because you wanted to come. That's the warrior's way. I have told you time and time again, the most effective way to live is as a warrior. Worry and think before you make any decision, but once you make it, be on your way free from worries or thoughts; there will be a million other decisions still awaiting you. That's the warrior's way."

"I believe I do that, don Juan, at least some of the time. It's very hard to keep on reminding myself, though."

"A warrior thinks of his death when things become unclear."

"That's even harder, don Juan. For most people death is very vague and remote. We never think of it."

"Why not?"

"Why should we?"

"Very simple," he said. "Because the idea of death is the only thing that tempers our spirit."

By the time we left Los Vidrios it was so dark that the jagged silhouette of the mountains had emerged into the darkness of the sky. We drove in silence for more than an hour. I felt tired. It was as though I didn't want to talk because there was nothing to talk about. The traffic was minimal. Few cars passed by from the opposite direction. It seemed as if we were the only people going south on the highway. I thought that was strange and I kept on looking in the rear-view mirror to see if there were other cars coming from behind, but there were none.

After a while I stopped looking for cars and began to dwell again on the prospect of our trip. Then I noticed that my headlights seemed extremely bright in contrast with the darkness all around and I looked again in the rear-view mirror. I saw a bright glare first and then two points of light that seemed to have emerged from the ground. They were the headlights of a car on a hilltop in the distance behind us. They remained visible for a while, then they disappeared into the darkness as if they had been scooped away; after a moment they appeared on another hilltop, and then they disappeared again. I followed their appearances and disappearances in the mirror for a long time. At one point it occurred to me that the car was gaining on us. It was definitely closing in. The lights were bigger and brighter. I deliberately stepped on the gas pedal. I had a sensation of uneasiness. Don Juan seemed to notice my concern, or perhaps he was only noticing that I was speeding up. He looked at me first, then he turned around and looked at the distant headlights.

He asked me if there was something wrong with me. I told him that I had not seen any cars behind us for hours and that suddenly I had noticed the lights of a car that seemed to be gaining on us all the time.

He chuckled and asked me if I really thought it was a car. I told him that it had to be a car and he said that my concern revealed to him that, somehow, I must have felt that whatever was behind us was something more than a mere car. I insisted that I thought it was just another car on the highway, or perhaps a truck.

"What else can it be?" I said loudly.

Don Juan's probing had put me on edge.

He turned and looked straight at me, then he nodded slowly, as if measuring what he was going to say.

"Those are the lights on the head of death," he said softly. "Death puts them on like a hat and then shoots off on a gallop. Those are the lights of death on the gallop gaining on us, getting closer and closer."

A chill ran up my back. After a while I looked in the rear-view mirror again, but the lights were not there any more.

I told don Juan that the car must have stopped or turned off the road. He did not look back; he just stretched his arms and yawned.

"No," he said. "Death never stops. Sometimes it turns off its lights, that's all."

We arrived in northeastern Mexico June 13. Two old Indian women, who looked alike and seemed to be sisters, and four girls were gathered at the door of a small adobe house. There was a hut behind the house and a dilapidated barn that had only part of its roof and one wall left. The women were apparently waiting for us; they must have spotted my car by the dust it raised on the dirt road after I left the paved highway a couple of miles away. The house was in a deep valley, and viewed from the door the highway looked like a long scar high up on the side of the green hills.

Don Juan got out of the car and talked with the old women for a moment. They pointed to some wooden stools in front of the door. Don Juan signaled me to come over and sit down. One of the old women sat with us; the rest went inside the house. Two of the girls remained by the door, examining me with curiosity. I waved at them; they giggled and ran inside. After a few minutes two young men came over and greeted don Juan. They did not speak to me or even look at me. They talked to don Juan briefly; then he got up and all of us, including the women, walked to another house, perhaps half a mile away.

We met there with another group of people. Don Juan

went inside but told me to stay by the door. I looked in and saw an old Indian man around don Juan's age sitting on a wooden stool.

It was not quite dark. A group of young Indian men and women were standing quietly around an old truck parked in front of the house. I talked to them in Spanish but they deliberately avoided answering me; the women giggled every time I said something and the men smiled politely and turned their eyes away. It was as if they did not understand me, yet I was sure all of them spoke Spanish because I had heard them talking among themselves.

After a while don Juan and the other old man came out and got into the truck and sat next to the driver. That appeared to be a signal for everyone to climb onto the flatbed of the truck. There were no side railings, and when the truck began to move we all hung onto a long rope that was tied to some hooks on the chassis.

The truck moved slowly on the dirt road. At one point, on a very steep slope, it stopped and everybody jumped down and walked behind it; then two young men hopped onto the flatbed again and sat on the edge without using the rope. The women laughed and encouraged them to maintain their precarious position. Don Juan and the old man, who was referred to as don Silvio, walked together and did not seem to be concerned with the young men's histrionics. When the road leveled off everybody got on the truck again.

We rode for about an hour. The floor was extremely hard and uncomfortable, so I stood up and held onto the roof of the cab and rode that way until we stopped in front of a group of shacks. There were more people there; it was very dark by then and I could see only a few of them in the dim, yellowish light of a kerosene lantern that hung by an open door.

Everybody got off the truck and mingled with the people in the houses. Don Juan told me again to stay outside. I leaned against the front fender of the truck and after a minute or two I was joined by three young men. I had met one of them four years before at a previous mitote. He embraced me by grabbing my forearms.

"You're fine," he whispered to me in Spanish.

We stayed very quietly by the truck. It was a warm, windy night. I could hear the soft rumble of a stream close by. My friend asked me in a whisper if I had any cigarettes. I passed a pack around. By the glow of the cigarettes I looked at my watch. It was nine o'clock.

A group of people emerged from inside the house soon afterwards and the three young men walked away. Don Juan came over to me and told me that he had explained my presence to everybody's satisfaction and that I was welcome to come and serve water at the mitote. He said we would be going right away.

A group of ten women and eleven men left the house. The man heading the party was rather husky; he was perhaps in his mid-fifties. They called him "Mocho," a nickname which means "cropped." He moved with brisk, firm steps. He carried a kerosene lantern and waved it from side to side as he walked. At first I thought he was moving it at random, but then I discovered that he waved the lantern to mark an obstacle or a difficult pass on the road. We walked for over an hour. The women chatted and laughed softly from time to time. Don Juan and the other old man were at the head of the line; I was at the very tail end of it. I kept my eyes down on the road, trying to see where I was walking.

It had been four years since don Juan and I had been in the hills at night, and I had lost a great deal of physical prowess. I kept stumbling and involuntarily kicking small rocks. My knees did not have any flexibility; the road seemed to come up at me when I encountered a high spot, or it seemed to give in under me when I hit a low spot. I was the noisiest walker and that made me into an unwilling clown. Someone in the group said, "Woo," every time I stumbled and everyone laughed. At one point, one of the rocks I kicked hit a woman's heel and she said out loud, to everyone's delight, "Give a candle to that poor boy!" But the final mortification was when I tripped and had to hold onto the person in front of me; he nearly lost his balance with my weight on him and let out a deliberate scream that was out of all proportion. Everyone laughed so hard that the whole group had to stop for a while.

At a certain moment the man who was leading jerked his lantern up and down. It seemed that was the sign we had arrived at our destination. There was a dark silhouette of a low house to my right, a short distance away. Everyone in the group scrambled in different directions. I looked for don Juan. It was difficult to find him in the darkness. I stumbled noisily for a while before noticing that he was sitting on a rock.

He again told me that my duty was to bring water for the men who were going to participate. He had taught me the procedure years before. I remembered every detail of it but he insisted on refreshing my memory and showed me again how to do it.

Afterwards we walked to the back of the house where all the men had gathered. They had built a fire. There was a cleared area covered with straw mats perhaps fifteen feet away from the fire. Mocho, the man who had led us, sat on a mat first; I noticed that the upper edge of his left ear was missing, which accounted for his nickname. Don Silvio sat to his right and don Juan to his left. Mocho was sitting facing the fire. A young man advanced toward him and placed a flat basket with peyote buttons in front of him; then the young man sat down between Mocho and don Silvio. Another young man carried two small baskets and placed them next to the peyote buttons and then sat between Mocho and don Juan. Then two other young men flanked don Silvio and don Juan, closing a circle of seven persons. The women remained inside the house. Two young men were in charge of keeping the fire burning all night, and one teenager and I kept the water that was going to be given to the seven participants after their all-night ritual. The boy and I sat by a rock. The fire and the receptacle with water were opposite each other and at an equal distance from the circle of participants.

Mocho, the headman, sang his peyote song; his eyes were closed; his body bobbed up and down. It was a very long song. I did not understand the language. Then all of them, one by one, sang their peyote songs. They did not seem to follow any preconceived order. They apparently sang whenever they felt like doing it. Then Mocho held the basket with peyote buttons, took two of them, and placed it back again in the center of the circle; don Silvio was next and then don Juan. The four young men, who seemed to be a separate unit, took two peyote buttons each, following a counter-clockwise direction.

Each of the seven participants sang and ate two peyote buttons four consecutive times, then they passed the other two baskets, which contained dried fruit and meat.

They repeated this cycle at various times during the night, yet I could not detect any underlying order to their individual movements. They did not speak to one another; they seemed rather to be by themselves and to themselves. I did not see any of them, not even once, paying attention to what the other men were doing.

Before daybreak they got up and the young man and I gave them water. Afterwards I walked around to orient myself. The house was a one-room shack, a low adobe construction with a thatched roof. The scenery that surrounded it was quite oppressive. The shack was located in a harsh plain with mixed vegetation. Shrubs and cacti grew together, but there were no trees at all. I did not feel like venturing beyond the house.

The women left during the morning. The men moved silently in the area immediately surrounding the house. Around midday all of us sat down again in the same order we had sat the night before. A basket with pieces of dried meat cut to the same size as a peyote button was passed around. Some of the men sang their peyote songs. After an hour or so all of them stood up and went off in different directions.

The women had left a pot of gruel for the fire and water attendants. I ate some of it and then I slept most of the afternoon.

After dark the young men in charge of the fire built another one and the cycle of intaking peyote buttons began again. It followed roughly the same order as the preceding night, ending at daybreak.

During the course of the night I struggled to observe

and record every single movement performed by each of the seven participants, in hopes of discovering the slightest form of a detectable system of verbal or nonverbal communication among them. There was nothing in their actions, however, that revealed an underlying system.

In the early evening the cycle of intaking peyote was renewed. By morning I knew that I had completely failed to find clues that would point out the covert leader, or to discover any form of covert communication among them or any traces of their system of agreement. For the rest of the day I sat by myself and tried to arrange my notes.

When the men gathered again for the fourth night I knew somehow that this was to be the last meeting. Nobody had mentioned anything about it to me, yet I knew they would disband the next day. I sat by the water again and everyone else resumed his position in the order that had already been established.

The behavior of the seven men in the circle was a replica of what I had observed during the three previous nights. I became absorbed in their movements as I had done before. I wanted to record everything they did, every movement, every utterance, every gesture.

At a certain moment I heard a sort of beep in my ear; it was a common sort of buzzing in the ear and I did not pay attention to it. The beep became louder, yet it was still within the range of my ordinary bodily sensations. I remembered dividing my attention between watching the men and listening to the buzzing I was hearing. Then, at a given instant, the faces of the men seemed to become brighter; it was as if a light had been turned on. But it was not quite like an electric light, or a lantern, or the reflection of the fire on their faces. It was rather an iridescence; a pink luminosity, very tenuous, yet detectable from where I was. The buzzing seemed to increase. I looked at the teenage boy who was with me but he had fallen asleep.

The pink luminosity became more noticeable by then. I looked at don Juan; his eyes were closed; so were don Silvio's and so were Mocho's. I could not see the eyes of the four younger men because two of them were bent forward and the other two had their backs turned to me.

I became even more involved in watching. Yet I had not fully realized that I was actually hearing a buzzing and was actually seeing a pinkish glow hovering over the men. After a moment I became aware that the tenuous pink light and the buzzing were very steady. I had a moment of intense bewilderment and then a thought crossed my mind, a thought that had nothing to do with the scene I was witnessing, nor with the purpose I had in mind for being there. I remembered something my mother had told me once when I was a child. The thought was distracting and very inappropriate; I tried to discard it and involve myself again in my assiduous watching, but I could not do it. The thought recurred; it was stronger, more demanding, and then I clearly heard my mother's voice calling me. I heard the shuffling of her slippers and then her laughter. I turned around looking for her; I conceived that I was going to be transported in time by some sort of hallucination or mirage and I was going to see her, but I saw only the boy sleeping beside me. To see him jolted me and I experienced a brief moment of ease, of sobriety.

I looked again at the group of men. They had not changed their positions at all. However, the luminosity was gone, and so was the buzzing in my ears. I felt relieved. I thought that the hallucination of hearing my mother's voice was over. Her voice had been so clear and vivid. I said to myself over and over that for an instant the voice had almost trapped me. I noticed vaguely that don Juan was looking at me, but that did not matter. It was the memory of my mother's voice calling me that was mesmerizing. I struggled desperately to think about something else. And then I heard her voice again, as clearly as if she had been behind me. She called my name. I turned quickly, but all I saw was the dark silhouette of the shack and the shrubs beyond it.

Hearing my name caused me the most profound anguish. I whined involuntarily. I felt cold and very lonely and I began to weep. At that moment I had the sensation that I needed someone to care for me. I turned my head to look at don Juan; he was staring at me. I did not want to see him so I closed my eyes. And then I saw my mother.

It was not the thought of my mother, the way I think of her ordinarily. This was a clear vision of her, standing by me. I felt desperate. I was trembling and wanted to escape. The vision of my mother was too disturbing, too alien to what I was pursuing in that peyote meeting. There was apparently no conscious way to avoid it. Perhaps I could have opened my eyes if I really wanted the vision to vanish, but instead I examined it in detail. My examination was more than merely looking at her; it was a compulsive scrutiny and assessment. A very peculiar feeling enveloped me as if it were an outside force, and I suddenly felt the horrendous burden of my mother's love. When I heard my name I was torn apart; the memory of my mother filled me with anguish and melancholy, but when I examined her I knew that I had never liked her. This was a shocking realization. Thoughts and images came to me as an avalanche. The vision of my mother must have vanished in the meantime; it was no longer important. I was no longer interested in what the Indians were doing either. In fact I had forgotten the mitote. I was absorbed in a series of extraordinary thoughts, extraordinary because they were more than thoughts; these were complete units of feeling that were emotional certainties, indisputable evidences about the nature of my relationship with my mother.

At a certain moment these extraordinary thoughts ceased to come. I noticed that they had lost their fluidity and their quality of being complete units of feeling. I had begun to think about other things. My mind was rambling. I thought of other members of my immediate family, but there were no images to accompany my thoughts. Then I looked at don Juan. He was standing; the rest of the men were also standing, and then they all walked toward the water. I moved aside and nudged the boy who was still asleep.

I related to don Juan the sequence of my astounding vision almost as soon as he got into my car. He laughed with great delight and said that my vision was a sign, an omen as important as my first experience with Mescalito.

I remembered that don Juan had interpreted the reactions I had when I first ingested peyote as an all-important omen; in fact he decided to teach me his knowledge because of it.

Don Juan said that during the last night of the mitote Mescalito had hovered over me so obviously that everyone was forced to turn toward me, and that was why he was staring at me when I looked at him.

I wanted to hear his interpretation of my vision, but he did not want to talk about it. He said that whatever I had experienced was nonsense in comparison to the omen.

Don Juan kept on talking about Mescalito's light hovering over me and how everyone had seen it.

"That was really something," he said. "I couldn't possibly ask for a better omen."

Don Juan and I were obviously on two different avenues of thought. He was concerned with the importance of the events he had interpreted as an omen and I was obsessed with the details of the vision I had had.

"I don't care about omens," I said. "I want to know what happened to me."

He frowned as if he were upset and remained very stiff and quiet for a moment. Then he looked at me. His tone was very forceful. He said that the only important issue was that Mescalito had been very gentle with me, had engulfed me with his light and had given me a lesson with no other effort on my part than being around.

4

On September 4, 1968, I went to Sonora to visit don Juan. Following a request he had made during my previous visit to him, I stopped on the way, in Hermosillo, to buy him a noncommercial tequila called *bacanora*. His request seemed very odd to me at the time, since I knew he disliked drinking, but I bought four bottles and put them in a box along with other things I had brought for him.

"Why, you got four bottles!" he said, laughing, when he opened the box. "I asked you to buy me one. I believe you thought the *bacanora* was for me, but it's for my grandson Lucio, and you have to give it to him as though it's a personal gift of your own."

I had met don Juan's grandson two years before; he was twenty-eight years old then. He was very tall, over six feet, and was always extravagantly well dressed for his means and in comparison to his peers. While the majority of Yaquis wear khakis and Levis, straw hats, and homemade sandals called *guaraches,* Lucio's outfit was an expensive black leather jacket with frills of turquoise beads, a Texan cowboy hat, and a pair of boots that were monogrammed and hand decorated.

Lucio was delighted to receive the liquor and immediately took the bottles inside his house, apparently to put them away. Don Juan made a casual comment that one should never hoard liquor and drink alone. Lucio said he was not really hoarding, but was putting it away until that evening, at which time he was going to invite his friends to drink with him.

That evening around seven o'clock I returned to Lucio's place. It was dark. I made out the vague silhouette of two people standing under a small tree; it was Lucio and one of his friends, who were waiting for me and guided me to the house with a flashlight.

Lucio's house was a flimsy, two-room, dirt-floor, wattle-and-daub construction. It was perhaps twenty feet long and supported by relatively thin beams of the mesquite tree. It had, as all the houses of the Yaquis have, a flat, thatched roof and a nine-foot-wide *ramada,* which is a sort of awning over the entire front part of the house. A *ramada* roof is never thatched; it is made of branches arranged in a loose fashion, giving enough shade and yet permitting the cooling breeze to circulate freely.

As I entered the house I turned on my tape recorder,

which I kept inside my brief case. Lucio introduced me to his friends. There were eight men inside the house, including don Juan. They were sitting casually around the center of the room under the bright light of a gasoline lantern that hung from a beam. Don Juan was sitting on a box. I sat facing him at the end of a six-foot bench made with a thick wooden beam nailed on two prongs planted in the ground.

Don Juan had placed his hat on the floor beside him. The light of the gasoline lantern made his short white hair look more brilliantly white. I looked at his face; the light had also enhanced the deep wrinkles on his neck and forehead, and made him look darker and older.

I looked at the other men; under the greenish-white light of the gasoline lantern all of them looked tired and old.

Lucio addressed the whole group in Spanish and said in a loud voice that we were going to drink one bottle of *bacanora* that I had brought for him from Hermosillo. He went into the other room, brought out a bottle, uncorked it, and gave it to me along with a small tin cup. I poured a very small amount into the cup and drank it. The *bacanora* seemed to be more fragrant and more dense than regular tequila, and stronger too. It made me cough. I passed the bottle and everyone poured himself a small drink, everyone except don Juan; he just took the bottle and placed it in front of Lucio, who was at the end of the line.

All of them made lively comments about the rich flavor of that particular bottle, and all of them agreed that the liquor must have come from the high mountains of Chihuahua.

The bottle went around a second time. The men smacked their lips, repeated their statements of praise, and engaged themselves in a lively discussion about the noticeable differences between the tequila made around Guadalajara and that made at a high altitude in Chihuahua.

During the second time around don Juan again did not drink and I poured only a dab for myself, but the rest of them filled the cup to the brim. The bottle went around once more and was finished.

"Get the other bottles, Lucio," don Juan said.

Lucio seemed to vacillate, and don Juan quite casually explained to the others that I had brought four bottles for Lucio.

Benigno, a young man of Lucio's age, looked at the brief case that I had placed inconspicuously behind me and asked if I was a tequila salesman. Don Juan answered that I was not, and that I had really come to Sonora to see him.

"Carlos is learning about Mescalito, and I'm teaching him," don Juan said.

All of them looked at me and smiled politely. Bajea, the woodcutter, a small, thin man with sharp features, looked at me fixedly for a moment and then said that the storekeeper had accused me of being a spy from an American company that was planning to do mining in the Yaqui land. They all reacted as if they were indignant at such an accusation. Besides, they all resented the storekeeper, who was a Mexican, or a *Yori* as the Yaquis say.

Lucio went into the other room and returned with another bottle of *bacanora*. He opened it, poured himself a large drink, and then passed it around. The conversation drifted to the probabilities of the American company coming to Sonora and its possible effect on the Yaquis. The bottle went back to Lucio. He lifted it and looked at its contents to see how much was left.

"Tell him not to worry," don Juan whispered to me. "Tell him you'll bring him more next time you come around."

I leaned over to Lucio and assured him that on my next visit I was going to bring him at least half a dozen bottles.

At one moment the topics of conversation seemed to wane away.

Don Juan turned to me and said loudly, "Why don't you tell the guys here about your encounters with Mescalito? I think that'll be much more interesting than this idle chat about what will happen if the American company comes to Sonora."

"Is Mescalito peyote, Grandpa?" Lucio asked curiously.

"Some people call it that way," don Juan said dryly. "I prefer to call it Mescalito."

"That confounded thing causes madness," said Genaro, a tall, husky, middle-aged man.

"I think it's stupid to say that Mescalito causes madness," don Juan said softly. "Because if that were the case, Carlos would be in a strait-jacket this very moment instead of being here talking to you. He has taken it and look at him. He is fine."

Bajea smiled and replied shyly, "Who can tell?" and everybody laughed.

"Look at me then," don Juan said. "I've known Mescalito nearly all my life and it has never hurt me."

The men did not laugh, but it was obvious that they were not taking him seriously.

"On the other hand," don Juan went on, "it's true that Mescalito drives people crazy, as you said, but that's only when they come to him without knowing what they're doing."

Esquere, an old man who seemed to be don Juan's age, chuckled softly as he shook his head from side to side.

"What do you mean by 'knowing,' Juan?" he asked. "The last time I saw you, you were saying the same thing."

"People go really crazy when they take that peyote stuff," Genaro continued. "I've seen the Huichol Indians eating it. They acted as if they had rabies. They frothed and puked and pissed all over the place. You could get epilepsy from taking that confounded thing. That's what Mr. Salas, the government engineer, told me once. And epilepsy is for life, you know."

"That's being worse than animals," Bajea added solemnly.

"You saw only what you wanted to see about the Huichol Indians, Genaro," don Juan said. "For one thing, you never took the trouble of finding out from them what it's like to get acquainted with Mescalito. Mescalito has never made anyone epileptic, to my knowledge. The government engineer is a Yori and I doubt that a Yori knows anything about it. You really don't think that all the thousands of people who know Mescalito are crazy, do you?"

"They must be crazy, or pretty nearly so, to do a thing like that," answered Genaro.

"But if all those thousands of people were crazy at the same time who would do their work? How would they manage to survive?" don Juan asked.

"Macario, who comes from the 'other side' "—the U.S.A.—"told me that whoever takes it there is marked for life," Esquere said.

"Macario is lying if he says that," don Juan said. "I'm sure he doesn't know what he's talking about."

"He really tells too many lies," said Benigno.

"Who's Macario?" I asked.

"He's a Yaqui Indian who lives here," Lucio said. "He says he's from Arizona and that he was in Europe during the war. He tells all kinds of stories."

"He says he was a colonel!" Benigno said.

Everyone laughed and the conversation shifted for a while to Macario's unbelievable tales, but don Juan returned again to the topic of Mescalito.

"If all of you know that Macario is a liar, how can you believe him when he talks about Mescalito?"

"Do you mean peyote, Grandpa?" Lucio asked, as if he were really struggling to make sense out of the term.

"God damn it! Yes!"

Don Juan's tone was sharp and abrupt. Lucio recoiled involuntarily, and for a moment I felt they were all afraid. Then don Juan smiled broadly and continued in a mild tone.

"Don't you fellows see that Macario doesn't know what he's talking about? Don't you see that in order to talk about Mescalito one has to know?"

"There you go again," Esquere said. "What the hell is this knowledge? You are worse than Macario. At least he says what's on his mind, whether he knows it or not. For years I've been listening to you say we have to know. What do we have to know?"

"Don Juan says there is a spirit in peyote," Benigno said.

"I have seen peyote in the field, but I have never seen spirits or anything of the sort," Bajea added.

"Mescalito is like a spirit, perhaps," don Juan explained. "But whatever he is doesn't become clear until one knows about him. Esquere complains that I have been saying this for years. Well, I have. But it's not my fault that you don't understand. Bajea says that whoever takes it becomes like an animal. Well, I don't see it that way. To me those who think they are above animals live worse than animals. Look at my grandson here. He works without rest. I would say he lives to work, like a mule. And all he does that is not animal-like is to get drunk."

Everybody laughed. Victor, a very young man who seemed to be still in adolescence, laughed in a pitch above everybody else.

Eligio, a young farmer, had not uttered a single word so far. He was sitting on the floor to my right, with his back against some sacks of chemical fertilizer that had been piled inside the house to protect them from the rain. He was one of Lucio's childhood friends, powerful looking and, although shorter than Lucio, more stocky and better built. Eligio seemed concerned about don Juan's words. Bajea was trying to come back with a comment, but Eligio interrupted him.

"In what way would peyote change all this?" he asked. "It seems to me that a man is born to work all his life, like mules do."

"Mescalito changes everything," don Juan said, "yet we still have to work like everybody else, like mules. I said there was a spirit inside Mescalito because it is something like a spirit which brings about the change in men. A spirit we can see and can touch, a spirit that changes us, sometimes even against our will."

"Peyote drives you out of your mind," Genaro said, "and then of course you believe you've changed. True?"

"How can it change us?" Eligio insisted.

"He teaches us the right way to live," don Juan said. "He helps and protects those who know him. The life you fellows are leading is no life at all. You don't know the happiness that comes from doing things deliberately. You don't have a protector!"

"What do you mean?" Genaro said indignantly. "We certainly have. Our Lord Jesus Christ, and our Mother the Virgin, and the little Virgin of Guadalupe. Aren't they our protectors?"

"Fine bunch of protectors!" don Juan said mockingly. "Have they taught you a better way to live?"

"That's because people don't listen to them," Genaro protested, "and they only pay attention to the devil."

"If they were real protectors they would force you to listen," don Juan said. "If Mescalito becomes your protector you will have to listen whether you like it or not, because you can see him and you must take heed of what he says. He will make you approach him with respect. Not the way you fellows are accustomed to approach your protectors."

"What do you mean, Juan?" Esquere asked.

"What I mean is that for you to come to your protectors means that one of you has to play a fiddle, and a dancer has to put on his mask and leggings and rattles and dance, while the rest of you drink. You, Benigno, you were a dancer once, tell us about it."

"I gave it up after three years," Benigno said. "It's hard work."

"Ask Lucio," Esquere said satirically. "He gave it up in one week!"

Everybody laughed except don Juan. Lucio smiled, seemingly embarrassed, and gulped down two huge swallows of *bacanora*.

"It is not hard, it is stupid," don Juan said. "Ask Valencio, the dancer, if he enjoys dancing. He does not! He got accustomed to it, that's all. I've seen him dance for years, and every time I have, I've seen the same movements badly executed. He takes no pride in his art except when he talks about it. He has no love for it, therefore year after year he repeats the same motions. What was bad about his dancing at the beginning has become fixed. He cannot see it any longer."

"He was taught to dance that way," Eligio said. "I was

also a dancer in the town of Torím. I know you must dance the way they teach you."

"Valencio is not the best dancer anyway," Esquere said. "There are others. How about Sacateca?"

"Sacateca is a man of knowledge, he is not in the same class with you fellows," don Juan said sternly. "He dances because that's the bent of his nature. All I wanted to say was that you, who are not dancers, do not enjoy it. Perhaps if the dances are well performed some of you will get pleasure. Not many of you know that much about dancing, though; therefore you are left with a very lousy piece of joy. This is why you fellows are all drunkards. Look at my grandson here!"

"Cut it out, Grandpa!" Lucio protested.

"He's not lazy or stupid," don Juan went on, "but what else does he do besides drink?"

"He buys leather jackets!" Genaro remarked, and the whole audience roared.

Lucio gulped down more *bacanora*.

"And how is peyote going to change that?" Eligio asked.

"If Lucio would seek the protector," don Juan said, "his life would be changed. I don't know exactly how, but I am sure it would be different."

"He would stop drinking, is that what you mean?" Eligio insisted.

"Perhaps he would. He needs something else besides tequila to make his life satisfying. And that something, whatever it may be, might be provided by the protector."

"Then peyote must taste very good," Eligio said.

"I didn't say that," don Juan said.

"How in the hell are you going to enjoy it if it doesn't taste good?" Eligio said.

"It makes one enjoy life better," don Juan said.

"But if it doesn't taste good, how could it make us enjoy our lives better?" Eligio persisted. "It doesn't make sense."

"Of course it makes sense," Genaro said with conviction. "Peyote makes you crazy and naturally you think you're having a great time with your life, no matter what you do."

They all laughed again.

"It does make sense," don Juan proceeded, undisturbed, "if you think how little we know and how much there is to see. Booze is what makes people crazy. It blurs the images. Mescalito, on the other hand, sharpens everything. It makes you see so very well. So very well!"

Lucio and Benigno looked at each other and smiled as though they had already heard the story before. Genaro and Esquere grew more impatient and began to talk at the same time. Victor laughed above all the other voices. The only one interested seemed to be Eligio.

"How can peyote do all that?" he asked.

"In the first place," don Juan explained, "you must want to become acquainted with him, and I think this is by far the most important thing. Then you must be offered to him, and you must meet with him many times before you can say you know him."

"And what happens then?" Eligio asked.

Genaro interrupted. "You crap on the roof with your ass on the ground."

The audience roared.

"What happens next is entirely up to you," don Juan went on without losing his self-control. "You must come to him without fear and, little by little, he will teach you how to live a better life."

There was a long pause. The men seemed to be tired. The bottle was empty. Lucio, with obvious reluctance, opened another.

"Is peyote Carlos' protector too?" Eligio asked in a joking tone.

"I wouldn't know that," don Juan said. "He has taken it three times, so ask him to tell you about it."

They all turned to me curiously and Eligio asked, "Did you really take it?"

"Yes. I did."

It seemed don Juan had won a round with his audience. They were either interested in hearing about my experience or too polite to laugh in my face.

"Didn't it hurt your mouth?" Lucio asked.

"It did. It also tasted terrible."

"Why did you take it, then?" Benigno asked.

I began to explain to them in elaborate terms that for a Western man don Juan's knowledge about peyote was one of the most fascinating things one could find. I said that everything he had said about it was true and that each one of us could verify that truth for ourselves.

I noticed that all of them were smiling as if they were concealing their contempt. I grew very embarrassed. I was aware of my awkwardness in conveying what I really had in mind. I talked for a while longer, but I had lost the impetus and only repeated what don Juan had already said.

Don Juan came to my aid and asked in a reassuring tone, "You were not looking for a protector when you first came to Mescalito, were you?"

I told them that I did not know that Mescalito could be a protector, and that I was moved only by my curiosity and a great desire to know him.

Don Juan reaffirmed that my intentions had been faultless and said that because of it Mescalito had had a beneficial effect on me.

"But it made you puke and piss all over the place, didn't it?" Genaro insisted.

I told him that it had in fact affected me in such a manner. They all laughed with restraint. I felt that they had become even more contemptuous of me. They didn't seem to be interested, except for Eligio, who was gazing at me.

"What did you see?" he asked.

Don Juan urged me to recount for them all or nearly all the salient details of my experiences, so I described the sequence and the form of what I had perceived. When I finished talking Lucio made a comment.

"If peyote is that weird, I'm glad I've never taken it."

"It is just like I said," Genaro said to Bajea. "That thing makes you insane."

"But Carlos is not insane now. How do you account for that?" don Juan asked Genaro.

"How do we know he isn't?" Genaro retorted.

They all broke out laughing, including don Juan.

"Were you afraid?" Benigno asked.

"I certainly was."

"Why did you do it, then?" Eligio asked.

"He said he wanted to know," Lucio answered for me. "I think Carlos is getting to be like my grandpa. Both have been saying they want to know, but nobody knows what in the hell they want to know."

"It is impossible to explain that knowing," don Juan said to Eligio, "because it is different for every man. The only thing which is common to all of us is that Mescalito reveals his secrets privately to each man. Being aware of how Genaro feels, I don't recommend that he meet Mescalito. Yet in spite of my words or his feelings, Mescalito could have a totally beneficial effect on him. But only *he* could find out, and *that* is the knowing I have been talking about."

Don Juan got up. "It's time to go home," he said. "Lucio is drunk and Victor is asleep."

Two days later, on September 6, Lucio, Benigno, and Eligio came over to the house where I was staying to go hunting with me. They remained silent for a while as I kept on writing my notes. Then Benigno laughed politely as a warning that he was going to say something important.

After a preliminary embarrassing silence he laughed again and said, "Lucio here says that he would take peyote."

"Would you really?" I asked.

"Yes. I wouldn't mind it."

Benigno's laughter came in spurts.

"Lucio says he will eat peyote if you buy him a motorcycle."

Lucio and Benigno looked at each other and broke out laughing.

"How much is a motorcycle in the United States?" Lucio asked.

"You could probably get one for a hundred dollars," I said.

"That isn't very much there, is it? You could easily get it for him, couldn't you?" Benigno asked.

"Well, let me ask your grandpa first," I said to Lucio.

"No, no," he protested. "Don't mention it to him. He'll spoil everything. He's a weirdo. And besides, he's too old and feeble-minded and he doesn't know what he's doing."

"He was a real sorcerer once," Benigno added. "I mean a real one. My folks say he was the best. But he took to peyote and became a nobody. Now he's too old."

"And he goes over and over the same crappy stories about peyote," Lucio said.

"That peyote is pure crap," Benigno said. "You know, we tried it once. Lucio got a whole sack of it from his grandpa. One night as we were going to town we chewed it. Son of a bitch! It cut my mouth to shreds. It tasted like hell!"

"Did you swallow it?" I asked.

"We spit it out," Lucio said, "and threw the whole damn sack away."

They both thought the incident was very funny. Eligio, in the meantime, had not said a word. He was withdrawn, as usual. He did not even laugh.

"Would you like to try it, Eligio?" I asked.

"No. Not me. Not even for a motorcycle."

Lucio and Benigno found the statement utterly funny and roared again.

"Nevertheless," Eligio continued, "I must admit that don Juan baffles me."

"My grandfather is too old to know anything," Lucio said with great conviction.

"Yeah, he's too old," Benigno echoed.

I thought the opinion the two young men had of don Juan was childish and unfounded. I felt it was my duty to defend his character and I told them that in my judgment don Juan was then, as he had been in the past, a great sorcerer, perhaps even the greatest of all. I said I felt there was something about him, something truly extraordinary.

I urged them to remember that he was over seventy years old and yet he was more energetic and stronger than all of us put together. I challenged the young men to prove it to themselves by trying to sneak up on don Juan.

"You just can't sneak up on my grandpa," Lucio said proudly. "He's a brujo."

I reminded them that they had said he was too old and feeble-minded, and that a feeble-minded person does not know what goes on around him. I said that I had marveled at don Juan's alertness time and time again.

"No one can sneak up on a brujo, even if he's old," Benigno said with authority. "They can gang up on him when he's asleep, though. That's what happened to a man named Cevicas. People got tired of his evil sorcery and killed him."

I asked them to give me all the details of that event, but they said it had taken place before their time, or when they were still very young. Eligio added that people secretly believed that Cevicas had been only a fool, and that no one could harm a real sorcerer. I tried to question them further on their opinions about sorcerers. They did not seem to have much interest in the subject; besides, they were eager to start out and shoot the .22 rifle I had brought.

We were silent for a while as we walked toward the thick chaparral, then Eligio, who was at the head of the line, turned around and said to me, "Perhaps we're the crazy ones. Perhaps don Juan is right. Look at the way we live."

Lucio and Benigno protested. I tried to mediate. I agreed with Eligio and told them that I myself had felt that the way I lived was somehow wrong. Benigno said that I had no business complaining about my life, that I had money and I had a car. I retorted that I could easily say that they themselves were better off because each owned a piece of land. They responded in unison that the owner of their land was the federal bank. I told them that I did not own my car either, that a bank in California owned it, and that my life was only different but not better than theirs. By that time we were already in the dense shrubs.

We did not find any deer or wild boars, but we got three jack rabbits. On our return we stopped at Lucio's house and he announced that his wife was going to make rabbit stew. Benigno went to the store to buy a bottle of tequila and get us some sodas. When we came back don Juan was with him.

"Did you find my grandpa at the store buying beer?" Lucio asked laughing.

"I haven't been invited to this reunion," don Juan said. "I've just dropped by to ask Carlos if he's leaving for Hermosillo."

I told him I was planning to leave the next day, and while we talked Benigno distributed the bottles. Eligio gave his to don Juan, and since among the Yaquis it is deadly impolite to refuse, even as a courtesy, don Juan took it quietly. I gave mine to Eligio, and he was obliged to take it. So Benigno in turn gave me his bottle. But Lucio, who had obviously visualized the entire scheme of Yaqui good manners, had already finished drinking his soda. He turned to Benigno, who had a pathetic look on his face, and said, laughing, "They've screwed you out of your bottle."

Don Juan said he never drank soda and placed his bottle in Benigno's hands. We sat under the *ramada* in silence.

Eligio seemed to be nervous. He fidgeted with the brim of his hat.

"I've been thinking about what you said the other night," he said to don Juan. "How can peyote change our life? How?"

Don Juan did not answer. He stared fixedly at Eligio for a moment and then began to sing in Yaqui. It was not a song proper but a short recitation. We remained quiet for a long time. Then I asked don Juan to translate the Yaqui words for me.

"That was only for Yaquis," he said matter-of-factly.

I felt dejected. I was sure he had said something of great importance.

"Eligio is an Indian," don Juan finally said to me, "and as an Indian Eligio has nothing. We Indians have nothing. All you see around here belongs to the Yoris. The Yaquis have only their wrath and what the land offers to them freely."

Nobody uttered a sound for quite some time, then don Juan stood up and said goodbye and walked away. We looked at him until he had disappeared behind a bend of the road. All of us seemed to be nervous. Lucio told us in a disoriented manner that his grandfather had not stayed because he hated rabbit stew. Eligio seemed to be immersed in thoughts. Benigno turned to me and said loudly, "I think the Lord is going to punish you and don Juan for what you're doing."

Lucio began to laugh and Benigno joined him.

"You're clowning, Benigno," Eligio said somberly. "What you've just said isn't worth a damn."

September 15, 1968

It was nine o'clock Saturday night. Don Juan sat in front of Eligio in the center of the *ramada* of Lucio's house. Don Juan placed his sack of peyote buttons between them and sang while rocking his body slightly back and forth. Lucio, Benigno, and I sat five or six feet behind Eligio with our backs against the wall. It was quite dark at first. We had been sitting inside the house under the gasoline lantern waiting for don Juan. He had called us out to the *ramada* when he arrived and had told us where to sit. After a while my eyes became accustomed to the dark. I could see everyone clearly. I noticed that Eligio seemed to be terrified. His entire body shook; his teeth chattered uncontrollably. He was convulsed with spasmodic jerks of his head and back.

Don Juan spoke to him, telling him not to be afraid, and to trust the protector, and to think of nothing else. He casually took a peyote button, offered it to Eligio, and ordered him to chew it very slowly. Eligio whined like a puppy and recoiled. His breathing was very rapid, it sounded like the whizzing of bellows. He took off his hat and wiped his forehead. He covered his face with his hands. I thought he was crying. It was a very long, tense moment before he regained some control over himself. He sat up straight and, still covering his face with one hand, took the peyote button and began chewing it.

I felt a tremendous apprehension. I had not realized until then that I was perhaps as scared as Eligio. My mouth had a dryness similar to that produced by peyote. Eligio chewed the button for a long time. My tension increased. I began to whine involuntarily as my respiration became more accelerated.

Don Juan began to chant louder, then he offered another button to Eligio and after Eligio had finished it he offered him dry fruit and told him to chew it very slowly.

Eligio got up repeatedly and went to the bushes. At one point he asked for water. Don Juan told him not to drink it but only swish it in his mouth.

Eligio chewed two more buttons and don Juan gave him dry meat.

By the time he had chewed his tenth button I was nearly sick with anxiety.

Suddenly Eligio slumped forward and his forehead hit the ground. He rolled on his left side and jerked convulsively. I looked at my watch. It was twenty after eleven. Eligio tossed, wobbled, and moaned for over an hour while he lay on the floor.

Don Juan maintained the same position in front of him. His peyote songs were almost a murmur. Benigno, who was sitting to my right, looked inattentive; Lucio, next to him, had slumped on his side and was snoring.

Eligio's body crumpled into a contorted position. He lay on his right side with his front toward me and his hands between his legs. His body gave a powerful jump and he turned on his back with his legs slightly curved. His left hand waved out and up with an extremely free and elegant motion. His right hand repeated the same pattern, and then both arms alternated in a wavering, slow movement, resembling that of a harpist. The movement became more vigorous by degrees. His arms had a perceptible vibration and went up and down like pistons.

At the same time his hands rotated onward at the wrist and his fingers quivered. It was a beautiful, harmonious, hypnotic sight. I thought his rhythm and muscular control were beyond comparison.

Eligio then rose slowly, as if he were stretching against an enveloping force. His body shivered. He squatted and then pushed himself up to an erect position. His arms, trunk, and head trembled as if an intermittent electric current were going through them. It was as though a force outside his control was setting him or driving him up.

Don Juan's chanting became very loud. Lucio and Benigno woke up and looked at the scene uninterestedly for a while and then went back to sleep.

Eligio seemed to be moving up and up. He was apparently climbing. He cupped his hands and seemed to grab onto objects beyond my vision. He pushed himself up and paused to catch his breath.

I wanted to see his eyes and moved closer to him, but don Juan gave me a fierce look and I recoiled to my place.

Then Eligio jumped. It was a final, formidable leap. He had apparently reached his goal. He puffed and sobbed with the exertion. He seemed to be holding onto a ledge. But something was overtaking him. He shrieked desperately. His grip faltered and he began to fall. His body arched backward and was convulsed from head to toe with the most beautiful, coordinated ripple. The ripple went through him perhaps a hundred times before his body collapsed like a lifeless burlap sack.

After a while he extended his arms in front of him as though he was protecting his face. His legs stretched out backward as he lay on his chest; they were arched a few inches above the ground, giving his body the very appearance of sliding or flying at an incredible speed. His head was arched as far back as possible, his arms locked over his eyes, shielding them. I could feel the wind hissing around him. I gasped and gave a loud involuntary shriek. Lucio and Benigno woke and looked at Eligio curiously.

"If you promise to buy me a motorcycle I will chew it now," Lucio said loudly.

I looked at don Juan. He made an imperative gesture with his head.

"Son of a bitch!" Lucio mumbled, and went back to sleep.

Eligio stood up and began walking. He took a couple of steps toward me and stopped. I could see him smiling with a beatific expression. He tried to whistle. There was no clear sound yet it had harmony. It was a tune. It had only a couple of bars, which he repeated over and over. After a while the whistling was distinctly audible, and then it became a sharp melody. Eligio mumbled unintelligible words. The words seemed to be the lyrics to the tune. He repeated it for hours. A very simple song, repetitious, monotonous, and yet strangely beautiful.

Eligio seemed to be looking at something while he sang. At one moment he got very close to me. I saw his eyes in the semidarkness. They were glassy, transfixed. He smiled and giggled. He walked and sat down and walked again, groaning and sighing.

Suddenly something seemed to have pushed him from behind. His body arched in the middle as though moved by a direct force. At one instant Eligio was balanced on the tips of his toes, making nearly a complete circle, his hands touching the ground. He dropped to the ground again, softly, on his back, and extended his whole length, acquiring a strange rigidity.

He whimpered and groaned for a while, then began to snore. Don Juan covered him with some burlap sacks. It was 5:35 A.M.

Lucio and Benigno had fallen asleep shoulder to shoulder with their backs against the wall. Don Juan and I sat quietly for a very long time. He seemed to be tired. I broke the silence and asked him about Eligio. He told me that Eligio's encounter with Mescalito had been exceptionally successful; Mescalito had taught him a song the first time they met and that was indeed extraordinary.

I asked him why he had not let Lucio take some for a

motorcycle. He said that Mescalito would have killed Lucio if he had approached him under such conditions. Don Juan admitted that he had prepared everything carefully to convince his grandson; he told me that he had counted on my friendship with Lucio as the central part of his strategy. He said that Lucio had always been his great concern, and that at one time they had lived together and were very close, but Lucio became gravely ill when he was seven and don Juan's son, a devout Catholic, made a vow to the Virgin of Guadalupe that Lucio would join a sacred dancing society if his life were spared. Lucio recovered and was forced to carry out the promise. He lasted one week as an apprentice, and then made up his mind to break the vow. He thought he would have to die as a result of it, braced himself, and for a whole day he waited for death to come. Everybody made fun of the boy and the incident was never forgotten.

Don Juan did not speak for a long time. He seemed to have become engulfed by thoughts.

"My setup was for Lucio," he said, "and I found Eligio instead. I knew it was useless, but when we like someone we should properly insist, as though it were possible to remake men. Lucio had courage when he was a little boy and then he lost it along the way."

"Can you bewitch him, don Juan?"

"Bewitch him? For what?"

"So he will change and regain his courage."

"You don't bewitch for courage. Courage is something personal. Bewitching is for rendering people harmless or sick or dumb. You don't bewitch to make warriors. To be a warrior you have to be crystal clear, like Eligio. There you have a man of courage!"

Eligio snored peacefully under the burlap sacks. It was already daylight. The sky was impeccably blue. There were no clouds in sight.

"I would give anything in this world," I said, "to know about Eligio's journey. Would you mind if I asked him to tell me?"

"You should not under any circumstances ask him to do that!"

"Why not? I tell you about my experiences."

"That's different. It is not your inclination to keep things to yourself. Eligio is an Indian. His journey is all he has. I wish it had been Lucio."

"Isn't there anything you can do, don Juan?"

"No. Unfortunately there is no way to make bones for a jellyfish. It was only my folly."

The sun came out. Its light blurred my tired eyes.

"You've told me time and time again, don Juan, that a sorcerer cannot have follies. I've never thought you could have any."

Don Juan looked at me piercingly. He got up, glanced at Eligio and then at Lucio. He tucked his hat on his head, patting it on its top.

"It's possible to insist, to properly insist, even though we know that what we're doing is useless," he said, smiling. "But we must know first that our acts are useless and yet we must proceed as if we didn't know it. That's a sorcerer's controlled folly."

5

I returned to don Juan's house on October 3, 1968, for the sole purpose of asking him about the events surrounding Eligio's initiation. An almost endless stream of questions had occurred to me while rereading the account of what took place then. I was after very precise explanations so I made a list of questions beforehand, carefully choosing the most appropriate words.

I began by asking him: "Did I *see* that night, don Juan?"

"You almost did."

"Did you *see* that I was *seeing* Eligio's movements?"

"Yes. I *saw* that Mescalito was allowing you to *see*

part of Eligio's lesson, otherwise you would've been looking at a man sitting there, or perhaps lying there. During
the last mitote you did not notice that the men were doing
anything, did you?"

At the last mitote I had not noticed any of the men
performing movements out of the ordinary. I told him I
could safely say that all I had recorded in my notes was
that some of them got up and went to the bushes more
often than others.

"But you nearly *saw* Eligio's entire lesson," don Juan
went on. "Think about that. Do you understand now how
generous Mescalito is with you? Mescalito has never been
so gentle with anyone, to my knowledge. Not anyone. And
yet you have no regard for his generosity. How can you
turn your back on him so bluntly? Or perhaps I should
say, in exchange for what are you turning your back on
Mescalito?"

I felt that don Juan was cornering me again. I was
unable to answer his question. I had always believed I
had quit the apprenticeship in order to save myself, yet I
had no idea from what I was saving myself, or for what.
I wanted to change the direction of our conversation
quickly, and to that end I abandoned my intention to
carry on with all my precalculated questions and brought
out my most important query.

"I wonder if you could tell me more about your controlled folly," I said.

"What do you want to know about it?"

"Please tell me, don Juan, what exactly is controlled
folly?"

Don Juan laughed loudly and made a smacking sound
by slapping his thigh with the hollow of his hand.

"This is controlled folly!" he said, and laughed and
slapped his thigh again.

"What do you mean . . . ?"

"I am happy that you finally asked me about my controlled folly after so many years, and yet it wouldn't have
mattered to me in the least if you had never asked. Yet I
have chosen to feel happy, as if I cared, that you asked,
as if it would matter that I care. *That* is controlled folly!"

We both laughed very loudly. I hugged him. I found his explanation delightful although I did not quite understand it.

We were sitting, as usual, in the area right in front of the door of his house. It was mid-morning. Don Juan had a pile of seeds in front of him and was picking the debris from them. I had offered to help him but he had turned me down; he said the seeds were a gift for one of his friends in central Mexico and I did not have enough power to touch them.

"With whom do you exercise controlled folly, don Juan?" I asked after a long silence.

He chuckled.

"With everybody!" he exclaimed, smiling.

"When do you choose to exercise it, then?"

"Every single time I act."

I felt I needed to recapitulate at that point and I asked him if controlled folly meant that his acts were never sincere but were only the acts of an actor.

"My acts are sincere," he said, "but they are only the acts of an actor."

"Then everything you do must be controlled folly!" I said truly surprised.

"Yes, everything," he said.

"But it can't be true," I protested, "that every one of your acts is only controlled folly."

"Why not?" he replied with a mysterious look.

"That would mean that nothing matters to you and you don't really care about anything or anybody. Take me, for example. Do you mean that you don't care whether or not I become a man of knowledge, or whether I live, or die, or do anything?"

"True! I don't. You are like Lucio, or everybody else in my life, my controlled folly."

I experienced a peculiar feeling of emptiness. Obviously there was no reason in the world why don Juan had to care about me, but on the other hand I had almost the certainty that he cared about me personally; I thought it could not be otherwise, since he had always given me his undivided attention during every moment I had spent with him. It occurred to me that perhaps don Juan was just saying that because he was annoyed with me. After all, I had quit his teachings.

"I have the feeling we are not talking about the same thing," I said. "I shouldn't have used myself as an example. What I meant to say was that there must be something in the world you care about in a way that is not controlled folly. I don't think it is possible to go on living if nothing really matters to us."

"That applies to *you*," he said. "Things matter to *you*. You asked me about my controlled folly and I told you that everything I do in regard to myself and my fellow men is folly, because nothing matters."

"My point is, don Juan, that if nothing matters to you, how can you go on living?"

He laughed and after a moment's pause, in which he seemed to deliberate whether or not to answer, he got up and went to the back of his house. I followed him.

"Wait, wait, don Juan." I said. "I really want to know; you must explain to me what you mean."

"Perhaps it's not possible to explain," he said. "Certain things in your life matter to you because they're important; your acts are certainly important to you, but for me, not a single thing is important any longer, neither my acts nor the acts of any of my fellow men. I go on living, though, because I have my will. Because I have tempered my will throughout my life until it's neat and wholesome and now it doesn't matter to me that nothing matters. My will controls the folly of my life."

He squatted and ran his fingers on some herbs that he had put to dry in the sun on a big piece of burlap.

I was bewildered. Never would I have anticipated the direction that my query had taken. After a long pause I thought of a good point. I told him that in my opinion some of the acts of my fellow men were of supreme importance. I pointed out that a nuclear war was definitely the most dramatic example of such an act. I said that for me destroying life on the face of the earth was an act of staggering enormity.

"You believe that because you're thinking. You're

thinking about life," don Juan said with a glint in his eyes. "You're not *seeing*."

"Would I feel differently if I could *see?*" I asked.

"Once a man learns to *see* he finds himself alone in the world with nothing but folly," don Juan said cryptically.

He paused for a moment and looked at me as if he wanted to judge the effect of his words.

"Your acts, as well as the acts of your fellow men in general, appear to be important to you because you have *learned* to think they are important."

He used the word "learned" with such a peculiar inflection that it forced me to ask what he meant by it.

He stopped handling his plants and looked at me.

"We learn to think about everything," he said, "and then we train our eyes to look as we think about the things we look at. We look at ourselves already thinking that we are important. And therefore we've got to *feel* important! But then when a man learns to *see,* he realizes that he can no longer think about the things he looks at, and if he cannot think about what he looks at everything becomes unimportant."

Don Juan must have noticed my puzzled look and repeated his statements three times, as if to make me understand them. What he said sounded to me like gibberish at first, but upon thinking about it, his words loomed more like a sophisticated statement about some facet of perception.

I tried to think of a good question that would make him clarify his point, but I could not think of anything. All of a sudden I felt exhausted and could not formulate my thoughts clearly.

Don Juan seemed to notice my fatigue and patted me gently.

"Clean these plants here," he said, "and then shred them carefully into this jar."

He handed me a large coffee jar and left.

He returned to his house hours later, in the late afternoon. I had finished shredding his plants and had had plenty of time to write my notes. I wanted to ask him some questions right off, but he was not in any mood to answer me. He said he was famished and had to fix his food first. He lit a fire in his earthen stove and set up a pot with bone-broth stock. He looked in the bag of groceries I had brought and took some vegetables, sliced them into small pieces, and dumped them into the pot. Then he lay on his mat, kicked off his sandals, and told me to sit closer to the stove so I could feed the fire.

It was almost dark; from where I sat I could see the sky to the west. The edges of some thick cloud formations were tinted with a deep buff, while the center of the clouds remained almost black.

I was going to make a comment on how beautiful the clouds were, but he spoke first.

"Fluffy edges and a thick core," he said, pointing at the clouds.

His statement was so perfectly apropos that it made me jump.

"I was just going to tell you about the clouds," I said.

"Then I beat you to it," he said, and laughed with childlike abandon.

I asked him if he was in a mood to answer some questions.

"What do you want to know?" he replied.

"What you told me this afternoon about controlled folly has disturbed me very much," I said. "I really cannot understand what you meant."

"Of course you cannot understand it," he said. "You are trying to think about it, and what I said does not fit with your thoughts."

"I'm trying to think about it," I said, "because that's the only way I personally can understand anything. For example, don Juan, do you mean that once a man learns to *see*, everything in the whole world is worthless?"

"I didn't say worthless. I said unimportant. Everything is equal and therefore unimportant. For example, there is no way for me to say that my acts are more important than yours, or that one thing is more essential than another, therefore all things are equal and by being equal they are unimportant."

I asked him if his statements were a pronouncement

that what he had called "seeing" was in effect a "better way" than merely "looking at things." He said that the eyes of man could perform both functions, but neither of them was better than the other; however, to train the eyes only to look was, in his opinion, an unnecessary loss.

"For instance, we need to look with our eyes to laugh," he said, "because only when we look at things can we catch the funny edge of the world. On the other hand, when our eyes *see*, everything is so equal that nothing is funny."

"Do you mean, don Juan, that a man who *sees* cannot ever laugh?"

He remained silent for some time.

"Perhaps there are men of knowledge who never laugh," he said. "I don't know any of them, though. Those I know *see* and also look, so they laugh."

"Would a man of knowledge cry as well?"

"I suppose so. Our eyes look so we may laugh, or cry, or rejoice, or be sad, or be happy. I personally don't like to be sad, so whenever I witness something that would ordinarily make me sad, I simply shift my eyes and *see* it instead of looking at it. But when I encounter something funny I look and I laugh."

"But then, don Juan, your laughter is real and not controlled folly."

Don Juan stared at me for a moment.

"I talk to you because you make me laugh," he said. "You remind me of some bushy-tailed rats of the desert that get caught when they stick their tails in holes trying to scare other rats away in order to steal their food. You get caught in your own questions. Watch out! Sometimes those rats yank their tails off trying to pull themselves free."

I found his comparison funny and I laughed. Don Juan had once shown me some small rodents with bushy tails that looked like fat squirrels; the image of one of those chubby rats yanking its tail off was sad and at the same time morbidly funny.

"My laughter, as well as everything I do, is real," he

said, "but it also is controlled folly because it is useless; it changes nothing and yet I still do it."

"But as I understand it, don Juan, your laughter is not useless. It makes you happy."

"No! I am happy because I choose to look at things that make me happy and then my eyes catch their funny edge and I laugh. I have said this to you countless times. One must always choose the path with heart in order to be at one's best, perhaps so one can always laugh."

I interpreted what he had said as meaning that crying was inferior to laughter, or at least perhaps an act that weakened us. He asserted that there was no intrinsic difference and that both were unimportant; he said, however, that his preference was laughter, because laughter made his body feel better than crying.

At that point I suggested that if one has a preference there is no equality; if he preferred laughing to crying, the former was indeed more important.

He stubbornly maintained that his preference did not mean they were not equal; and I insisted that our argument could be logically stretched to saying that if things were supposed to be so equal why not also choose death?

"Many men of knowledge do that," he said. "One day they may simply disappear. People may think that they have been ambushed and killed because of their doings. They choose to die because it doesn't matter to them. On the other hand, I choose to live, and to laugh, not because it matters, but because that choice is the bent of my nature. The reason I say I choose is because I *see*, but it isn't that I choose to live; my will makes me go on living in spite of anything I may *see*.

"You don't understand me now because of your habit of thinking as you look and thinking as you think."

This statement intrigued me very much. I asked him to explain what he meant by it.

He repeated the same construct various times, as if giving himself time to arrange it in different terms, and then delivered his point, saying that by "thinking" he meant the constant idea that we have of everything in the world. He

said that "seeing" dispelled that habit and until I learned
to "see" I could not really understand what he meant.

"But if nothing matters, don Juan, why should it matter
that I learn to *see*?"

"I told you once that our lot as men is to learn, for
good or bad," he said. "I have learned to *see* and I tell
you that nothing really matters; now it is your turn; perhaps some day you will *see* and you will know then
whether things matter or not. For me nothing matters, but
perhaps for you everything will. You should know by now
that a man of knowledge lives by acting, not by thinking
about acting, nor by thinking about what he will think
when he has finished acting. A man of knowledge chooses
a path with heart and follows it; and then he looks and
rejoices and laughs; and then he *sees* and knows. He
knows that his life will be over altogether too soon; he
knows that he, as well as everybody else, is not going
anywhere; he knows, because he *sees,* that nothing is more
important than anything else. In other words, a man of
knowledge has no honor, no dignity, no family, no name,
no country, but only life to be lived, and under these
circumstances his only tie to his fellow men is his controlled folly. Thus a man of knowledge endeavors, and
sweats, and puffs, and if one looks at him he is just like
any ordinary man, except that the folly of his life is under
control. Nothing being more important than anything else,
a man of knowledge chooses any act, and acts it out as if
it matters to him. His controlled folly makes him say that
what he does matters and makes him act as if it did, and
yet he knows that it doesn't; so when he fulfills his acts he
retreats in peace, and whether his acts were good or bad,
or worked or didn't, is in no way part of his concern.

"A man of knowledge may choose, on the other hand,
to remain totally impassive and never act, and behave as
if to be impassive really matters to him; he will be rightfully true at that too, because that would also be his controlled folly."

I involved myself at this point in a very complicated
effort to explain to don Juan that I was interested in knowing what would motivate a man of knowledge to act in a

particular way in spite of the fact that he knew nothing mattered.

He chuckled softly before answering.

"You think about your acts," he said. "Therefore you have to believe your acts are as important as you think they are, when in reality nothing of what one does is important. Nothing! But then if nothing really matters, as you asked me, how can I go on living? It would be simple to die; that's what you say and believe, because you're thinking about life, just as you're thinking now what *seeing* would be like. You wanted me to describe it to you so you could begin to think about it, the way you do with everything else. In the case of *seeing,* however, thinking is not the issue at all, so I cannot tell you what it is like to *see.* Now you want me to describe the reasons for my controlled folly and I can only tell you that controlled folly is very much like *seeing;* it is something you cannot think about."

He yawned. He lay on his back and stretched his arms and legs. His bones made a cracking sound.

"You have been away too long," he said. "You think too much."

He got up and walked into the thick chaparral at the side of the house. I fed the fire to keep the pot boiling. I was going to light a kerosene lantern but the semidarkness was very soothing. The fire from the stove, which supplied enough light to write, also created a reddish glow all around me. I put my notes on the ground and lay down. I felt tired. Out of the whole conversation with don Juan the only poignant thing in my mind was that he did not care about me; it disturbed me immensely. Over a period of years I had put my trust in him. Had I not had complete confidence in him I would have been paralyzed with fear at the prospect of learning his knowledge; the premise on which I had based my trust was the idea that he cared about me personally; actually I had always been afraid of him, but I had kept my fear in check because I trusted him. When he removed that basis I had nothing to fall back on and I felt helpless.

A very strange anxiety possessed me. I became extremely agitated and began pacing up and down in front of the stove. Don Juan was taking a long time. I waited for him impatiently.

He returned a while later; he sat down again in front of the fire and I blurted out my fears. I told him that I worried because I was incapable of changing directions in midstream; I explained to him that together with the trust I had in him, I had also learned to respect and to regard his way of life as being intrinsically more rational, or at least more functional, than mine. I said that his words had plunged me into a terrible conflict because they entailed my having to change my feelings. To illustrate my point I told don Juan the story of an old man of my culture, a very wealthy, conservative lawyer who lived his life convinced that he upheld the truth. In the early thirties, with the advent of the New Deal, he found himself passionately involved in the political drama of that time. He was categorically sure that change was deleterious to the country, and out of devotion to his way of life and the conviction that he was right, he vowed to fight what he thought to be a political evil. But the tide of the time was too strong, it overpowered him. He struggled for ten years against it in the political arena and in the realm of his personal life; then the Second World War sealed his efforts into total defeat. His political and ideological downfall resulted in a profound bitterness; he became a self-exile for twenty-five years. When I met him he was eighty-four years old and had come back to his home town to spend his last years in a home for the aged. It seemed inconceivable to me that he had lived that long, considering the way he had squandered his life in bitterness and self-pity. Somehow he found my company amenable and we used to talk at great length.

The last time I saw him he had concluded our conversation with the following: "I have had time to turn around and examine my life. The issues of my time are today only a story; not even an interesting one. Perhaps I threw away years of my life chasing something that never existed. I've had the feeling lately that I believed in something farcical. It wasn't worth my while. I think I know that. However, I can't retrieve the forty years I've lost."

I told don Juan that my conflict arose from the doubts into which his words about controlled folly had thrown me.

"If nothing really matters," I said, "upon becoming a man of knowledge one would find oneself, perforce, as empty as my friend and in no better position."

"That's not so," don Juan said cuttingly. "Your friend is lonely because he will die without *seeing*. In his life he just grew old and now he must have more self-pity than ever before. He feels he threw away forty years because he was after victories and found only defeats. He'll never know that to be victorious and to be defeated are equal.

"So now you're afraid of me because I've told you that you're equal to everything else. You're being childish. Our lot as men is to learn and one goes to knowledge as one goes to war; I have told you this countless times. One goes to knowledge or to war with fear, with respect, aware that one is going to war, and with absolute confidence in oneself. Put your trust in yourself, not in me.

"And so you're afraid of the emptiness of your friend's life. But there's no emptiness in the life of a man of knowledge, I tell you. Everything is filled to the brim."

Don Juan stood up and extended his arms as if feeling things in the air.

"Everything is filled to the brim," he repeated, "and everything is equal. I'm not like your friend who just grew old. When I tell you that nothing matters I don't mean it the way he does. For him, his struggle was not worth his while, because he was defeated; for me there is no victory, or defeat, or emptiness. Everything is filled to the brim and everything is equal and my struggle was worth my while.

"In order to become a man of knowledge one must be a warrior, not a whimpering child. One must strive without giving up, without a complaint, without flinching, until one *sees,* only to realize then that nothing matters."

Don Juan stirred the pot with a wooden spoon. The food

was ready. He took the pot off the fire and placed it on an
adobe rectangular block, which he had built against the
wall and which he used as a shelf or a table. With his foot
he shoved two small boxes that served as comfortable
chairs, especially if one sat with his back against the sup-
porting beams of the wall. He signaled me to sit down and
then he poured a bowl of soup. He smiled; his eyes were
shining as if he were truly enjoying my presence. He
pushed the bowl gently toward me. There was such a
warmth and kindness in his gesture that it seemed to be an
appeal to restore my trust in him. I felt idiotic; I tried to
disrupt my mood by looking for my spoon, but I couldn't
find it. The soup was too hot to be drunk directly from
the bowl, and while it cooled off I asked don Juan if controlled folly meant that a man of knowledge could not
like anybody any more.

He stopped eating and laughed.

"You're too concerned with liking people or with being
liked yourself," he said. "A man of knowledge likes, that's
all. He likes whatever or whoever he wants, but he uses his
controlled folly to be unconcerned about it. The opposite
of what you are doing now. To like people or to be liked
by people is not all one can do as a man."

He stared at me for a moment with his head tilted a
little to one side.

"Think about that," he said.

"There is one more thing I want to ask, don Juan. You
said that we need to look with our eyes to laugh, but I
believe we laugh because we think. Take a blind man, he
also laughs."

"No," he said. "Blind men don't laugh. Their bodies
jerk a little with the ripple of laughter. They have never
looked at the funny edge of the world and have to
imagine it. Their laughter is not roaring."

We did not speak any more. I had a sensation of well-
being, of happiness. We ate in silence; then don Juan
began to laugh. I was using a dry twig to spoon the vegetables into my mouth.

October 4, 1968

At a certain moment today I asked don Juan if he minded talking a bit more about "seeing." He seemed to deliberate for an instant, then he smiled and said that I was again involved in my usual routine, trying to talk instead of doing.

"If you want to *see* you have to let the smoke guide you," he said emphatically. "I won't talk about this any more."

I was helping him clean some dry herbs. We worked in complete silence for a long time. When I am forced into a prolonged silence I always feel apprehensive, especially around don Juan. At a given moment I brought up a question to him in a sort of compulsive, almost belligerent outburst.

"How does a man of knowledge exercise controlled folly when it comes to the death of a person he loves?" I asked.

Don Juan was taken aback by my question and looked at me quizzically.

"Take your grandson Lucio," I said. "Would your acts be controlled folly at the time of his death?"

"Take my son Eulalio, that's a better example," don Juan replied calmly. "He was crushed by rocks while working in the construction of the Pan-American Highway. My acts toward him at the moment of his death were controlled folly. When I came down to the blasting area he was almost dead, but his body was so strong that it kept on moving and kicking. I stood in front of him and told the boys in the road crew not to move him any more; they obeyed me and stood there surrounding my son, looking at his mangled body. I stood there too, but I did not look. I shifted my eyes so I would *see* his personal life disintegrating, expanding uncontrollably beyond its limits, like a fog of crystals, because that is the way life and death mix and expand. That is what I did at the time of my son's death. That's all one could ever do, and that is controlled folly. Had I looked at him I would have watched him becoming immobile and I would have felt a cry inside of me, because never again would I look at his fine figure pacing the earth. I *saw* his death instead, and there was no sadness, no feeling. His death was equal to everything else."

Don Juan was quiet for a moment. He seemed to be sad, but then he smiled and tapped my head.

"So you may say that when it comes to the death of a person I love, my controlled folly is to shift my eyes."

I thought about the people I love myself and a terribly oppressive wave of self-pity enveloped me.

"Lucky you, don Juan," I said. "You can shift your eyes, while I can only look."

He found my statement funny and laughed.

"Lucky, bull!" he said. "It's hard work."

We both laughed. After a long silence I began probing him again, perhaps only to dispel my own sadness.

"If I have understood you correctly then, don Juan," I said, "the only acts in the life of a man of knowledge which are not controlled folly are those he performs with his ally or with Mescalito. Isn't that right?"

"That's right," he said, chuckling. "My ally and Mescalito are not on a par with us human beings. My controlled folly applies only to myself and to the acts I perform while in the company of my fellow men."

"However, it is a logical possibility," I said, "to think that a man of knowledge may also regard his acts with his ally or with Mescalito as controlled folly, true?"

He stared at me for a moment.

"You're thinking again," he said. "A man of knowledge doesn't think, therefore he cannot encounter that possibility. Take me, for example. I say that my controlled folly applies to the acts I performed while in the company of my fellow men; I say that because I can *see* my fellow men. However, I cannot *see* through my ally and that makes it incomprehensible to me, so how could I control my folly if I don't *see* through it? With my ally or with Mescalito I am only a man who knows how to *see* and finds that he's baffled by what he *sees;* a man who knows that he'll never understand all that is around him.

"Take your case, for instance. It doesn't matter to me

whether you become a man of knowledge or not; however, it matters to Mescalito. Obviously it matters to him or he wouldn't take so many steps to show his concern about you. I can notice his concern and I act toward it, yet his reasons are incomprehensible to me."

6

Just as we were getting into my car to start on a trip to central Mexico, on October 5, 1968, don Juan stopped me.

"I have told you before," he said with a serious expression, "that one should never reveal the name nor the whereabouts of a sorcerer. I believe you understood that you should never reveal my name nor the place where my body is. Now I am going to ask you to do the same with a friend of mine, a friend you will call Genaro. We are going to his house; we will spend some time there."

I assured don Juan that I had never betrayed his confidence.

"I know that," he said without changing his serious expression. "Yet I am concerned with your becoming thoughtless."

I protested and don Juan said his aim was only to remind me that every time one was careless in matters of sorcery, one was playing with an imminent and senseless death that could be averted by being thoughtful and aware.

"We will not touch upon this matter any longer," he said. "Once we leave my house we will not mention Genaro, nor will we think about him. I want you to put your thoughts in order now. When you meet him you must be clear and have no doubts in your mind."

"What kinds of doubts are you referring to, don Juan?"

"Any kinds of doubts whatever. When you meet him you ought to be crystal clear. He will *see* you!"

His strange admonitions made me very apprehensive. I mentioned that perhaps I should not meet his friend at all but only drive to the vicinity of his friend's house and leave him there.

"What I've told you was only a precaution," he said. "You've met one sorcerer already, Vicente, and he nearly killed you. Watch out this time!"

After we arrived in central Mexico it took us two days to walk from where I left my car to his friend's house, a little shack perched on the side of a mountain. Don Juan's friend was at the door, as if he had been waiting for us. I recognized him immediately. I had already made his acquaintance, although very briefly, when I brought my book to don Juan. I had not really looked at him at that time, except in a glancing fashion, so I had had the feeling he was as old as don Juan. As he stood at the door of his house, however, I noticed that he was definitely younger. He was perhaps in his early sixties. He was shorter than don Juan and slimmer, very dark and wiry. His hair was thick and graying and a bit long; it ran over his ears and forehead. His face was round and hard. A very prominent nose made him look like a bird of prey with small dark eyes.

He talked to don Juan first. Don Juan nodded affirmatively. They conversed briefly. They were not speaking Spanish so I did not understand what they were saying. Then don Genaro turned to me.

"You're welcome to my humble little shack," he said apologetically in Spanish.

His words were a polite formula I had heard before in various rural areas of Mexico. Yet as he said the words he laughed joyously for no overt reason, and I knew he was exercising his controlled folly. He did not care in the least that his house was a shack. I liked don Genaro very much.

For the next two days we went into the mountains to collect plants. Don Juan, don Genaro, and I left each day at the crack of dawn. The two old men went together to some specific but unidentified part of the mountains and left me alone in one area of the woods. I had an exquisite feeling there. I did not notice the passage of time, nor was I apprehensive at staying alone; the extraordinary experience I had both days was an uncanny capacity to concentrate on the delicate task of finding the specific plants don Juan had entrusted me to collect.

We returned to the house in the late afternoon and both days I was so tired that I fell asleep immediately.

The third day, however, was different. The three of us worked together, and don Juan asked don Genaro to teach me how to select certain plants. We returned around noon and the two old men sat for hours in front of the house, in complete silence, as if they were in a state of trance. Yet they were not asleep. I walked around them a couple of times; don Juan followed my movements with his eyes, and so did don Genaro.

"You must talk to the plants before you pick them," don Juan said. He dropped his words casually and repeated his statement three times, as if to catch my attention. Nobody had said a word until he spoke.

"In order to *see* the plants you must talk to them personally," he went on. "You must get to know them individually; then the plants can tell you anything you care to know about them."

It was late in the afternoon. Don Juan was sitting on a flat rock facing the western mountains; don Genaro was sitting by him on a straw mat with his face toward the north. Don Juan had told me, the first day we were there, that those were their "positions" and that I had to sit on the ground at any place opposite to both of them. He added that while we sat in those positions I had to keep my face toward the southeast and look at them only in brief glances.

"Yes, that's the way it is with plants, isn't it?" don Juan said and turned to don Genaro, who agreed with an affirmative gesture.

I told him that the reason I had not followed his instructions was because I felt a little stupid talking to plants.

"You fail to understand that a sorcerer is not joking," he said severely. "When a sorcerer attempts to *see*, he attempts to gain power."

Don Genaro was staring at me. I was taking notes and that seemed to baffle him. He smiled at me, shook his head, and said something to don Juan. Don Juan shrugged his shoulders. To see me writing must have been quite odd for don Genaro. Don Juan was, I suppose, habituated to my taking notes, and the fact that I wrote while he spoke was no longer odd to him; he could carry on talking without appearing to notice my acts. Don Genaro, however, kept on laughing, and I had to stop writing in order not to disrupt the mood of the conversation.

Don Juan affirmed again that a sorcerer's acts were not to be taken as jokes because a sorcerer played with death at every turn of the way. Then he proceeded to relate to don Genaro the story of how one night I had looked at the lights of death following me during one of our trips. The story proved to be utterly funny; don Genaro rolled on the ground laughing.

Don Juan apologized to me and said that his friend was given to explosions of laughter. I glanced at don Genaro, who I thought was still rolling on the ground, and saw him performing a most unusual act. He was standing on his head without the aid of his arms or hands, and his legs were crossed as if he were sitting. The sight was so incongruous that it made me jump. When I realized he was doing something almost impossible, from the point of view of body mechanics, he had gone back again to a normal sitting position. Don Juan, however, seemed to be cognizant of what was involved and celebrated don Genaro's performance with roaring laughter.

Don Genaro seemed to have noticed my confusion; he clapped his hands a couple of times and rolled on the ground again; apparently he wanted me to watch him. What had at first appeared to be rolling on the ground was actually leaning over in a sitting position, and touching the ground with his head. He seemingly attained his illogical posture by gaining momentum, leaning over several times, until the inertia carried his body to a vertical stand, so that for an instant he "sat on his head."

When their laughter subsided don Juan continued talking; his tone was very severe. I shifted the position of my body in order to be at ease and give him all my attention. He did not smile at all, as he usually does, especially when I try to pay deliberate attention to what he is saying. Don Genaro kept looking at me as if he were expecting me to start writing again, but I did not take notes any more. Don Juan's words were a reprimand for not talking to the plants I had collected, as he had always told me to do. He said the plants I had killed could also have killed me; he said he was sure they would, sooner or later, make me get ill. He added that if I became ill as a result of hurting plants, I would, however, slough it off and believe I had only a touch of the flu.

The two of them had another moment of mirth, then don Juan became serious again and said that if I did not think of my death, my entire life would be only a personal chaos. He looked very stern.

"What else can a man have, except his life and his death?" he said to me.

At that point I felt it was indispensable to take notes and I began writing again. Don Genaro stared at me and smiled. Then he tilted his head back a little and opened his nostrils. He apparently had remarkable control over the muscles operating his nostrils, because they opened up to perhaps twice their normal size.

What was most comical about his clowning was not so much his gestures as his own reactions to them. After he enlarged his nostrils he tumbled down, laughing, and worked his body again into the same, strange, sitting-on-his-head, upside-down posture.

Don Juan laughed until tears rolled down his cheeks. I felt a bit embarrassed and laughed nervously.

"Genaro doesn't like writing," don Juan said as an explanation.

I put my notes away, but don Genaro assured me that it was all right to write, because he did not really mind it. I gathered my notes again and began writing. He repeated the same hilarious motions and both of them had the same reactions again.

Don Juan looked at me, still laughing, and said that his friend was portraying me; that my tendency was to open my nostrils whenever I wrote; and that don Genaro thought that trying to become a sorcerer by taking notes was as absurd as sitting on one's head and thus he had made up the ludicrous posture of resting the weight of his sitting body on his head.

"Perhaps you don't think it's funny," don Juan said, "but only Genaro can work his way up to sitting on his head, and only you can think of learning to be a sorcerer by writing your way up."

They both had another explosion of laughter and don Genaro repeated his incredible movement.

I liked him. There was so much grace and directness in his acts.

"My apologies, don Genaro," I said, pointing to the writing pad.

"It's all right," he said and chuckled again.

I could not write any more. They went on talking for a very long time about how plants could actually kill and how sorcerers used plants in that capacity. Both of them kept staring at me while they talked, as if they expected me to write.

"Carlos is like a horse that doesn't like to be saddled," don Juan said. "You have to be very slow with him. You scared him and now he won't write."

Don Genaro expanded his nostrils and said in a mocking plea, frowning and puckering his mouth. "Come on, Carlitos, write! Write until your thumb falls off."

Don Juan stood up, stretching his arms and arching his back. In spite of his advanced age his body seemed to be powerful and limber. He went to the bushes at the side of the house and I was left alone with don Genaro. He looked at me and I moved my eyes away because he made me feel embarrassed.

"Don't tell me you're not even going to look at me?" he said with a most hilarious intonation.

He opened his nostrils and made them quiver; then he

stood up and repeated don Juan's movements, arching his back and stretching his arms but with his body contorted into a most ludicrous position; it was truly an indescribable gesture that combined an exquisite sense of pantomime and a sense of the ridiculous. It enthralled me. It was a masterful caricature of don Juan.

Don Juan came back at that moment and caught the gesture and obviously the meaning also. He sat down chuckling.

"Which direction is the wind?" don Genaro asked casually.

Don Juan pointed to the west with a movement of his head.

"I'd better go where the wind blows," don Genaro said with a serious expression.

He then turned and shook his finger at me.

"And don't you pay any attention if you hear strange noises," he said. "When Genaro shits the mountains tremble."

He leaped into the bushes and a moment later I heard a very strange noise, a deep, unearthly rumble. I did not know what to make of it. I looked at don Juan for a clue but he was doubled over with laughter.

October 17, 1968

I don't remember what prompted don Genaro to tell me about the arrangement of the "other world," as he called it. He said that a master sorcerer was an eagle, or rather that he could make himself into an eagle. On the other hand, an evil sorcerer was a "tecolote," an owl. Don Genaro said that an evil sorcerer was a child of the night and for such a man the most useful animals were the mountain lion or other wild cats, or the night birds, especially the owl. He said that the "brujos liricos," lyric sorcerers, meaning the dilettante sorcerers, preferred other animals—a crow, for example. Don Juan laughed; he had been listening in silence.

Don Genaro turned to him and said, "That's true, you know that, Juan."

Then he said that a master sorcerer could take his disciple on a journey with him and actually pass through the ten layers of the other world. The master, provided that he was an eagle, could start at the very bottom layer and then go through each successive world until he reached the top. Evil sorcerers and dilettantes could at best, he said, go through only three layers.

Don Genaro gave a description of what those steps were by saying, "You start at the very bottom and then your teacher takes you with him in his flight and soon, boom! You go through the first layer. Then a little while later, boom! You go through the second; and boom! You go through the third . . ."

Don Genaro took me through ten booms to the last layer of the world. When he had finished talking don Juan looked at me and smiled knowingly.

"Talking is not Genaro's predilection," he said, "but if you care to get a lesson, he will teach you about the equilibrium of things."

Don Genaro nodded affirmatively; he puckered up his mouth and closed his eyelids halfway.

I thought his gesture was delightful.

Don Genaro stood up and so did don Juan.

"All right," don Genaro said. "Let's go, then. We could go and wait for Nestor and Pablito. They're through now. On Thursdays they're through early."

Both of them got into my car; don Juan sat in the front. I did not ask them anything but simply started the engine. Don Juan directed me to a place he said was Nestor's home; don Genaro went into the house and a while later came out with Nestor and Pablito, two young men who were his apprentices. They all got in my car and don Juan told me to take the road toward the western mountains.

We left my car on the side of the dirt road and walked along the bank of a river, which was perhaps fifteen or twenty feet across, to a waterfall that was visible from where I had parked. It was late afternoon. The scenery was quite impressive. Directly above us there was a huge, dark, bluish cloud that looked like a floating roof; it had a well-defined edge and was shaped like an enormous half-

circle. To the west, on the high mountains of the Cor-
dillera Central, the rain seemed to be descending on the
slopes. It looked like a whitish curtain falling on the green
peaks. To the east there was the long, deep valley; there
were only scattered clouds over the valley and the sun was
shining there. The contrast between the two areas was
magnificent. We stopped at the bottom of the waterfall; it
was perhaps a hundred and fifty feet high; the roar was
very loud.

Don Genaro fastened a belt around his waist. He had
at least seven items hanging from it. They looked like
small gourds. He took off his hat and let it hang on his
back from a cord tied around his neck. He put on a headband that he took from a pouch made of a thick wool
fabric. The headband was also made of wool of various
colors; a sharp yellow was the most prominent of them.
He inserted three feathers in the headband. They seemed
to be eagle feathers. I noticed that the places where he had
inserted them were not symmetrical. One feather was
above the back curve of his right ear, the other was a few
inches to the front, and the third was over his left temple.
Then he took off his sandals, hooked or tied them to the
waist of his trousers, and fastened his belt over his poncho. The belt seemed to be made of woven strips of
leather. I could not see whether he tied it or buckled it.
Don Genaro walked toward the waterfall.

Don Juan manipulated a round rock into a steady
position and sat down on it. The other two young men did
the same with some rocks and sat down to his left. Don
Juan pointed to the place next to him, on his right side,
and told me to bring a rock and sit by him.

"We must make a line here," he said, showing me that
the three were sitting in a row.

By then don Genaro had reached the very bottom of
the waterfall and had begun climbing a trail on the right
side of it. From where we were sitting the trail looked
fairly steep. There were a lot of shrubs he used as railings.
At one moment he seemed to lose his footing and almost
slid down, as if the dirt were slippery. A moment later the
same thing happened and the thought crossed my mind

that perhaps don Genaro was too old to be climbing. I
saw him slipping and stumbling several times before he
reached the spot where the trail ended.

I experienced a sort of apprehension when he began to
climb the rocks. I could not figure out what he was going
to do.

"What's he doing?" I asked don Juan in a whisper.

Don Juan did not look at me. "Obviously he's climbing," he said.

Don Juan was looking straight at don Genaro. His gaze
was fixed. His eyelids were half-closed. He was sitting very
erect with his hands resting between his legs, on the edge
of the rock.

I leaned over a little bit to see the two young men. Don
Juan made an imperative gesture with his hand to make
me get back in line. I retreated immediately. I had only a
glimpse of the young men. They seemed to be as attentive
as he was.

Don Juan made another gesture with his hand and
pointed to the direction of the waterfall.

I looked again. Don Genaro had climbed quite a way
on the rocky wall. At the moment I looked he was perched
on a ledge, inching his way slowly to circumvent a huge
boulder. His arms were spread, as if he were embracing
the rock. He moved slowly toward his right and suddenly
he lost his footing. I gasped involuntarily. For a moment
his whole body hung in the air. I was sure he was going to
fall but he did not. His right hand had grabbed onto something and very agilely his feet went back on the ledge
again. But before he moved on he turned to us and looked.
It was only a glance. There was, however, such a styl-
ization to the movement of turning his head that I began
to wonder. I remembered then that he had done the same
thing, turning to look at us, every time he slipped. I had
thought that don Genaro must have felt embarrassed by
his clumsiness and turned to see if we were looking.

He climbed a bit more toward the top, suffered another
loss of footing, and hung perilously on the overhanging
rock face. This time he was supported by his left hand.
When he regained his balance he turned and looked at us

again. He slipped twice more before he reached the top. From where we were sitting, the crest of the waterfall seemed to be twenty to twenty-five feet across.

Don Genaro stood motionless for a moment. I wanted to ask don Juan what don Genaro was going to do up there, but don Juan seemed to be so absorbed in watching that I did not dare disturb him.

Suddenly don Genaro jumped onto the water. It was such a thoroughly unexpected action that I felt a vacuum in the pit of my stomach. It was a magnificent, outlandish leap. For a second I had the clear sensation that I had seen a series of superimposed images of his body making an elliptical flight to the middle of the stream.

When my surprise receded I noticed that he had landed on a rock on the edge of the fall, a rock which was hardly visible from where we were sitting.

He stayed perched there for a long time. He seemed to be fighting the power of the onrushing water. Twice he hung over the precipice and I could not determine what he was clinging to. He gained his balance and squatted on the rock. Then he leaped again, like a tiger. I could barely see the next rock where he landed; it was like a small cone on the very edge of the fall.

He remained there almost ten minutes. He was motionless. His immobility was so impressive to me that I was shivering. I wanted to get up and walk around. Don Juan noticed my nervousness and told me imperatively to be calm.

Don Genaro's stillness plunged me into an extraordinary and mysterious terror. I felt that if he remained perched there any longer I could not control myself.

Suddenly he jumped again, this time all the way to the other bank of the waterfall. He landed on his feet and hands, like a feline. He remained in a squat position for a moment, then he stood up and looked across the fall, to the other side, and then down at us. He stayed dead still looking at us. His hands were clasped at his sides, as if he were holding onto an unseen railing.

There was something truly exquisite about his posture; his body seemed so nimble, so frail. I thought that don

Genaro with his headband and feathers, his dark poncho and his bare feet was the most beautiful human being I had ever seen.

He threw his arms up suddenly, lifted his head, and flipped his body swiftly in a sort of lateral somersault to his left. The boulder where he had been standing was round and when he jumped he disappeared behind it.

Huge drops of rain began to fall at that moment. Don Juan got up and so did the two young men. Their movement was so abrupt that it confused me. Don Genaro's masterful feat had thrown me into a state of profound emotional excitement. I felt he was a consummate artist and I wanted to see him right then to applaud him.

I strained to look on the left side of the waterfall to see if he was coming down, but he was not. I insisted on knowing what had happened to him. Don Juan did not answer.

"We better hurry out of here," he said. "It's a real downpour. We have to take Nestor and Pablito to their house and then we'll have to start on our trip back."

"I didn't even say goodbye to don Genaro," I complained.

"He already said goodbye to you," don Juan answered harshly.

He peered at me for an instant and then softened his frown and smiled.

"He has also wished you well," he said. "He felt happy with you."

"But aren't we going to wait for him?"

"No!" don Juan said sharply. "Let him be, wherever he is. Perhaps he is an eagle flying to the other world, or perhaps he has died up there. It doesn't matter now."

October 23, 1968

Don Juan casually mentioned that he was going to make another trip to central Mexico in the near future.

"Are you going to visit don Genaro?" I asked.

"Perhaps," he said without looking at me.

"He's all right, isn't he, don Juan? I mean nothing bad happened to him up there on top of the waterfall, did it?"

"Nothing happened to him; he is sturdy."

We talked about his projected trip for a while and then I said I had enjoyed don Genaro's company and his jokes. He laughed and said that don Genaro was truly like a child. There was a long pause; I struggled in my mind to find an opening line to ask about his lesson. Don Juan looked at me and said in a mischievous tone: "You're dying to ask me about Genaro's lesson, aren't you?"

I laughed with embarrassment. I had been obsessed with everything that took place at the waterfall. I had been hashing and rehashing all the details I could remember and my conclusions were that I had witnessed an incredible feat of physical prowess. I thought don Genaro was beyond doubt a peerless master of equilibrium; every single movement he had performed was highly ritualized and, needless to say, must have had some inextricable, symbolic meaning.

"Yes," I said. "I admit I'm dying to know what his lesson was."

"Let me tell you something," don Juan said. "It was a waste of time for you. His lesson was for someone who can *see*. Pablito and Nestro got the gist of it, although they don't *see* very well. But you, you went there to look. I told Genaro that you are a very strange plugged-up fool and that perhaps you'd get unplugged with his lesson, but you didn't. It doesn't matter, though. *Seeing* is very difficult.

"I didn't want you to speak to Genaro afterwards, so we had to leave. Too bad. Yet it would have been worse to stay. Genaro risked a great deal to show you something magnificent. Too bad you can't *see*."

"Perhaps, don Juan, if you tell me what the lesson was I may find out that I really *saw*."

Don Juan doubled up with laughter.

"Your best feature is asking questions," he said.

He was apparently going to drop the subject again. We were sitting, as usual, in the area in front of his house; he suddenly got up and walked inside. I trailed behind him and insisted on describing to him what I had seen. I faithfully followed the sequence of events as I remembered it. Don Juan kept on smiling while I spoke. When I had finished he shook his head.

"*Seeing* is very difficult," he said.

I begged him to explain his statement.

"*Seeing* is not a matter of talk," he said imperatively.

Obviously he was not going to tell me anything more, so I gave up and left the house to run some errands for him.

When I returned it was already dark; we had something to eat and afterwards we walked out to the *ramada;* we had no sooner sat down than don Juan began to talk about don Genaro's lesson. He did not give me any time to prepare myself for it. I did have my notes with me, but it was too dark to write and I did not want to alter the flow of his talk by going inside the house for the kerosene lantern.

He said that don Genaro, being a master of balance, could perform very complex and difficult movements. Sitting on his head was one of such movements and with it he had attempted to show me that it was impossible to "see" while I took notes. The action of sitting on his head without the aid of his hands was, at best, a freakish stunt that lasted only an instant. In don Genaro's opinion, writing about "seeing" was the same; that is, it was a precarious maneuver, as odd and as unnecessary as sitting on one's head.

Don Juan peered at me in the dark and in a very dramatic tone said that while don Genaro was horsing around, sitting on his head, I was on the very verge of "seeing." Don Genaro noticed it and repeated his maneuvers over and over, to no avail, because I had lost the thread right away.

Don Juan said that afterwards don Genaro, moved by his personal liking for me, attempted in a very dramatic way to bring me back to that verge of "seeing." After very careful deliberation he decided to show me a feat of equilibrium by crossing the waterfall. He felt that the waterfall was like the edge on which I was standing and was confident I could also make it across.

Don Juan then explained don Genaro's feat. He said that he had already told me that human beings were, for those who "saw," luminous beings composed of something like fibers of light, which rotated from the front to the back and maintained the appearance of an egg. He said that he had also told me that the most astonishing part of the egg-like creatures was a set of long fibers that came out of the area around the navel; don Juan said that those fibers were of the uttermost importance in the life of a man. Those fibers were the secret of don Genaro's balance and his lesson had nothing to do with acrobatic jumps across the waterfall. His feat of equilibrium was in the way he used those "tentacle-like" fibers.

Don Juan dropped the subject as suddenly as he had started it and began to talk about something thoroughly unrelated.

October 24, 1968

I cornered don Juan and told him I intuitively felt that I was never going to get another lesson in equilibrium and that he had to explain to me all the pertinent details, which I would otherwise never discover by myself. Don Juan said I was right, in so far as knowing that don Genaro would never give me another lesson.

"What else do you want to know?" he asked.

"What are those tentacle-like fibers, don Juan?"

"They are the tentacles that come out of a man's body which are apparent to any sorcerer who *sees*. Sorcerers act toward people in accordance to the way they *see* their tentacles. Weak persons have very short, almost invisible fibers; strong persons have bright, long ones. Genaro's, for instance, are so bright that they resemble thickness. You can tell from the fibers if a person is healthy, or if he is sick, or if he is mean, or kind, or treacherous. You can also tell from the fibers if a person can *see*. Here is a baffling problem. When Genaro *saw* you he knew, just like my friend Vicente did, that you could *see;* when I *see* you I *see* that you can *see* and yet I know myself that you can't. How baffling! Genaro couldn't get over that. I told him that you were a strange fool. I think he wanted to *see* that for himself and took you to the waterfall."

"Why do you think I give the impression I can *see?*"

Don Juan did not answer me. He remained silent for a long time. I did not want to ask him anything else. Finally he spoke to me and said that he knew why but did not know how to explain it.

"You think everything in the world is simple to understand," he said, "because everything you do is a routine that is simple to understand. At the waterfall, when you looked at Genaro moving across the water, you believed that he was a master of somersaults, because somersaults was all you could think about. And that is all you will ever believe he did. Yet Genaro never jumped across that water. If he had jumped he would have died. Genaro balanced himself on his superb, bright fibers. He made them long, long enough so that he could, let's say, roll on them across the waterfall. He demonstrated the proper way to make those tentacles long, and how to move them with precision.

"Pablito *saw* nearly all of Genaro's movements. Nestor, on the other hand, *saw* only the most obvious maneuvers. He missed the delicate details. But you, you *saw* nothing at all."

"Perhaps if you had told me beforehand, don Juan, what to look for . . ."

He interrupted me and said that giving me instructions would only have hindered don Genaro. Had I known what was going to take place, my fibers would have been agitated and would have interfered with don Genaro's.

"If you could *see*," he said, "it would have been obvious to you, from the first step that Genaro took, that he was not slipping as he went up the side of the waterfall. He was loosening his tentacles. Twice he made them go around boulders and held to the sheer rock like a fly. When he got to the top and was ready to cross the water he focused them onto a small rock in the middle of the stream, and when they were secured there, he let the fibers pull him. Genaro never jumped, therefore he could land on the slippery surfaces of small boulders at the very edge of the water. His fibers were at all times neatly wrapped around every rock he used.

"He did not stay on the first boulder very long, because he had the rest of his fibers tied onto another one, even smaller, at the place where the onrush of water was the greatest. His tentacles pulled him again and he landed on it. That was the most outstanding thing he did. The surface was too small for a man to hold onto; and the onrush of the water would have washed his body over the precipice had he not had some of his fibers still focused on the first rock.

"He stayed in that second position for a long time, because he had to draw out his tentacles again and send them across to the other side of the fall. When he had them secured he had to release the fibers focused on the first rock. That was very tricky. Perhaps only Genaro could do that. He nearly lost his grip; or maybe he was only fooling us, we'll never know that for sure. Personally, I really think he nearly lost his grip. I know that, because he became rigid and sent out a magnificent shoot, like a beam of light across the water. I feel that beam alone could have pulled him through. When he got to the other side he stood up and let his fibers glow like a cluster of lights. That was the one thing he did just for you. If you had been able to *see,* you would have *seen* that.

"Genaro stood there looking at you, and then he knew that you had not *seen.*"

PART TWO

The Task of "Seeing"

7

Don Juan was not at his house when I arrived there at midday on November 8, 1968. I had no idea where to look for him, so I sat and waited. For some unknown reason I knew he would soon be home. A short while later don Juan walked into his house. He nodded at me. We exchanged greetings. He seemed to be tired and lay down on his mat. He yawned a couple of times.

The idea of "seeing" had become an obsession with me and I had made up my mind to use his hallucinogenic smoking mixture again. It had been a terribly difficult decision to make, so I still wanted to argue the point a bit further.

"I want to learn to *see,* don Juan," I said bluntly. "But I really don't want to take anything; I don't want to smoke your mixture. Do you think there is any chance I could learn to *see* without it?"

He sat up, stared at me for a moment, and lay down again.

"No!" he said. "You will have to use the smoke."

"But you said I was on the verge of *seeing* with don Genaro."

"I meant that something in you was glowing as though you were really aware of Genaro's doings, but you were just looking. Obviously there is something in you that resembles *seeing,* but isn't; you're plugged up and only the smoke can help you."

"Why does one have to smoke? Why can't one simply learn to *see* by oneself? I have a very earnest desire. Isn't that enough?"

"No, it's not enough. *Seeing* is not so simple and only

the smoke can give you the speed you need to catch a glimpse of that fleeting world. Otherwise you will only look."

"What do you mean by a fleeting world?"

"The world, when you *see*, is not as you think it is now. It's rather a fleeting world that moves and changes. One may perhaps learn to apprehend that fleeting world by oneself, but it won't do any good, because the body decays with the stress. With the smoke, on the other hand, one never suffers from exhaustion. The smoke gives the necessary speed to grasp the fleeting movement of the world and at the same time it keeps the body and its strength intact."

"All right!" I said dramatically. "I don't want to beat around the bush any longer. I'll smoke."

He laughed at my display of histrionics.

"Cut it out," he said. "You always hook onto the wrong thing. Now you think that just deciding to let the smoke guide you is going to make you *see*. There's much more to it. There is always much more to anything."

He became serious for a moment.

"I have been very careful with you, and my acts have been deliberate," he said, "because it is Mescalito's desire that you understand my knowledge. But I know that I won't have time to teach you all I want. I will only have time to put you on the road and trust that you will seek in the same fashion I did. I must admit that you are more indolent and more stubborn than I. You have other views, though, and the direction that your life will take is something I cannot foresee."

His deliberate tone of voice, something in his attitude, summoned up an old feeling in me, a mixture of fear, loneliness, and expectation.

"We'll soon know where you stand," he said cryptically.

He did not say anything else. After a while he went outside the house. I followed him and stood in front of him, not knowing whether to sit down or to unload some packages I had brought for him.

"Would it be dangerous?" I asked, just to say something.

"Everything is dangerous," he said.

Don Juan did not seem to be inclined to tell me anything else; he gathered some small bundles that were piled in a corner and put them inside a carrying net. I did not offer to help him because I knew that if he had wished my help he would have asked me. Then he lay down on his straw mat. He told me to relax and rest. I lay down on my mat and tried to sleep but I was not tired; the night before I had stopped at a motel and slept until noon, knowing that I had only a three-hour drive to don Juan's place. He was not sleeping either. Although his eyes were closed, I noticed an almost imperceptible, rhythmical movement of his head. The thought occurred to me that he was perhaps chanting to himself.

"Let's eat something," don Juan said suddenly, and his voice made me jump. "You're going to need all your energy. You should be in good shape."

He made some soup, but I wasn't hungry.

The next day, November 9, don Juan let me eat only a morsel of food and told me to rest. I lay around all morning but I could not relax. I had no idea what don Juan had in mind, but, worst of all, I was not certain what I had in mind myself.

We were sitting under his *ramada* around 3:00 P.M. I was very hungry. I had suggested various times that we should eat, but he had refused.

"You haven't prepared your mixture for three years," he said suddenly. "You'll have to smoke my mixture, so let's say that I have collected it for you. You will need only a bit of it. I will fill the pipe's bowl once. You will smoke all of it and then rest. Then the keeper of the other world will come. You will do nothing but observe it. Observe how it moves; observe everything it does. Your life may depend on how well you watch."

Don Juan had dropped his instructions so abruptly that I did not know what to say or even what to think. I mumbled incoherently for a moment. I could not organize my thoughts. Finally I asked the first clear thing that came to my mind. "Who's this guardian?"

Don Juan flatly refused to involve himself in conversation, but I was too nervous to stop talking and I insisted desperately that he tell me about this guardian.

"You'll *see* it," he said casually. "It guards the other world."

"What world? The world of the dead?"

"It's not the world of the dead or the world of anything. It's just another world. There's no use telling you about it. *See* it for yourself."

With that don Juan went inside the house. I followed him into his room.

"Wait, wait, don Juan. What are you going to do?"

He did not answer. He took his pipe out of a bundle and sat down on a straw mat in the center of the room, looking at me inquisitively. He seemed to be waiting for my consent.

"You're a fool," he said softly. "You're not afraid. You just say you're afraid."

He shook his head slowly from side to side. Then he took the little bag with the smoking mixture and filled the pipe bowl.

"I am afraid, don Juan. I am really afraid."

"No, it's not fear."

I desperately tried to gain time and began a long discussion about the nature of my feelings. I sincerely maintained that I was afraid, but he pointed out that I was not panting, nor was my heart beating faster than usual.

I thought for a while about what he had said. He was wrong; I did have many of the physical changes ordinarily associated with fear, and I was desperate. A sense of impending doom permeated everything around me. My stomach was upset and I was sure I was pale; my hands were sweating profusely; and yet I really thought I was not afraid. I did not have the feeling of fear I had been accustomed to throughout my life. The fear which has always been idiosyncratically mine was not there. I was talking as I paced up and down the room in front of don Juan, who was still sitting on his mat, holding his pipe, and looking at me inquisitively; and upon considering the matter I arrived at the conclusion that what I felt instead of my usual fear was a profound sense of displeasure, a discomfort at the mere thought of the confusion created by the intake of hallucinogenic plants.

Don Juan stared at me for an instant, then he looked past me, squinting as if he were struggling to detect something in the distance.

I kept walking back and forth in front of him until he forcefully told me to sit down and relax. We sat quietly for a few minutes.

"You don't want to lose your clarity, do you?" he said abruptly.

"That's very right, don Juan," I said.

He laughed with apparent delight.

"Clarity, the second enemy of a man of knowledge, has loomed upon you.

"You're not afraid," he said reassuringly, "but now you hate to lose your clarity, and since you're a fool, you call that fear."

He chuckled.

"Get me some charcoals," he ordered.

His tone was kind and reassuring. I got up automatically and went to the back of the house and gathered some small pieces of burning charcoal from the fire, put them on top of a small stone slab, and returned to the room.

"Come out here to the porch," don Juan called loudly from outside.

He placed a straw mat on the spot where I usually sit. I put the charcoals next to him and he blew on them to activate the fire. I was about to sit down but he stopped me and told me to sit on the right edge of the mat. He then put a piece of charcoal in the pipe and handed it to me. I took it. I was amazed at the silent forcefulness with which don Juan had steered me. I could not think of anything to say. I had no more arguments. I was convinced that I was not afraid, but only unwilling to lose my clarity.

"Puff, puff," he ordered me gently. "Just one bowl this time."

I sucked on the pipe and heard the chirping of the mixture catching on fire. I felt an instantaneous coat of ice inside my mouth and my nose. I took another puff and the coating extended to my chest. When I had taken the last puff I felt that the entire inside of my body was coated with a peculiar sensation of cold warmth.

Don Juan took the pipe away from me and tapped the bowl on his palm to loosen the residue. Then, as he always does, he wet his finger with saliva and rubbed it inside the bowl.

My body was numb, but I could move. I changed positions to sit more comfortably.

"What's going to happen?" I asked.

I had some difficulty vocalizing.

Don Juan very carefully put his pipe inside its sheath and rolled it up in a long piece of cloth. Then he sat up straight, facing me. I felt dizzy; my eyes were closing involuntarily. Don Juan shook me vigorously and ordered me to stay awake. He said I knew very well that if I fell asleep I would die. That jolted me. It occurred to me that don Juan was probably just saying that to keep me awake, but on the other hand, it also occurred to me that he might be right. I opened my eyes as wide as I could and that made don Juan laugh. He said that I had to wait for a while and keep my eyes open all the time and that at a given moment I would be able to see the guardian of the other world.

I felt a very annoying heat all over my body; I tried to change positions, but I could not move any more. I wanted to talk to don Juan; the words seemed to be so deep inside of me that I could not bring them out. Then I tumbled on my left side and found myself looking at don Juan from the floor.

He leaned over and ordered me in a whisper not to look at him but to stare fixedly at a point on my mat which was directly in front of my eyes. He said that I had to look with one eye, my left eye, and that sooner or later I would *see* the guardian.

I fixed my stare on the spot he had pointed to but I did not see anything. At a certain moment, however, I noticed a gnat flying in front of my eyes. It landed on the mat. I followed its movements. It came very close to me, so close that my visual perception blurred. And then, all of a sudden, I felt as if I had stood up. It was a very puzzling sensation that deserved some pondering, but there was no time for that. I had the total sensation that I was looking straight onward from my usual eye level, and what I saw shook up the last fiber of my being. There is no other way to describe the emotional jolt I experienced. Right there facing me, a short distance away, was a gigantic, monstrous animal. A truly monstrous thing! Never in the wildest fantasies of fiction had I encountered anything like it. I looked at it in complete, utmost bewilderment.

The first thing I really noticed was its size. I thought, for some reason, that it must be close to a hundred feet tall. It seemed to be standing erect, although I could not figure out how it stood. Next, I noticed that it had wings, two short, wide wings. At that point I became aware that I insisted on examining the animal as if it were an ordinary sight; that is, I looked at it. However, I could not really look at it in the way I was accustomed to looking. I realized that I was, rather, noticing things about it, as if the picture were becoming more clear as parts were added. Its body was covered with tufts of black hair. It had a long muzzle and was drooling. Its eyes were bulgy and round, like two enormous white balls.

Then it began to beat its wings. It was not the flapping motion of a bird's wings, but a kind of flickering, vibratory tremor. It gained speed and began circling in front of me; it was not flying, but rather skidding with astounding speed and agility, just a few inches above the ground. For a moment I found myself engrossed in watching it move. I thought that its movements were ugly and yet its speed and easiness were superb.

It circled twice in front of me, vibrating its wings, and whatever was drooling out of its mouth flew in all directions. Then it turned around and skidded away at an incredible speed until it disappeared in the distance. I stared fixedly in the direction it had gone because there was nothing else I could do. I had a most peculiar sensation of being incapable of organizing my thoughts coherently. I could not move away. It was as if I were glued to the spot.

Then I saw something like a cloud in the distance; an instant later the gigantic beast was circling again at full speed in front of me. Its wings cut closer and closer to my eyes until they hit me. I felt that its wings had actually hit whatever part of me was there. I yelled with all my might in the midst of one of the most excruciating pains I have ever had.

The next thing I knew I was seated on my mat and don Juan was rubbing my forehead. He rubbed my arms and legs with leaves, then he took me to an irrigation ditch behind his house, took off my clothes, and submerged me completely, then pulled me out and submerged me over and over again.

As I lay on the shallow bottom of the irrigation ditch, don Juan pulled up my left foot from time to time and tapped the sole gently. After a while I felt a ticklishness. He noticed it and said that I was all right. I put on my clothes and we returned to his house. I sat down again on my straw mat and tried to talk, but I felt I could not concentrate on what I wanted to say, although my thoughts were very clear. I was amazed to realize how much concentration was necessary to talk. I also noticed that in order to say something I had to stop looking at things. I had the impression that I was entangled at a very deep level and when I wanted to talk I had to surface like a diver; I had to ascend as if pulled by my words. Twice I went as far as clearing my throat in a fashion which was perfectly ordinary. I could have said then whatever I wanted to, but I did not. I preferred to remain at the strange level of silence where I could just look. I had the feeling that I was beginning to tap what don Juan had called "seeing" and that made me very happy.

Afterwards don Juan gave me some soup and tortillas and ordered me to eat. I was able to eat without any trouble and without losing what I thought to be my "power of seeing." I focused my gaze on everything around me. I was convinced I could "see" everything, and yet the world looked the same to the best of my assessment. I struggled to "see" until it was quite dark. I finally got tired and lay down and went to sleep.

I woke up when don Juan covered me with a blanket. I had a headache and I was sick to my stomach. After a while I felt better and slept soundly until the next day.

In the morning I was myself again. I asked don Juan eagerly, "What happened to me?"

Don Juan laughed coyly. "You went to look for the keeper and of course you found it," he said.

"But what was it, don Juan?"

"The guardian, the keeper, the sentry of the other world," don Juan said factually.

I intended to relate to him the details of the portentous and ugly beast, but he disregarded my attempt, saying that my experience was nothing special, that any man could do that.

I told him that the guardian had been such a shock to me that I really had not yet been able to think about it.

Don Juan laughed and made fun of what he called an overdramatic bent of my nature.

"That thing, whatever it was, hurt me," I said. "It was as real as you and I."

"Of course it was real. It caused you pain, didn't it?"

As I recollected my experience I grew more excited. Don Juan told me to calm down. Then he asked me if I had really been afraid of it; he stressed the word "really."

"I was petrified," I said. "Never in my life have I experienced such an awesome fright."

"Come on," he said, laughing. "You were not that afraid."

"I swear to you," I said with genuine fervor, "that if I could have moved I would have run hysterically."

He found my statement very funny and roared with laughter.

"What was the point of making me see that monstrosity, don Juan?"

He became serious and gazed at me.

"That was the guardian," he said. "If you want to *see* you must overcome the guardian."

"But how am I to overcome it, don Juan? It is perhaps a hundred feet tall."

Don Juan laughed so hard that tears rolled down his cheeks.

"Why don't you let me tell you what I saw, so there won't be any misunderstanding?" I said.

"If that makes you happy, go ahead, tell me."

I narrated everything I could remember, but that did not seem to change his mood.

"Still, that's nothing new," he said, smiling.

"But how do you expect me to overcome a thing like that? With what?"

He was silent for quite a while. Then he turned to me and said, "You were not afraid, not really. You were hurt, but you were not afraid."

He reclined against some bundles and put his arms behind his head. I thought he had dropped the subject.

"You know," he said suddenly, looking at the roof of the *ramada*, "every man can *see* the guardian. And the guardian is sometimes for some of us an awesome beast as high as the sky. You're lucky; for you it was only a hundred feet tall. And yet its secret is so simple."

He paused for a moment and hummed a Mexican song.

"The guardian of the other world is a gnat," he said slowly, as if he were measuring the effect of his words.

"I beg your pardon."

"The guardian of the other world is a gnat," he repeated. "What you encountered yesterday was a gnat; and that little gnat will keep you away until you overcome it."

For a moment I did not want to believe what don Juan was saying, but upon recollecting the sequence of my vision I had to admit that at a certain moment I was looking at a gnat, and an instant later a sort of mirage had taken place and I was looking at the beast.

"But how could a gnat hurt me, don Juan?" I asked, truly bewildered.

"It was not a gnat when it hurt you," he said, "it was the guardian of the other world. Perhaps some day you will have the courage to overcome it. Not now, though; now it is a hundred-foot-tall drooling beast. But there is no point in talking about it. It's no feat to stand in front of it, so if you want to know more about it, find the guardian again."

Two days later, on November 11, I smoked don Juan's mixture again.

I had asked don Juan to let me smoke once more to find the guardian. I had not asked him on the spur of the moment, but after long deliberation. My curiosity about the guardian was disproportionately greater than my fear, or the discomfort of losing my clarity.

The procedure was the same. Don Juan filled the pipe bowl once and when I had finished the entire contents he cleaned it and put it away.

The effect was markedly slower; when I began to feel a bit dizzy don Juan came to me and, holding my head in his hands, helped me to lie down on my left side. He told me to stretch my legs and relax and then helped me put my right arm in front of my body, at the level of my chest. He turned my hand so the palm was pressing against the mat, and let my weight rest on it. I did not do anything to help or hinder him, for I did not know what he was doing.

He sat in front of me and told me not to be concerned with anything. He said that the guardian was going to come, and that I had a ringside seat to *see* it. He also told me, in a casual way, that the guardian could cause great pain, but that there was one way to avert it. He said that two days before he had made me sit up when he judged I had had enough. He pointed to my right arm and said that he had deliberately put it in that position so I could use it as a lever to push myself up whenever I wanted to.

By the time he had finished telling me all that, my body was quite numb. I wanted to call to his attention the fact that it would be impossible for me to push myself up because I had lost control of my muscles. I tried to vocalize the words but I could not. He seemed to have anticipated me, however, and explained that the trick was in the will. He urged me to remember the time, years before, when I had first smoked the mushrooms. On that occasion I had fallen to the ground and sprung up to my feet again by an act of what he called, at that time, my "will"; I had "thought myself up." He said that was in fact the only possible way to get up.

What he was saying was useless to me because I did not remember what I had really done years before. I had an overwhelming sense of despair and closed my eyes.

Don Juan grabbed me by the hair, shook my head vigorously, and ordered me imperatively not to close my eyes. I not only opened my eyes but I did something I thought was astonishing. I actually said, "I don't know how I got up that time."

I was startled. There was something very monotonous about the rhythm of my voice, but it was plainly my voice, and yet I honestly believed I could not have said that, because a minute before I had been incapable of speaking.

I looked at don Juan. He turned his face to one side and laughed.

"I didn't say that," I said.

And again I was startled by my voice. I felt elated. Speaking under these conditions became an exhilarating process. I wanted to ask don Juan to explain my talking, but I found I was again incapable of uttering one single word. I struggled fiercely to voice my thoughts, but it was useless. I gave up and at that moment, almost involuntarily, I said, "Who's talking, who's talking?"

That question made don Juan laugh so hard that at one point he bobbed on his side.

Apparently it was possible for me to say simple things, as long as I knew exactly what I wanted to say.

"Am I talking? Am I talking?" I asked.

Don Juan told me that if I did not stop horsing around he was going to go out and lie down under the *ramada* and leave me alone with my clowning.

"It isn't clowning," I said.

I was very serious about that. My thoughts were very clear; my body, however, was numb; I did not feel it. I was not suffocated, as I had once been in the past under similar conditions; I was comfortable because I could not feel anything; I had no control whatever over my voluntary system and yet I could talk. The thought occurred to me that if I could talk I could probably stand up as don Juan had said.

"Up," I said in English, and in a flicker of an eye I was up.

Don Juan shook his head in disbelief and walked out of the house.

"Don Juan!" I called out three times.

He came back.

"Put me down," I said.

"Put yourself down," he said. 'You seem to be doing very well."

I said, "Down," and suddenly I lost sight of the room. I could not see anything. After a moment the room and don Juan came back again into my field of vision. I thought that I must have lain down with my face to the ground and he had grabbed me by the hair and lifted my head.

"Thank you," I said in a very slow monotone.

"You are welcome," he replied, mocking my tone of voice, and had another attack of laughter.

Then he took some leaves and began rubbing my arms and feet with them.

"What are you doing?" I asked.

"I am rubbing you," he said, imitating my painful mono-tone.

His body convulsed with laughter. His eyes were shiny and very friendly. I liked him. I felt that don Juan was compassionate and fair and funny. I could not laugh with him, but I would have liked to. Another feeling of ex-hilaration invaded me and I laughed; it was such an awful sound that don Juan was taken aback for an instant.

"I better take you to the ditch," he said, "or you're going to kill yourself clowning."

He put me up on my feet and made me walk around the room. Little by little I began to feel my feet, and my legs, and finally my entire body. My ears were bursting with a strange pressure. It was like the sensation of a leg or an arm that has fallen asleep. I felt a tremendous weight on the back of my neck and under the scalp on the top of my head.

Don Juan rushed me to the irrigation ditch at the back

of his house; he dumped me there fully clothed. The cold water reduced the pressure and the pain, by degrees, until it was all gone.

I changed my clothes in the house and sat down and I again felt the same kind of aloofness, the same desire to stay quiet. I noticed this time, however, that it was not clarity of mind, or a power to focus; rather, it was a sort of melancholy and a physical fatigue. Finally I fell asleep.

November 12, 1968

This morning don Juan and I went to the nearby hills to collect plants. We walked about six miles on extremely rough terrain. I became very tired. We sat down to rest, at my initiative, and he began a conversation, saying that he was pleased with my progress.

"I know now that it was I who talked," I said, "but at the time I could have sworn it was someone else."

"It was you, of course," he said.

"How come I couldn't recognize myself?"

"That's what the little smoke does. One can talk and not notice it; or one can move thousands of miles and not notice that either. That's also how one can go through things. The little smoke removes the body and one is free, like the wind; better than the wind, the wind can be stopped by a rock or a wall or a mountain. The little smoke makes one as free as the air; perhaps even freer, the air can be locked in a tomb and become stale, but with the aid of the little smoke one cannot be stopped or locked in."

Don Juan's words unleashed a mixture of euphoria and doubt. I felt an overwhelming uneasiness, a sensation of undefined guilt.

"Then one can really do all those things, don Juan?"

"What do you think? You would rather think you're crazy, wouldn't you?" he said cuttingly.

"Well, it's easy for you to accept all those things. For me it's impossible."

"It's not easy for me. I don't have any more privileges

than you. Those things are equally hard for you or for me or for anyone else to accept."

"But you are at home with all this, don Juan."

"Yes, but it cost me plenty. I had to struggle, perhaps more than you ever will. You have a baffling way of getting everything to work for you. You have no idea how hard I had to toil to do what you did yesterday. You have something that helps you every inch of the way. There is no other possible explanation for the manner in which you learn about the powers. You did it before with Mescalito, now you have done it with the little smoke. You should concentrate on the fact that you have a great gift, and leave other considerations on the side."

"You make it sound so easy, but it isn't. I'm torn inside."

"You'll be in one piece again soon enough. You have not taken care of your body, for one thing. You're too fat. I didn't want to say anything to you before. One must always let others do what they have to do. You were away for years. I told you that you would come back, though, and you did. The same thing happened to me. I quit for five and a half years."

"Why did you stay away, don Juan?"

"For the same reason you did. I didn't like it."

"Why did you come back?"

"For the same reason you have come back yourself, because there is no other way to live."

That statement had a great impact on me, for I had found myself thinking that perhaps there was no other way to live. I had never voiced this thought to anyone, yet don Juan had surmised it correctly.

After a very long silence I asked him, "What did I do yesterday, don Juan?"

"You got up when you wanted to."

"But I don't know how I did that."

"It takes time to perfect that technique. The important thing, however, is that you know how to do it."

"But I don't. That's the point, I really don't."

"Of course you do."

"Don Juan, I assure you, I swear to you . . ."

He did not let me finish; he got up and walked away.

Later on we talked again about the guardian of the other world.

"If I believe that whatever I have experienced is actually real," I said, "then the guardian is a gigantic creature that can cause unbelievable physical pain; and if I believe that one can actually travel enormous distances by an act of will, then it's logical to conclude that I could also will the monster to disappear. Is that correct?"

"Not exactly," he said. "You cannot will the guardian to disappear. Your will can stop it from harming you, though. Of course if you ever accomplish that, the road is open to you. You can actually go by the guardian and there's nothing that it can do, not even whirl around madly."

"How can I accomplish that?"

"You already know how. All you need now is practice."

I told him that we were having a misunderstanding that stemmed from our differences in perceiving the world. I said that for me to know something meant that I had to be fully aware of what I was doing and that I could repeat what I knew at will, but in this case I was neither aware of what I had done under the influence of the smoke, nor could I repeat it if my life depended on it.

Don Juan looked at me inquisitively. He seemed to be amused by what I was saying. He took off his hat and scratched his temples as he does when he wants to pretend bewilderment.

"You really know how to talk and say nothing, don't you?" he said laughing. "I have told you, you have to have an unbending intent in order to become a man of knowledge. But you seem to have an unbending intent to confuse yourself with riddles. You insist on explaining everything as if the whole world were composed of things that can be explained. Now you are confronted with the guardian and with the problem of moving by using your will. Has it ever occurred to you that only a few things in this world can be explained your way? When I say that the guardian is really blocking your passing and could actually knock the devil out of you, I know what I mean. When I say that one can move by one's will, I also know what I mean. I wanted to teach you, little by little, how to move, but then I realized that you know how to do it even though you say you don't."

"But I really don't know how," I protested.

"You do, you fool," he said sternly, and then smiled. "It reminds me of the time when someone put that kid Julio on a harvesting machine; he knew how to run it although he had never done it before."

"I know what you mean, don Juan; however, I still feel that I could not do it again, because I am not sure of what I did."

"A phony sorcerer tries to explain everything in the world with explanations he is not sure about," he said, "and so everything is witchcraft. But then you're no better. You also want to explain everything your way but you're not sure of your explanations either."

8

Don Juan asked me abruptly if I was planning to leave for home during the weekend. I said I intended to leave Monday morning. We were sitting under his *ramada* around midday on Saturday, January 18, 1969, taking a rest after a long walk in the nearby hills. Don Juan got up and went into the house. A few moments later he called me inside. He was sitting in the middle of his room and had placed my straw mat in front of his. He motioned me to sit down and without saying a word he unwrapped his pipe, took it out of its sheath, filled its bowl with his smoking mixture, and lit it. He had even brought into his room a clay tray filled with small charcoals.

He did not ask me whether I was willing to smoke. He just handed me the pipe and told me to puff. I did not hesitate. Don Juan had apparently assessed my mood correctly; my overwhelming curiosity about the guardian must have been obvious to him. I did not need any coaxing and eagerly smoked the entire bowl.

The reactions I had were identical to those I had had before. Don Juan also proceeded in very much the same manner. This time, however, instead of helping me to do it, he just told me to prop my right arm on the mat and lie down on my left side. He suggested that I should make a fist if that would give me a better leverage.

I did make a fist with my right hand, because I found it was easier than turning my palm against the floor while lying with my weight on it. I was not sleepy; I felt very warm for a while, then I lost all feeling.

Don Juan lay down on his side facing me; his right forearm rested on his elbow and propped his head up like a pillow. Everything was perfectly placid, even my body, which by then lacked tactile sensations. I felt very content.

"It's nice," I said.

Don Juan got up hurriedly.

"Don't you dare start with this crap," he said forcefully. "Don't talk. You'll waste every bit of energy talking, and then the guardian will mash you down, like you would smash a gnat."

He must have thought that his simile was funny because he began to laugh, but he stopped suddenly.

"Don't talk, please don't talk," he said with a serious look on his face.

"I wasn't about to say anything," I said, and I really did not want to say that.

Don Juan got up. I saw him walking away toward the back of his house. A moment later I noticed that a gnat had landed on my mat and that filled me with a kind of anxiety I had never experienced before. It was a mixture of elation, anguish, and fear. I was totally aware that something transcendental was about to unfold in front of me; a gnat who guarded the other world. It was a ludicrous thought; I felt like laughing out loud, but then I realized that my elation was distracting me and I was going to miss a transition period I wanted to clarify. In my previous attempt to see the guardian I had looked at the gnat first with my left eye, and then I felt that I had stood up and looked at it with both eyes, but I was not aware how that transition had occurred.

I saw the gnat whirling around on the mat in front of my face and realized that I was looking at it with both eyes. It came very close; at a given moment I could not see it with both eyes any longer and shifted the view to my left eye, which was level with the ground. The instant I changed focus I also felt that I had straightened my body to a fully vertical position and I was looking at an unbelievably enormous animal. It was brilliantly black. Its front was covered with long, black, insidious hair, which looked like spikes coming through the cracks of some slick, shiny scales. The hair was actually arranged in tufts. Its body was massive, thick and round. Its wings were wide and short in comparison to the length of its body. It had two white, bulging eyes and a long muzzle. This time it looked more like an alligator. It seemed to have long ears, or perhaps horns, and it was drooling.

I strained myself to fix my gaze on it and then became fully aware that I could not look at it in the same way I ordinarily look at things. I had a strange thought; looking at the guardian's body I felt that every single part of it was independently alive, as the eyes of men are alive. I realized then for the first time in my life that the eyes were the only part of a man that could show, to me, whether or not he was alive. The guardian, on the other hand, had a "million eyes."

I thought this was a remarkable finding. Before this experience I had speculated on the similes that could describe the "distortions" that rendered a gnat as a gigantic beast; and I had thought that a good simile was "as if looking at an insect through the magnifying lens of a microscope." But that was not so. Apparently viewing the guardian was much more complex than looking at a magnified insect.

The guardian began to whirl in front of me. At one moment it stopped and I felt it was looking at me. I noticed then that it made no sound. The dance of the guardian was silent. The awesomeness was in its appearance: its bulging eyes; its horrendous mouth; its drooling; its insidious hair; and above all its incredible size. I watched very closely the way it moved its wings, how it made them vibrate without sound. I watched how it skidded over the ground like a monumental ice skater.

Looking at that nightmarish creature in front of me, I actually felt elated. I really believed I had discovered the secret of overpowering it. I thought the guardian was only a moving picture on a silent screen; it could not harm me; it only looked terrifying.

The guardian was standing still, facing me; suddenly it fluttered its wings and turned around. Its back looked like brilliantly colored armor; its shine was dazzling but the hue was nauseating; it was my unfavorable color. The guardian remained with its back turned to me for a while and then, fluttering its wings, again skidded out of sight.

I was confronted with a very strange dilemma. I honestly believed that I had overpowered it by realizing that it presented only a picture of wrath. My belief was perhaps due to don Juan's insistence that I knew more than I was willing to admit. At any rate, I felt I had overcome the guardian and the path was free. Yet I did not know how to proceed. Don Juan had not told me what to do in such a case. I tried to turn and look behind me, but I was unable to move. However, I could see very well over the major part of a 180-degree range in front of my eyes. And what I saw was a cloudy, pale-yellow horizon; it seemed gaseous. A sort of lemon hue uniformly covered all I could see. It seemed that I was on a plateau filled with vapors of sulphur.

Suddenly the guardian appeared again at a point on the horizon. It made a wide circle before stopping in front of me; its mouth was wide open, like a huge cavern; it had no teeth. It vibrated its wings for an instant and then it charged at me. It actually charged at me like a bull, and with its gigantic wings it swung at my eyes. I screamed with pain and then I flew up, or rather I felt I had ejected myself up, and went soaring beyond the guardian, beyond the yellowish plateau, into another world, the world of men, and I found myself standing in the middle of don Juan's room.

January 19, 1969

"I really thought I had overpowered the guardian," I said to don Juan.

"You must be kidding," he said.

Don Juan had not spoken one word to me since the day before and I did not mind it. I had been immersed in a sort of reverie and again I had felt that if I looked intently I would be able to "see." But I did not see anything that was different. Not talking, however, had relaxed me tremendously.

Don Juan asked me to recount the sequence of my experience, and what particularly interested him was the hue I had seen on the guardian's back. Don Juan sighed and seemed to be really concerned.

"You were lucky that the color was on the guardian's back," he said with a serious face. "Had it been on the front part of its body, or worse yet, on its head, you would be dead by now. You must not try to *see* the guardian ever again. It's not your temperament to cross that plain; yet I was convinced that you could go through it. But let's not talk about it any more. This was only one of a variety of roads."

I detected an unaccustomed heaviness in don Juan's tone.

"What will happen to me if I try to *see* the guardian again?"

"The guardian will take you away," he said. "It will pick you up in its mouth and carry you into that plain and leave you there forever. It is obvious that the guardian knew that it is not your temperament and warned you to stay away."

"How do you think the guardian knew that?"

Don Juan gave me a long, steadfast look. He tried to say something, but gave up as though he was unable to find the right words.

"I always fall for your questions," he said, smiling. "You were not really thinking when you asked me that, were you?"

I protested and reaffirmed that it puzzled me that the guardian knew my temperament.

Don Juan had a strange glint in his eye when he said, "And you had not even mentioned anything about your temperament to the guardian, had you?"

His tone was so comically serious that we both laughed. After a while, however, he said that the guardian, being the keeper, the watchman of that world, knew many secrets that a brujo was entitled to share.

"That's one way a brujo gets to *see*," he said. "But that will not be your domain, so there is no point in talking about it."

"Is smoking the only way to *see* the guardian?" I asked.

"No. You could also *see* it without it. There are scores of people who could do that. I prefer the smoke because it is more effective and less dangerous to oneself. If you try to *see* the guardian without the aid of the smoke, chances are that you may delay in getting out of its way. In your case, for instance, it is obvious that the guardian was warning you when it turned its back so you would look at your enemy color. Then it went away; but when it came back you were still there, so it charged at you. You were prepared, however, and jumped. The little smoke gave you the protection you needed; had you gone into that world without its aid you wouldn't have been able to extricate yourself from the guardian's grip."

"Why not?"

"Your movements would have been too slow. To survive in that world you need to be as fast as lightning. It was my mistake to leave the room, but I didn't want you to talk any more. You are a blabbermouth, so you talk even against your desire. Had I been there with you I would've pulled your head up. You jumped up by yourself, which was even better; however, I would rather not run a risk like that; the guardian is not something you can fool around with."

9

For three months don Juan systematically avoided talking about the guardian. I paid him four visits during these months; he involved me in running errands for him every time, and when I had performed the errands he simply told me to go home. On April 24, 1969, the fourth time I was at his house, I finally confronted him after we had eaten dinner and were sitting next to his earthen stove. I told him that he was doing something incongruous to me; I was ready to learn and yet he did not even want me around. I had had to struggle very hard to overcome my aversion to using his hallucinogenic mushrooms and I felt, as he had said himself, that I had no time to lose.

Don Juan patiently listened to my complaints.

"You're too weak," he said. "You hurry when you should wait, but you wait when you should hurry. You think too much. Now you think that there is no time to waste. A while back you thought you didn't want to smoke any more. Your life is too damn loose; you're not tight enough to meet the little smoke. I am responsible for you and I don't want you to die like a goddamn fool."

I felt embarrassed.

"What can I do, don Juan? I'm very impatient."

"Live like a warrior! I've told you already, a warrior takes responsibility for his acts; for the most trivial of his acts. You act out your thoughts and that's wrong. You failed with the guardian because of your thoughts."

"How did I fail, don Juan?"

"You think about everything. You thought about the guardian and thus you couldn't overcome it.

"First you must live like a warrior. I think you understand that very well."

I wanted to interject something in my defense, but he gestured with his hand to be quiet.

"Your life is fairly tight," he continued. "In fact, your life is tighter than Pablito's or Nestor's, Genaro's apprentices, and yet they *see* and you don't. Your life is tighter than Eligio's and he'll probably *see* before you do. This baffles me. Even Genaro cannot get over that. You've faithfully carried out everything I have told you to do. Everything that my benefactor taught me, in the first stage of learning, I have passed on to you. The rule is right, the steps cannot be changed. You have done everything one has to do and yet you don't *see;* but to those who *see,* like Genaro, you appear as though you *see.* I rely on that and I am fooled. You always turn around and behave like an idiot who doesn't *see,* which of course is right for you."

Don Juan's words distressed me profoundly. I don't know why but I was close to tears. I began to talk about my childhood and a wave of self-pity enveloped me. Don Juan stared at me for a brief moment and then moved his eyes away. It was a penetrating glance. I felt he had actually grabbed me with his eyes. I had the sensation of two fingers gently clasping me and I acknowledged a weird agitation, an itching, a pleasant despair in the area of my solar plexus. I became aware of my abdominal region. I sensed its heat. I could not speak coherently any more and I mumbled, then stopped talking altogether.

"Perhaps it's the promise," don Juan said after a long pause.

"I beg your pardon."

"A promise you once made, long ago."

"What promise?"

"Maybe you can tell me that. You do remember it, don't you?"

"I don't."

"You promised something very important once. I

thought that perhaps your promise was keeping you from *seeing*."

"I don't know what you're talking about."

"I'm talking about a promise you made! You must remember it."

"If you know what the promise was, why don't you tell me, don Juan?"

"No. It won't do any good to tell you."

"Was it a promise I made to myself?"

For a moment I thought he might be referring to my resolution to quit the apprenticeship.

"No. This is something that took place a long time ago," he said.

I laughed because I was certain don Juan was playing some sort of game with me. I felt mischievous. I had a sensation of elation at the idea that I could fool don Juan, who, I was convinced, knew as little as I did about the alleged promise. I was sure he was fishing in the dark and trying to improvise. The idea of humoring him delighted me.

"Was it something I promised to my grandpa?"

"No," he said, and his eyes glittered. "Neither was it something you promised to your little grandma."

The ludicrous intonation he gave to the word "grandma" made me laugh. I thought don Juan was setting some sort of trap for me, but I was willing to play the game to the end. I began enumerating all the possible individuals to whom I could have promised something of great importance. He said no to each. Then he steered the conversation to my childhood.

"Why was your childhood sad?" he asked with a serious expression.

I told him that my childhood had not really been sad, but perhaps a bit difficult.

"Everybody feels that way," he said, looking at me again. "I too was very unhappy and afraid when I was a child. To be an Indian is hard, very hard. But the memory of that time no longer has meaning for me, beyond that it was hard. I had ceased to think about the hardship of my life even before I had learned to *see*."

"I don't think about my childhood either," I said.

"Why does it make you sad, then? Why do you want to weep?"

"I don't know. Perhaps when I think of myself as a child I feel sorry for myself and for all my fellow men. I feel helpless and sad."

He looked at me fixedly and again my abdominal region registered the weird sensation of two gentle fingers clasping it. I moved my eyes away and then glanced back at him. He was looking into the distance, past me; his eyes were foggy, out of focus.

"It was a promise of your childhood," he said after a moment's silence.

"What did I promise?"

He did not answer. His eyes were closed. I smiled involuntarily; I knew he was feeling his way in the dark; however, I had lost some of my original impetus to humor him.

"I was a skinny child," he went on, "and I was always afraid."

"So was I," I said.

"What I remember the most is the terror and sadness that fell upon me when the Mexican soldiers killed my mother," he said softly, as if the memory was still painful. "She was a poor and humble Indian. Perhaps it was better that her life was over then. I wanted to be killed with her, because I was a child. But the soldiers picked me up and beat me. When I grabbed onto my mother's body they hit my fingers with a horsewhip and broke them. I didn't feel any pain, but I couldn't grasp any more, and then they dragged me away."

He stopped talking. His eyes were still closed and I could detect a very slight tremor in his lips. A profound sadness began to overtake me. Images of my own childhood started to flood my mind.

"How old were you, don Juan?" I asked, just to offset the sadness in me.

"Maybe seven. That was the time of the great Yaqui wars. The Mexican soldiers came upon us unexpectedly while my mother was cooking some food. She was a helpless woman. They killed her for no reason at all. It doesn't make any difference that she died that way, not really, and yet for me it does. I cannot tell myself why, though; it just does. I thought they had killed my father too, but they hadn't. He was wounded. Later on they put us in a train like cattle and closed the door. For days they kept us there in the dark, like animals. They kept us alive with bits of food they threw into the wagon from time to time.

"My father died of his wounds in that wagon. He became delirious with pain and fever and went on telling me that I had to survive. He kept on telling me that until the very last moment of his life.

"The people took care of me; they gave me food; an old woman curer fixed the broken bones of my hand. And as you can see, I lived. Life has been neither good nor bad to me; life has been hard. Life is hard and for a child it is sometimes horror itself."

We did not speak for a very long time. Perhaps an hour went by in complete silence. I had very confusing feelings. I was somewhat dejected and yet I could not tell why. I experienced a sense of remorse. A while before I had been willing to humor don Juan, but he had suddenly turned the tables with his direct account. It had been simple and concise and had produced a strange feeling in me. The idea of a child undergoing pain had always been a touchy subject for me. In an instant my feelings of empathy for don Juan gave way to a sensation of disgust with myself. I had actually taken notes, as if don Juan's life were merely a clinical case. I was on the verge of ripping up my notes when don Juan poked my calf with his toe to attract my attention. He said he was "seeing" a light of violence around me and wondered whether I was going to start beating him. His laughter was a delightful break. He said that I was given to outbursts of violent behavior but that I was not really mean and that most of the time the violence was against myself.

"You're right, don Juan," I said.

"Of course," he said, laughing.

He urged me to talk about my childhood. I began to tell him about my years of fear and loneliness and got involved in describing to him what I thought to be my overwhelming struggle to survive and maintain my spirit. He laughed at the metaphor of "maintaining my spirit."

I talked for a long time. He listened with a serious expression. Then, at a given moment his eyes "clasped" me again and I stopped talking. After a moment's pause he said that nobody had ever humiliated me and that was the reason I was not really mean.

"You haven't been defeated yet," he said.

He repeated the statement four or five times so I felt obliged to ask him what he meant by that. He explained that to be defeated was a condition of life which was unavoidable. Men were either victorious or defeated and, depending on that, they became persecutors or victims. These two conditions were prevalent as long as one did not "see"; "seeing" dispelled the illusion of victory, or defeat, or suffering. He added that I should learn to "see" while I was victorious to avoid ever having the memory of being humiliated.

I protested that I was not and had never been victorious at anything; and that my life was, if anything, a defeat.

He laughed and threw his hat on the floor.

"If your life is such a defeat, step on my hat," he dared me in jest.

I sincerely argued my point. Don Juan became serious. His eyes squinted to a fine slit. He said that I thought my life was a defeat for reasons other than defeat itself. Then in a very quick and thoroughly unexpected manner he took my head in his hands by placing his palms against my temples. His eyes became fierce as he looked into mine. Out of fright I took an involuntary deep breath through my mouth. He let my head go and reclined against the wall, still gazing at me. He had performed his movements with such a speed that by the time he had relaxed and reclined comfortably against the wall, I was still in the middle of my deep breath. I felt dizzy, ill at ease.

"I *see* a little boy crying," don Juan said after a pause.

He repeated it various times as if I did not understand. I had the feeling he was talking about me as a little boy crying, so I did not really pay attention to it.

"Hey!" he said, demanding my full concentration. "I *see* a little boy crying."

I asked him if that boy was me. He said no. Then I asked him if it was a vision of my life or just a memory of his own life. He did not answer.

"I *see* a little boy," he continued saying. "And he is crying and crying."

"Is he a boy I know?" I asked.

"Yes."

"Is he my little boy?"

"No."

"Is he crying now?"

"He's crying now," he said with conviction.

I thought don Juan was having a vision of someone I knew who was a little boy and who was at that very moment crying. I voiced the names of all the children I knew, but he said those children were irrelevant to my promise and the child who was crying was very important to it.

Don Juan's statements seemed to be incongruous. He had said that I had promised something to someone during my childhood, and that the child who was crying at that very moment was important to my promise. I told him he was not making sense. He calmly repeated that he "saw" a little boy crying at that moment, and that the little boy was hurt.

I seriously struggled to fit his statements into some sort of orderly pattern, but I could not relate them to anything I was aware of.

"I give up," I said, "because I can't remember making an important promise to anybody, least of all to a child."

He squinted his eyes again and said that this particular child who was crying at that precise moment was a child of my childhood.

"He was a child during my childhood and is still crying now?" I asked.

"He is a child crying now," he insisted.

"Do you realize what you're saying, don Juan?"

"I do."

"It doesn't make sense. How can he be a child now if he was one when I was a child myself?"

"He's a child and he's crying now," he said stubbornly.

"Explain it to me, don Juan."

"No. *You* must explain it to me."

For the life of me I could not fathom what he was referring to.

"He's crying! He's crying!" don Juan kept on saying in a mesmerizing tone. "And he's hugging you now. He's hurt! He's hurt! And he's looking at you. Do you feel his eyes? He's kneeling and hugging you. He's younger than you. He has come running to you. But his arm is broken. Do you feel his arm? That little boy has a nose that looks like a button. Yes! That's a button nose."

My ears began to buzz and I lost the sensation of being at don Juan's house. The words "button nose" plunged me at once into a scene out of my childhood. I knew a button-nose boy! Don Juan had edged his way into one of the most recondite places of my life. I knew then the promise he was talking about. I had a sensation of elation, of despair, of awe for don Juan and his splendid maneuver. How in the devil did he know about the button-nose boy of my childhood? I became so agitated by the memory don Juan had evoked in me that my power to remember took me back to a time when I was eight years old. My mother had left two years before and I had spent the most hellish years of my life circulating among my mother's sisters, who served as dutiful mother surrogates and took care of me a couple of months at a time. Each of my aunts had a large family, and no matter how careful and protective the aunts were toward me, I had twenty-two cousins to contend with. Their cruelty was sometimes truly bizarre. I felt then that I was surrounded by enemies, and in the excruciating years that followed I waged a desperate and sordid war. Finally, through means I still do not know to this day, I succeeded in subduing all my cousins. I was indeed victorious. I had no more competitors who counted. However, I did not know that, nor did I know how to stop my war, which logically was extended to the school grounds.

The classrooms of the rural school where I went were mixed and the first and third grades were separated only by a space between the desks. It was there that I met a little boy with a flat nose, who was teased with the nickname "Button-nose." He was a first-grader. I used to pick on him haphazardly, not really intending to. But he seemed to like me in spite of everything I did to him. He used to follow me around and even kept the secret that I was responsible for some of the pranks that baffled the principal. And yet I still teased him. One day I deliberately toppled over a heavy standing blackboard; it fell on him; the desk in which he was sitting absorbed some of the impact, but still the blow broke his collarbone. He fell down. I helped him up and saw the pain and fright in his eyes as he looked at me and held onto me. The shock of seeing him in pain, with a mangled arm, was more than I could bear. For years I had viciously battled against my cousins and I had won; I had vanquished my foes; I had felt good and powerful up to the moment when the sight of the button-nose little boy crying demolished my victories. Right there I quit the battle. In whatever way I was capable of, I made a resolution not to win ever again. I thought his arm would have to be cut off, and I promised that if the little boy was cured I would never again be victorious. I gave up my victories for him. That was the way I understood it then.

Don Juan had opened a festered sore in my life. I felt dizzy, overwhelmed. A well of unmitigated sadness beckoned me and I succumbed to it. I felt the weight of my acts on me. The memory of that little button-nose boy, whose name was Joaquín, produced in me such a vivid anguish that I wept. I told don Juan of my sadness for that boy who never had anything, that little Joaquín who did not have money to go to a doctor and whose arm never set properly. And all I had to give him were my childish victories. I felt so ashamed.

"Be in peace, you funny bird," don Juan said imperatively. "You gave enough. Your victories were strong and they were yours. You gave enough. Now you must change your promise."

"How do I change it? Do I just say so?"

"A promise like that cannot be changed by just saying

so. Perhaps very soon you'll be able to know what to do about changing it. Then perhaps you'll even get to *see*."

"Can you give me any suggestions, don Juan?"

"You must wait patiently, knowing that you're waiting, and knowing what you're waiting for. That is the warrior's way. And if it is a matter of fulfilling your promise then you must be aware that you are fulfilling it. Then a time will come when your waiting will be over and you will no longer have to honor your promise. There is nothing you can do for that little boy's life. Only he could cancel that act."

"But how can he?"

"By learning to reduce his wants to nothing. As long as he thinks that he was a victim, his life will be hell. And as long as you think the same your promise will be valid. What makes us unhappy is to want. Yet if we would learn to cut our wants to nothing, the smallest thing we'd get would be a true gift. Be in peace, you made a good gift to Joaquín. To be poor or wanting is only a thought; and so is to hate, or to be hungry, or to be in pain."

"I cannot truly believe that, don Juan. How could hunger and pain be only thoughts?"

"They are only thoughts for me now. That's all I know. I have accomplished that feat. The power to do that is all we have, mind you, to oppose the forces of our lives; without that power we are dregs, dust in the wind."

"I have no doubt that you have done it, don Juan, but how can a simple man like myself or little Joaquín accomplish that?"

"It is up to us as single individuals to oppose the forces of our lives. I have said this to you countless times: Only a warrior can survive. A warrior knows that he is waiting and what he is waiting for; and while he waits he wants nothing and thus whatever little thing he gets is more than he can take. If he needs to eat he finds a way, because he is not hungry; if something hurts his body he finds a way to stop it, because he is not in pain. To be hungry or to be in pain means that the man has abandoned himself and is no longer a warrior; and the forces of his hunger and pain will destroy him."

I wanted to go on arguing my point, but I stopped because I realized that by arguing I was making a barrier to protect myself from the devastating force of don Juan's superb feat which had touched me so deeply and with such a power. How did he know? I thought that perhaps I had told him the story of the button-nose boy during one of my deep states of nonordinary reality. I did not recollect telling him, but my not remembering under such conditions was understandable.

"How did you know about my promise, don Juan?"

"I *saw* it."

"Did you *see* it when I had taken Mescalito, or when I had smoked your mixture?"

"I *saw* it now. Today."

"Did you *see* the whole thing?"

"There you go again. I've told you, there's no point in talking about what *seeing* is like. It is nothing."

I did not pursue the point any longer. Emotionally I was convinced.

"I also made a vow once," don Juan said suddenly.

The sound of his voice made me jump.

"I promised my father that I would live to destroy his assassins. I carried that promise with me for years. Now the promise is changed. I'm no longer interested in destroying anybody. I don't hate the Mexicans. I don't hate anyone. I have learned that the countless paths one traverses in one's life are all equal. Oppressors and oppressed meet at the end, and the only thing that prevails is that life was altogether too short for both. Today I feel sad not because my mother and father died the way they did; I feel sad because they were Indians. They lived like Indians and died like Indians and never knew that they were, before anything else, men."

10

I went back to visit don Juan on May 30, 1969, and
bluntly told him that I wanted to take another crack at
"seeing." He shook his head negatively and laughed, and
I felt compelled to protest. He told me I had to be patient
and the time was not right, but I doggedly insisted I was
ready.

He did not seem annoyed with my nagging requests. He
tried, nevertheless, to change the subject. I did not let go
and asked him to advise me what to do in order to overcome my impatience.

"You must act like a warrior," he said.

"How?"

"One learns to act like a warrior by acting, not by
talking."

"You said that a warrior thinks about his death. I do
that all the time; obviously that isn't enough."

He seemed to have an outburst of impatience and made
a smacking sound with his lips. I told him that I had not
meant to make him angry and that if he did not need me
there at his house, I was ready to go back to Los Angeles.
Don Juan patted me gently on the back and said that he
never got angry with me; he had simply assumed I knew
what it meant to be a warrior.

"What can I do to live like a warrior?" I asked.

He took off his hat and scratched his temples. He looked
at me fixedly and smiled.

"You like everything spelled out, don't you?"

"My mind works that way."

"It doesn't have to."

"I don't know how to change. That is why I ask you to tell me exactly what to do to live like a warrior; if I knew that, I could find a way to adapt myself to it."

He must have thought my statements were humorous; he patted me on the back as he laughed.

I had the feeling he was going to ask me to leave any minute, so I quickly sat down on my straw mat facing him and began asking him more questions. I wanted to know why I had to wait.

He explained that if I were to try to "see" in a helter-skelter manner, before I had "healed the wounds" I received battling the guardian, chances were that I would encounter the guardian again even though I was not looking for it. Don Juan assured me that no man in that position would be capable of surviving such an encounter.

"You must completely forget the guardian before you can again embark on the quest of *seeing,*" he said.

"How can anyone forget the guardian?"

"A warrior has to use his will and his patience to forget. In fact, a warrior has only his will and his patience and with them he builds anything he wants."

"But I'm not a warrior."

"You have started learning the ways of sorcerers. You have no more time for retreats or for regrets. You only have time to live like a warrior and work for patience and will, whether you like it or not."

"How does a warrior work for them?"

Don Juan thought for a long time before answering.

"I think there is no way of talking about it," he finally said. "Especially about will. Will is something very special. It happens mysteriously. There is no real way of telling how one uses it, except that the results of using the will are astounding. Perhaps the first thing that one should do is to know that one can develop the will. A warrior knows that and proceeds to wait for it. Your mistake is not to know that you are waiting for your will.

"My benefactor told me that a warrior knows that he is waiting and knows what he is waiting for. In your case, you know that you're waiting. You've been here with me for years, yet you don't know what you are waiting for. It is very difficult, if not impossible, for the average man to know what he is waiting for. A warrior, however, has no problems; he knows that he is waiting for his will."

"What exactly is the will? Is it determination, like the determination of your grandson Lucio to have a motor-cycle?"

"No," don Juan said softly and giggled. "That's not will. Lucio only indulges. Will is something else, something very clear and powerful which can direct our acts. Will is something a man uses, for instance, to win a battle which he, by all calculations, should lose."

"Then will must be what we call courage," I said.

"No. Courage is something else. Men of courage are dependable men, noble men perennially surrounded by people who flock around them and admire them; yet very few men of courage have will. Usually they are fearless men who are given to performing daring common-sense acts; most of the time a courageous man is also fearsome and feared. Will, on the other hand, has to do with aston-ishing feats that defy our common sense."

"Is will the control we may have over ourselves?" I asked.

"You may say that it is a kind of control."

"Do you think I can exercise my will, for instance, by denying myself certain things?"

"Such as asking questions?" he interjected.

He said it in such a mischievous tone that I had to stop writing to look at him. We both laughed.

"No," he said. "Denying yourself is an indulgence and I don't recommend anything of the kind. That is the reason why I let you ask all the questions you want. If I told you to stop asking questions, you might warp your will trying to do that. The indulgence of denying is by far the worst; it forces us to believe we are doing great things, when in effect we are only fixed within ourselves. To stop asking questions is not the will I'm talking about. Will is a power. And since it is a power it has to be controlled and tuned and that takes time. I know that and I'm

patient with you. When I was your age I was as impulsive
as you. Yet I have changed. Our will operates in spite of
our indulgence. For example, your will is already opening
your gap, little by little."

"What gap are you talking about?"

"There is a gap in us; like the soft spot on the head of
a child which closes with age, this gap opens as one de-
velops one's will."

"Where is that gap?"

"At the place of your luminous fibers," he said, pointing
to his abdominal area.

"What is it like? What is it for?"

"It's an opening. It allows a space for the will to shoot
out, like an arrow."

"Is the will an object? Or like an object?"

"No. I just said that to make you understand. What a
sorcerer calls will is a power within ourselves. It is not a
thought, or an object, or a wish. To stop asking questions
is not will because it needs thinking and wishing. Will is
what can make you succeed when your thoughts tell you
that you're defeated. Will is what makes you invulnerable.
Will is what sends a sorcerer through a wall; through
space; to the moon, if he wants."

There was nothing else I wanted to ask. I was tired and
somewhat tense. I was afraid don Juan was going to ask
me to leave and that annoyed me.

"Let's go to the hills," he said abruptly, and stood up.

On the way he started talking about will again and
laughed at my dismay over not being able to take notes.

He described will as a force which was the true link
between men and the world. He was very careful to establish that the world was whatever we perceive, in any
manner we may choose to perceive. Don Juan maintained
that "perceiving the world" entails a process of apprehend-
ing whatever presents itself to us. This particular "perceiving" is done with our senses and with our will.

I asked him if will was a sixth sense. He said it was
rather a relation between ourselves and the perceived
world.

I suggested that we halt so I could take notes. He laughed and kept on walking.

He did not make me leave that night, and the next day after eating breakfast he himself brought up the subject of will.

"What you yourself call will is character and strong disposition," he said. "What a sorcerer calls will is a force that comes from within and attaches itself to the world out there. It comes out through the belly, right here, where the luminous fibers are."

He rubbed his navel to point out the area.

"I say that it comes out through here because one can feel it coming out."

"Why do you call it will?"

"I don't call it anything. My benefactor called it will, and other men of knowledge call it will."

"Yesterday you said that one can perceive the world with the senses as well as with the will. How is that possible?"

"An average man can 'grab' the things of the world only with his hands, or his eyes, or his ears, but a sorcerer can grab them also with his nose, or his tongue, or his will, especially with his will. I cannot really describe how it is done, but you yourself, for instance, cannot describe to me how you hear. It happens that I am also capable of hearing, so we can talk about what we hear, but not about how we hear. A sorcerer uses his will to perceive the world. That perceiving, however, is not like hearing. When we look at the world or when we hear it, we have the impression that it is out there and that it is real. When we perceive the world with our will we know that it is not as 'out there' or 'as real' as we think."

"Is will the same as *seeing*?"

"No. Will is a force, a power. *Seeing* is not a force, but rather a way of getting through things. A sorcerer may have a very strong will and yet he may not *see*; which means that only a man of knowledge perceives the world with his senses and with his will and also with his *seeing*."

I told him that I was more confused than ever about

how to use my will to forget the guardian. That statement and my mood of perplexity seemed to delight him.

"I've told you that when you talk you only get confused," he said and laughed. "But at least now you know you are waiting for your will. You still don't know what it is, or how it could happen to you. So watch carefully everything you do. The very thing that could help you develop your will is amidst all the little things you do."

Don Juan was gone all morning; he returned in the early afternoon with a bundle of dry plants. He signaled me with his head to help him and we worked in complete silence for hours, sorting the plants. When we finished we sat down to rest and he smiled at me benevolently.

I said to him in a very serious manner that I had been reading my notes and I still could not understand what being a warrior entailed or what the idea of will meant.

"Will is not an idea," he said.

This was the first time he had spoken to me the whole day.

After a long pause he continued: "We are different, you and I. Our characters are not alike. Your nature is more violent than mine. When I was your age I was not violent but mean; you are the opposite. My benefactor was like that; he would have been perfectly suited to be your teacher. He was a great sorcerer but he did not *see;* not the way I *see* or the way Genaro *sees.* I understand the world and live guided by my *seeing.* My benefactor, on the other hand, had to live as a warrior. If a man *sees* he doesn't have to live like a warrior, or like anything else, for he can *see* things as they really are and direct his life accordingly. But, considering your character, I would say that you may never learn to *see,* in which case you will have to live your entire life like a warrior.

"My benefactor said that when a man embarks on the paths of sorcery he becomes aware, in a gradual manner, that ordinary life has been forever left behind; that knowledge is indeed a frightening affair; that the means of the ordinary world are no longer a buffer for him; and that he must adopt a new way of life if he is going to survive. The first thing he ought to do, at that point, is to want to become a warrior, a very important step and decision. The frightening nature of knowledge leaves one no alternative but to become a warrior.

"By the time knowledge becomes a frightening affair the man also realizes that death is the irreplaceable partner that sits next to him on the mat. Every bit of knowledge that becomes power has death as its central force. Death lends the ultimate touch, and whatever is touched by death indeed becomes power.

"A man who follows the paths of sorcery is confronted with imminent annihilation every turn of the way, and unavoidably he becomes keenly aware of his death. Without the awareness of death he would be only an ordinary man involved in ordinary acts. He would lack the necessary potency, the necessary concentration that transforms one's ordinary time on earth into magical power.

"Thus to be a warrior a man has to be, first of all, and rightfully so, keenly aware of his own death. But to be concerned with death would force any one of us to focus on the self and that would be debilitating. So the next thing one needs to be a warrior is detachment. The idea of imminent death, instead of becoming an obsession, becomes an indifference."

Don Juan stopped talking and looked at me. He seemed to be waiting for a comment.

"Do you understand?" he asked.

I understood what he had said but I personally could not see how anyone could arrive at a sense of detachment. I said that from the point of view of my own apprenticeship I had already experienced the moment when knowledge became such a frightening affair. I could also truthfully say that I no longer found support in the ordinary premises of my daily life. And I wanted, or perhaps even more than wanted, I needed, to live like a warrior.

"Now you must detach yourself," he said.

"From what?"

"Detach yourself from everything."

"That's impossible. I don't want to be a hermit."

"To be a hermit is an indulgence and I never meant

that. A hermit is not detached, for he willfully abandons himself to being a hermit.

"Only the idea of death makes a man sufficiently detached so he is incapable of abandoning himself to anything. Only the idea of death makes a man sufficiently detached so he can't deny himself anything. A man of that sort, however, does not crave, for he has acquired a silent lust for life and for all things of life. He knows his death is stalking him and won't give him time to cling to anything, so he tries, without craving, all of everything.

"A detached man, who knows he has no possibility of fencing off his death, has only one thing to back himself with: the power of his decisions. He has to be, so to speak, the master of his choices. He must fully understand that his choice is his responsibility and once he makes it there is no longer time for regrets or recriminations. His decisions are final, simply because his death does not permit him time to cling to anything.

"And thus with an awareness of his death, with his detachment, and with the power of his decisions a warrior sets his life in a strategical manner. The knowledge of his death guides him and makes him detached and silently lusty; the power of his final decisions makes him able to choose without regrets and what he chooses is always strategically the best; and so he performs everything he has to with gusto and lusty efficiency.

"When a man behaves in such a manner one may rightfully say that he is a warrior and has acquired patience!"

Don Juan asked me if I had anything to say, and I remarked that the task he had described would take a lifetime. He said I protested too much in front of him and that he knew I behaved, or at least tried to behave, in terms of a warrior in my day-to-day life.

"You have pretty good claws," he said, laughing. "Show them to me from time to time. It's good practice."

I made a gesture of claws and growled, and he laughed. Then he cleared his throat and went on talking.

"When a warrior has acquired patience he is on his way to will. He knows how to wait. His death sits with him on his mat, they are friends. His death advises him, in mys-

terious ways, how to choose, how to live strategically. And
the warrior waits! I would say that the warrior learns
without any hurry because he knows he is waiting for his
will; and one day he succeeds in performing something
ordinarily quite impossible to accomplish. He may not
even notice his extraordinary deed. But as he keeps on
performing impossible acts, or as impossible things keep
on happening to him, he becomes aware that a sort of
power is emerging. A power that comes out of his body as
he progresses on the path of knowledge. At first it is like
an itching on the belly, or a warm spot that cannot be
soothed; then it becomes a pain, a great discomfort. Sometimes the pain and discomfort are so great that the warrior
has convulsions for months, the more severe the convulsions the better for him. A fine power is always heralded
by great pain.

"When the convulsions cease the warrior notices he has
strange feelings about things. He notices that he can
actually touch anything he wants with a feeling that comes
out of his body from a spot right below or right above his
navel. That feeling is the will, and when he is capable of
grabbing with it, one can rightfully say that the warrior is
a sorcerer, and that he has acquired will."

Don Juan stopped talking and seemed to await my comments or questions. I had nothing to say. I was deeply
concerned with the idea that a sorcerer had to experience
pain and convulsions but I felt embarrassed about asking
him if I also had to go through that. Finally, after a long
silence, I asked him, and he giggled as if he had been
anticipating my question. He said that pain was not absolutely necessary; he, for example, had never had it and will
had just happened to him.

"One day I was in the mountains," he said, "and I
stumbled upon a puma, a female one; she was big and
hungry. I ran and she ran after me. I climbed a rock and
she stood a few feet away ready to jump. I threw rocks at
her. She growled and began to charge me. It was then that
my will fully came out, and I stopped her with it before
she jumped on me. I caressed her with my will. I actually

rubbed her tits with it. She looked at me with sleepy eyes and lay down and I ran like a son of a bitch before she got over it."

Don Juan made a very comical gesture to portray a man running for dear life, holding onto his hat.

I told him that I hated to think I had only female mountain lions or convulsions to look forward to, if I wanted will.

"My benefactor was a sorcerer of great powers," he went on. "He was a warrior through and through. His will was indeed his most magnificent accomplishment. But a man can go still further than that; a man can learn to *see*. Upon learning to *see* he no longer needs to live like a warrior, nor be a sorcerer. Upon learning to *see* a man becomes everything by becoming nothing. He, so to speak, vanishes and yet he's there. I would say that this is the time when a man can be or can get anything he desires. But he desires nothing, and instead of playing with his fellow men like they were toys, he meets them in the midst of their folly. The only difference between them is that a man who *sees* controls his folly, while his fellow men can't. A man who *sees* has no longer an active interest in his fellow men. *Seeing* has already detached him from absolutely everything he knew before."

"The sole idea of being detached from everything I know gives me the chills," I said.

"You must be joking! The thing which should give you the chills is not to have anything to look forward to but a lifetime of doing that which you have always done. Think of the man who plants corn year after year until he's too old and tired to get up, so he lies around like an old dog. His thoughts and feelings, the best of him, ramble aimlessly to the only things he has ever done, to plant corn. For me that is the most frightening waste there is.

"We are men and our lot is to learn and to be hurled into inconceivable new worlds."

"Are there any new worlds for us really?" I asked half in jest.

"We have exhausted nothing, you fool," he said imperatively. *"Seeing* is for impeccable men. Temper your spirit now, become a warrior, learn to *see,* and then you'll know that there is no end to the new worlds for our vision."

11

Don Juan did not make me leave after I had run his errands, as he had been doing lately. He said I could stay, and the next day, June 28, 1969, just before noon he told me I was going to smoke again.

"Am I going to try to *see* the guardian again?"

"No, that's out. This is something else."

Don Juan calmly filled his pipe with smoking mixture, lighted it, and handed it to me. I experienced no apprehension. A pleasant drowsiness enveloped me right away. When I had finished smoking the whole bowl of mixture, don Juan put his pipe away and helped me stand up. We had been sitting facing each other on two straw mats he had placed in the center of his room. He said that we were going for a short walk and encouraged me to walk, shoving me gently. I took a step and my legs sagged. I did not feel any pain when my knees hit the ground. Don Juan held my arm and pushed me up on my feet again.

"You have to walk," he said, "the same way you got up the other time. You must use your will."

I seemed to be stuck to the ground. I attempted a step with my right foot and almost lost my balance. Don Juan held my right arm at the armpit and gently catapulted me forward, but my legs did not support me and I would have collapsed on my face had don Juan not caught my arm and buffered my fall. He held me by the right armpit and made me lean on him. I could not feel anything but I was certain that my head was resting on his shoulder; I was seeing the room from a slanted perspective. He dragged me in that position around the porch. We circled it twice in a most painful fashion; finally, I suppose, my weight became so great that he had to drop me on the ground. I knew he could not move me. In a certain way it was as if part of myself deliberately wanted to become lead-heavy. Don Juan did not make any effort to pick me up. He looked at me for an instant; I was lying on my back facing him. I tried to smile at him and he began to laugh; then he bent over and slapped me on the belly. I had a most peculiar sensation. It was not painful or pleasurable or anything I could think of. It was rather a jolt. Don Juan immediately began to roll me around. I did not feel anything; I assumed he was rolling me around because my view of the porch changed in accordance with a circular motion. When don Juan had me in the position he wanted he stepped back.

"Stand up!" he ordered me imperatively. "Stand up the way you did it the other day. Don't piddle around. You know how to get up. Now get up!"

I intently tried to recollect the actions I had performed on that occasion, but I could not think clearly; it was as if my thoughts had a will of their own no matter how hard I tried to control them. Finally the thought occurred to me that if I said "up" as I had done before I would certainly get up. I said, "Up," loud and clear but nothing happened.

Don Juan looked at me with obvious displeasure and then walked around me toward the door. I was lying on my left side and had a full view of the area in front of his house; my back was to the door, so when he walked around me I immediately assumed he had gone inside.

"Don Juan!" I called loudly, but he did not answer.

I had an overpowering feeling of impotence and despair. I wanted to get up. I said, "Up," again and again, as if that were the magic word that would make me move. Nothing happened. I had an attack of frustration and I went through a sort of tantrum. I wanted to beat my head against the floor and weep. I spent excruciating moments in which I wanted to move or talk and I could not do either. I was truly immobile, paralyzed.

"Don Juan, help me!" I finally managed to bellow.

Don Juan came back and sat in front of me, laughing. He said that I was getting hysterical and that whatever I was experiencing was inconsequential. He lifted my head and, looking straight at me, said that I was having an attack of sham fear. He told me not to fret.

"Your life is getting complicated," he said. "Get rid of whatever it is that's causing you to lose your temper. Stay here quietly and rearrange yourself."

He placed my head on the ground. He stepped over me and all I could perceive was the shuffling of his sandals as he walked away.

My first impulse was to fret again, but I could not gather the energy to work myself into it. Instead, I found myself slipping into a rare state of serenity; a great feeling of ease enveloped me. I knew what the complexity of my life was. It was my little boy. I wanted to be his father more than anything else on this earth. I liked the idea of molding his character and taking him hiking and teaching him "how to live," and yet I abhorred the idea of coercing him into my way of life, but that was precisely what I would have to do, coerce him with force or with that artful set of arguments and rewards we call understanding.

"I must let him go," I thought. "I must not cling to him. I must set him free."

My thoughts brought on a terrifying feeling of melancholy. I began to weep. My eyes filled with tears and my view of the porch blurred. Suddenly I had a great urge to get up and look for don Juan to explain to him about my little boy; and the next thing I knew, I was looking at the porch from an upright position. I turned around to face the house and found don Juan standing in front of me. Apparently he had been standing there behind me all the time.

Although I could not feel my steps, I must have walked toward him, because I moved. Don Juan came to me smiling and held me up by the armpits. His face was very close to mine.

"Good, good work," he said reassuringly.

At that instant I became aware that something extraordinary was taking place right there. I had the feeling at first that I was only recollecting an event that had taken place years before. At one time in the past I had seen don Juan's face at very close range; I had smoked his mixture and I had had the feeling then that don Juan's face was submerged in a tank of water. It was enormous and it was luminous and it moved. The image had been so brief that I did not have time to really take stock of it. This time, however, don Juan was holding me and his face was no more than a foot away from mine and I had time to examine it. When I stood up and turned around I definitely saw don Juan; "the don Juan I know" definitely walked toward me and held me. But when I focused my eyes on his face I did not see don Juan as I am accustomed to seeing him; instead, I saw a large object in front of my eyes. I knew it was don Juan's face, yet that knowledge was not guided by my perception; it was, rather, a logical conclusion on my part; after all, my memory confirmed that the instant before, "the don Juan I know" was holding me by the armpits. Therefore the strange, luminous object in front of me had to be don Juan's face; there was a familiarity to it; yet it had no resemblance to what I would call don Juan's "real" face. What I was looking at was a round object which had a luminosity of its own. Every part in it moved. I perceived a contained, undulatory, rhythmical flow; it was as if the flowing was enclosed within itself, never moving beyond its limits, and yet the object in front of my eyes was oozing with movement at any place on its surface. The thought that occurred to me was that it oozed life. In fact it was so alive that I became engrossed looking at its movement. It was a mesmerizing fluttering. It became more and more engrossing, until I could no longer tell what the phenomenon in front of my eyes was.

I experienced a sudden jolt; the luminous object became blurry, as if something were shaking it, and then it lost its glow and became solid and fleshy. I was then looking at don Juan's familiar dark face. He was smiling placidly.

The view of his "real" face lasted an instant and then the
face again acquired a glow, a shine, an iridescence. It was
not light as I am accustomed to perceiving light, or even
a glow; rather it was movement, an incredibly fast flickering of something. The glowing object began to bobble up
and down again and that disrupted its undulatory con-
tinuity. Its shine diminished as it shook, until it again
became the "solid" face of don Juan, as I see him in
everyday life. At that moment I vaguely realized that don
Juan was shaking me. He was also speaking to me. I did
not understand what he was saying, but as he kept on
shaking me I finally heard him.

"Don't stare at me. Don't stare at me," he kept saying.
"Break your gaze. Break your gaze. Move your eyes
away."

Shaking my body seemed to force me to dislodge my
steady gaze; apparently when I did not peer intently into
don Juan's face I did not see the luminous object. When I
moved my eyes away from his face and looked at it with
the corner of my eye, so to speak, I could perceive his
solidity; that is to say, I could perceive a three-dimensional
person; without really looking at him I could, in fact, perceive his whole body. but when I focused my gaze, the
face became at once the luminous object.

"Don't look at me at all," don Juan said gravely.

I moved my eyes away and looked at the ground.

"Don't fix your gaze on anything," don Juan said imperatively, and stepped aside in order to help me walk.

I did not feel my steps and could not figure out how I
performed the act of walking, yet with don Juan holding
me by the armpit, we moved all the way to the back of his
house. We stopped by the irrigation ditch.

"Now gaze at the water," don Juan ordered me.

I looked at the water but I could not gaze at it. Somehow the movement of the current distracted me. Don Juan
kept on urging me in a joking manner to exercise my
"gazing powers," but I could not concentrate. I gazed at
don Juan's face once again but the glow did not become
apparent any more.

I began to experience a strange itching on my body, the

sensation of a limb that has fallen asleep; the muscles of my legs began to twitch. Don Juan shoved me into the water and I tumbled down all the way to the bottom. He had apparently held my right hand as he pushed me, and when I hit the shallow bottom he pulled me up again.

It took a long time for me to regain control over myself. When we got back to his house hours later, I asked him to explain my experience. As I put on my dry clothes I excitedly described what I had perceived, but he discarded my entire account, saying that there was nothing of importance in it.

"Big deal!" he said, mocking me. "You saw a glow, big deal."

I insisted on an explanation and he got up and said he had to leave. It was almost five in the afternoon.

The next day I insisted again on discussing my peculiar experience.

"Was it *seeing*, don Juan?" I asked.

He remained quiet, smiling mysteriously, as I kept pressing him to answer me.

"Let's say that *seeing* is somewhat like that," he finally said. "You were gazing at my face and saw it shining, but it was still my face. It just happens that the little smoke makes one gaze like that. Nothing to it."

"But in what way would *seeing* be different?"

"When you *see* there are no longer familiar features in the world. Everything is new. Everything has never happened before. The world is incredible!"

"Why do you say incredible, don Juan? What makes it incredible?"

"Nothing is any longer familiar. Everything you gaze at becomes nothing! Yesterday you didn't *see*. You gazed at my face and, since you like me, you noticed my glow. I was not monstrous, like the guardian, but beautiful and interesting. But you did not *see* me. I didn't become nothing in front of you. And yet you did well. You took the first real step toward *seeing*. The only drawback was that you focused on me, and in that case I'm no better than the guardian for you. You succumbed in both instances and didn't *see*."

"Do things disappear? How do they become nothing?"

"Things don't disappear. They don't vanish, if that's what you mean; they simply become nothing and yet they are still there."

"How can that be possible, don Juan?"

"You have the damnedest insistence on talking!" don Juan exclaimed with a serious face. "I think we didn't hit it right about your promise. Perhaps what you really promised was to never, ever stop talking."

Don Juan's tone was severe. The look in his face was concerned. I wanted to laugh but I did not dare. I believed that don Juan was serious, but he was not. He began to laugh. I told him that if I did not talk I got very nervous.

"Let's walk, then," he said.

He took me to the mouth of a canyon at the bottom of the hills. It was about an hour's walk. We rested for a short while and then he guided me through the thick desert underbrush to a water hole; that is, to a spot he said was a water hole. It was as dry as any other spot in the surrounding area.

"Sit in the middle of the water hole," he ordered me.

I obeyed and sat down.

"Are you going to sit here too?" I asked.

I saw him fixing a place to sit some twenty yards from the center of the water hole, against the rocks on the side of the mountain.

He said he was going to watch me from there. I was sitting with my knees against my chest. He corrected my position and told me to sit with my left leg tucked under my seat and my right one bent, with the knee in an upward position. My right arm had to be by my side with my fist resting on the ground, while my left arm was crossed over my chest. He told me to face him and stay there, relaxed but not "abandoned." He then took a sort of whitish cord from his pouch. It looked like a big loop. He looped it around his neck and stretched it with his left hand until it was taut. He plucked the tight string with his right hand. It made a dull, vibratory sound.

He relaxed his grip and looked at me and told me that I had to yell a specific word if I began to feel that something was coming at me when he plucked the string.

I asked what was supposed to come at me and he told me to shut up. He signaled me with his hand that he was going to commence. He said that if something came at me in a very menacing way I had to adopt a fighting form that he had taught me years before, which consisted of dancing, beating the ground with the tip of the left foot, while I slapped my right thigh vigorously. The fighting form was part of a defense technique used in cases of extreme distress and danger.

I had a moment of genuine apprehension. I wanted to inquire about the reason for our being there, but he did not give me time and began plucking the string. He did it various times at regular intervals of perhaps twenty seconds. I noticed that as he kept plucking the string he augmented the tension. I could clearly see that his arms and neck were shivering under the stress. The sound became more clear and I realized then that he added a peculiar yell every time he plucked the string. The combined sound of the tense string and the human voice produced a weird, unearthly reverberation.

I did not feel anything coming at me, but the sight of don Juan's exertion and the eerie sound he was producing had me almost in a state of trance.

Don Juan relaxed his grip and looked at me. While he played, his back was turned to me and he was facing the southeast, as I was; when he relaxed, he faced me.

"Don't look at me when I play," he said. "Don't close your eyes, though. Not for anything. Look at the ground in front of you and listen."

He tensed the string again and began playing. I looked at the ground and concentrated on the sound he was making. I had never heard the sound before in my life.

I became very frightened. The eerie reverberation filled the narrow canyon and began to echo. In fact the sound don Juan was making was coming back to me as an echo from all around the canyon walls. Don Juan must have also noticed that and increased the tension of his string. Although don Juan had changed the pitch, the echo seemed to subside, and then it seemed to concentrate on one point, toward the southeast.

Don Juan reduced the tension of the string by degrees, until I heard a final dull twang. He put the string inside his pouch and walked toward me. He helped me stand up. I noticed then that the muscles of my arms and legs were stiff, like rocks; I was literally soaked in perspiration. I had no idea I had been perspiring so heavily. Drops of sweat ran into my eyes and made them burn.

Don Juan practically dragged me out of the place. I tried to say something but he put his hand over my mouth.

Instead of leaving the canyon the way we had come in, don Juan made a detour. We climbed the side of the mountain and ended up in some hills very far from the mouth of the canyon.

We walked in dead silence to his house. It was already dark by the time we got there. I tried to talk again but don Juan put his hand on my mouth once more.

We did not eat and did not light the kerosene lantern. Don Juan put my mat in his room and pointed at it with his chin. I understood it as a gesture that I should lie down and go to sleep.

"I have the proper thing for you to do," don Juan said to me as soon as I woke up the next morning. "You will start it today. There isn't much time, you know."

After a very long, uneasy pause I felt compelled to ask him, "What did you have me doing in the canyon yesterday?"

Don Juan giggled like a child.

"I just tapped the spirit of that water hole," he said. "That type of spirit should be tapped when the water hole is dry, when the spirit has retreated into the mountains. Yesterday I, let us say, woke him up from his slumber. But he didn't mind it and pointed to your lucky direction. His voice came from that direction." Don Juan pointed toward the southeast.

"What was the string you played, don Juan?"

"A spirit catcher."

"Can I look at it?"

"No. But I'll make you one. Or better yet, you will make one for yourself some day, when you learn to *see*."

"What is it made of, don Juan?"

"Mine is a wild boar. When you get one you will realize that it is alive and can teach you the different sounds it likes. With practice you will get to know your spirit catcher so well that together you will make sounds full of power."

"Why did you take me to look for the spirit of the water hole, don Juan?"

"You will know that very soon."

Around 11:30 A.M. we sat under his *ramada*, where he prepared his pipe for me to smoke.

He told me to stand up when my body was quite numb; I did that with great ease. He helped me walk around. I was surprised at my control; I actually walked twice around the *ramada* by myself. Don Juan stayed by my side but did not guide me or support me. Then he took me by the arm and walked me to the irrigation ditch. He made me sit on the edge of the bank and ordered me imperatively to gaze at the water and think of nothing else.

I tried to focus my gaze on the water but its movement distracted me. My mind and my eyes began to wander onto other features of the immediate surroundings. Don Juan bobbed my head up and down and ordered me again to gaze only at the water and not think at all. He said it was difficult to stare at the moving water and that one had to keep on trying. I tried three times and every time I became distracted by something else. Don Juan very patiently shook my head every time. Finally I noticed that my mind and my eyes were focusing on the water; in spite of its movement I was becoming immersed in my view of its liquidness. The water became slightly different. It seemed to be heavier and uniformly grayish green. I could notice the ripples it made as it moved. The ripples were extremely sharp. And then, suddenly, I had the sensation that I was not looking at a mass of moving water but at a picture of water; what I had in front of my eyes was a frozen segment of the running water. The ripples were immobile. I could look at every one of them. Then they began to acquire a green phosphorescence and a sort of green fog oozed out of them. The fog expanded in ripples and as it moved, its greenness became more brilliant until it was a dazzling radiance that covered everything.

I don't know how long I stayed by the irrigation ditch. Don Juan did not interrupt me. I was immersed in the green glow of the fog. I could sense it all around me. It soothed me. I had no thoughts, no feelings. All I had was a quiet awareness, the awareness of a brilliant, soothing greenness.

Being extremely cold and damp was the next thing I became aware of. Gradually I realized that I was submerged in the irrigation ditch. At one moment the water slipped inside my nose, and I swallowed it and it made me cough. I had an annoying itch inside my nose and I sneezed repeatedly. I stood up and had such a forceful and loud sneeze that I also farted. Don Juan clapped his hands and laughed.

"If a body farts, it's alive," he said.

He signaled me to follow him and we walked to his house.

I thought of keeping quiet. In a way, I expected to be in a detached and morose mood, but I really did not feel tired or melancholy. I felt rather buoyant and changed my clothes very rapidly. I began to whistle. Don Juan looked at me curiously and pretended to be surprised; he opened his mouth and his eyes. His gesture was very funny and I laughed quite a bit longer than it called for.

"You're cracking up," he said, and laughed very hard himself.

I explained to him that I did not want to fall into the habit of feeling morose after using his smoking mixture. I told him that after he had taken me out of the irrigation ditch, during my attempts to meet the guardian, I had become convinced that I could "see" if I stared at things around me long enough.

"*Seeing* is not a matter of looking and keeping quiet,"

he said. "*Seeing* is a technique one has to learn. Or maybe it is a technique some of us already know."

He peered at me as if to insinuate that I was one of those who already knew the technique.

"Are you strong enough to walk?" he asked.

I said I felt fine, which I did. I was not hungry, although I had not eaten all day. Don Juan put some bread and some pieces of dry meat in a knapsack, handed it to me, and gestured with his head for me to follow.

"Where are we going?" I asked.

He pointed toward the hills with a slight movement of his head. We headed for the same canyon where the water hole was, but we did not enter it. Don Juan climbed onto the rocks to our right, at the very mouth of the canyon. We went up the hill. The sun was almost on the horizon. It was a mild day but I felt hot and suffocated. I could hardly breathe.

Don Juan was quite a way ahead of me and had to stop to let me catch up with him. He said I was in terrible physical condition and that it was perhaps not wise to go any further. He let me rest for about an hour. He selected a slick, almost round boulder and told me to lie there. He arranged my body on the rock. He told me to stretch my arms and legs and let them hang loose. My back was slightly arched and my neck relaxed, so that my head also hung loose. He made me stay in that position for perhaps fifteen minutes. Then he told me to uncover my abdominal region. He carefully selected some branches and leaves and heaped them over my naked belly. I felt an instantaneous warmth all over my body. Don Juan then took me by the feet and turned me until my head was toward the southeast.

"Now let us call that spirit of the water hole," he said.

I tried to turn my head to look at him. He held me vigorously by the hair and said that I was in a very vulnerable position and in a terribly weak physical state and had to remain quiet and motionless. He had put all those special branches on my belly to protect me and was going to remain next to me in case I could not take care of myself.

He was standing next to the top of my head, and if I

rolled my eyes I could see him. He took his string and tensed it and then realized I was looking at him by rolling my eyes way into my forehead. He gave me a snappy tap on the head with his knuckles and ordered me to look at the sky, not to close my eyes, and to concentrate on the sound. He added, as if on second thought, that I should not hesitate to yell the word he had taught me if I felt something was coming at me.

Don Juan and his "spirit catcher" began with a low-tension twang. He slowly increased the tension, and I began to hear a sort of reverberation first, and then a definite echo which came consistently from a southeasterly direction. The tension increased. Don Juan and his "spirit catcher" were perfectly matched. The string produced a low-range note and don Juan magnified it, increasing its intensity until it was a penetrating cry, a howling call. The apex was an eerie shriek, inconceivable from the point of view of my own experience.

The sound reverberated in the mountains and echoed back to us. I fancied it was coming directly toward me. I felt it had something to do with the temperature of my body. Before don Juan started his calls I had been very warm and comfortable, but during the highest point of his calls I became chilled; my teeth chattered uncontrollably and I truly had the sensation that something was coming at me. At one point I noticed that the sky had become very dark. I had not been aware of the sky although I was looking at it. I had a moment of intense panic and I yelled the word don Juan had taught me.

Don Juan immediately began to decrease the tension of his eerie calls, but that did not bring me any relief.

"Cover your ears," don Juan mumbled imperatively.

I covered them with my hands. After some minutes don Juan stopped altogether and came around to my side. After he had taken the branches and leaves off my belly, he helped me up and carefully put them on the rock where I had been lying. He made a fire with them, and while it burned he rubbed my stomach with other leaves from his pouch.

He put his hand on my mouth when I was about to tell him that I had a terrible headache.

We stayed there until all the leaves had burned. It was fairly dark by then. We walked down the hill and I got sick to my stomach.

While we were walking along the irrigation ditch, don Juan said that I had done enough and I should not stay around. I asked him to explain what the spirit of the water hole was, but he gestured me to be quiet. He said that we would talk about it some other time, then he deliberately changed the subject and gave me a long explanation about "seeing." I said it was regrettable that I could not write in the darkness. He seemed very pleased and said that most of the time I did not pay attention to what he had to say because I was so determined to write everything down.

He spoke about "seeing" as a process independent of the allies and the techniques of sorcery. A sorcerer was a person who could command an ally and could thus manipulate an ally's power to his advantage, but the fact that he commanded an ally did not mean that he could "see." I reminded him that he had told me before that it was impossible to "see" unless one had an ally. Don Juan very calmly replied that he had come to the conclusion it was possible to "see" and yet not command an ally. He felt there was no reason why not, since "seeing" had nothing to do with the manipulatory techniques of sorcery, which served only to act upon our fellow men. The techniques of "seeing," on the other hand, had no effect on men.

My thoughts were very clear. I experienced no fatigue or drowsiness and no longer had an uncomfortable feeling in my stomach, as I walked with don Juan. I was terribly hungry, and when we got to his house I gorged myself with food.

Afterwards I asked him to tell me more about the techniques of "seeing." He smiled broadly at me and said that I was again myself.

"How is it," I said, "that the techniques of *seeing* have no effect on our fellow men?"

"I've told you already," he said. "*Seeing* is not sorcery. Yet one may easily confuse them, because a man who *sees* can learn, in no time at all, to manipulate an ally and may become a sorcerer. On the other hand, a man may learn certain techniques in order to command an ally and thus become a sorcerer, and yet he may never learn to *see*.

"Besides, *seeing* is contrary to sorcery. *Seeing* makes one realize the unimportance of it all."

"The unimportance of what, don Juan?"

"The unimportance of everything."

We did not say anything else. I felt very relaxed and did not want to speak any more. I was lying on my back on a straw mat. I had made a pillow with my windbreaker. I felt comfortable and happy and wrote my notes for hours in the light of the kerosene lantern.

Suddenly don Juan spoke again.

"Today you did very well," he said. "You did very well at the water. The spirit of the water hole likes you and helped you all the way."

I realized then that I had forgotten to recount my experience to him. I began to describe the way I had perceived the water. He did not let me continue. He said that he knew I had perceived a green fog.

I felt compelled to ask, "How did you know that, don Juan?"

"I *saw* you."

"What did I do?"

"Nothing, you sat there and gazed into the water and finally you perceived the green mist."

"Was it *seeing?*"

"No. But it was very close. You're getting close."

I got very excited. I wanted to know more about it. He laughed and made fun of my eagerness. He said that anyone could perceive the green fog because it was like the guardian, something that was unavoidably there, so there was no great accomplishment in perceiving it.

"When I said you did well, I meant that you did not fret," he said, "as you did with the guardian. If you had become restless I would have had to shake your head and bring you back. Whenever a man goes into the green fog his benefactor has to stay by him in case it begins to trap him. You can jump out of the guardian's reach by yourself, but you can't escape the clutches of the green fog by yourself. At least not at the beginning. Later on you may learn a way to do it. Now we're trying to find out something else."

"What are we trying to find out?"

"Whether you can *see* the water."

"How will I know that I have *seen* it, or that I am *seeing* it?"

"You will know. You get confused only when you talk."

12

Working on my notes I had come across various questions.

"Is the green fog, like the guardian, something that one has to overcome in order to *see?*" I asked don Juan as soon as we sat down under his *ramada* on August 8, 1969.

"Yes. One must overcome everything," he said.

"How can I overcome the green fog?"

"The same way you should have overcome the guardian, by letting it turn into nothing."

"What should I do?"

"Nothing. For you, the green fog is something much easier than the guardian. The spirit of the water hole likes you, while it certainly was not your temperament to deal with the guardian. You never really *saw* the guardian."

"Maybe that was because I didn't like it. What if I were to meet a guardian I liked? There must be some people who would regard the guardian I saw as being beautiful. Would they overcome it because they liked it?"

"No! You still don't understand. It doesn't matter whether you like or dislike the guardian. As long as you have a feeling toward it, the guardian will remain the same, monstrous, beautiful, or whatever. If you have no feeling toward it, on the other hand, the guardian will become nothing and will still be there in front of you."

The idea that something as colossal as the guardian could become nothing and still be in front of my eyes made absolutely no sense. I felt it was one of the alogical premises of don Juan's knowledge. However, I also felt that if he wanted to he could explain it to me. I insisted on asking him what he meant by that.

"You thought the guardian was something you knew, that's what I mean."

"But I didn't think it was something I knew."

"You thought it was ugly. Its size was awesome. It was a monster. You know what all those things are. So the guardian was always something you knew, and as long as it was something you knew you did not *see* it. I have told you already, the guardian had to become nothing and yet it had to stand in front of you. It had to be there and it had, at the same time, to be nothing."

"How could that be, don Juan? What you say is absurd."

"It is. But that is *seeing*. There is really no way to talk about it. *Seeing,* as I said before, is learned by *seeing*.

"Apparently you have no problem with water. You nearly *saw* it the other day. Water is your 'hinge.' All you need now is to perfect your technique of *seeing*. You have a powerful helper in the spirit of the water hole."

"That's another burning question I have, don Juan."

"You may have all the burning questions you want, but we cannot talk about the spirit of the water hole in this vicinity. In fact, it is better not to think about it at all. Not at all. Otherwise the spirit will trap you and if that happens there is nothing a living man can do to help you. So keep your mouth shut and keep your thoughts on something else."

Around ten o'clock the next morning don Juan took his pipe out of its sheath, filled it with smoking mixture, then handed it to me and told me to carry it to the bank of the stream. Holding the pipe with both hands, I managed to unbutton my shirt and put the pipe inside and hold it tight. Don Juan carried two straw mats and a small tray with coals. It was a warm day. We sat on the mats in the shade of a small grove of *brea* trees at the very edge of the water. Don Juan placed a charcoal inside the pipe bowl and told me to smoke. I did not have any apprehension or any feeling of elation. I remembered that during my second attempt to "see" the guardian, after don Juan had explained its nature, I had had a unique sensation of wonder and awe. This time, however, although don Juan had made me cognizant of the possibility of actually "seeing" the water, I was not involved emotionally; I was only curious.

Don Juan made me smoke twice the amount I had smoked during previous attempts. At a given moment he leaned over and whispered in my right ear that he was going to teach me how to use the water in order to move. I felt his face very close, as if he had put his mouth next to my ear. He told me not to gaze into the water, but to focus my eyes on the surface and keep them fixed until the water turned into a green fog. He repeated over and over that I had to put all my attention on the fog until I could not detect anything else.

"Look at the water in front of you," I heard him saying, "but don't let its sound carry you anywhere. If you let the sound of the water carry you I may never be able to find you and bring you back. Now get into the green fog and listen to my voice."

I heard and understood him with extraordinary clarity. I began looking at the water fixedly, and had a very peculiar sensation of physical pleasure; an itch; an undefined happiness. I stared for a long time but did not detect the green fog. I felt that my eyes were getting out of focus and I had to struggle to keep looking at the water; finally I could not control my eyes any longer and I must have closed them, or blinked, or perhaps I just lost my capacity to focus; at any rate, at that very moment the water became fixed; it ceased to move. It seemed to be a painting. The ripples were immobile. Then the water began to fizzle;

it was as if it had carbonated particles that exploded at once. For an instant I saw the fizzling as a slow expansion of green matter. It was a silent explosion; the water burst into a brilliant green mist, which expanded until it had enveloped me.

I remained suspended in it until a very sharp, sustained, shrill noise shook everything; the fog seemed to congeal into the usual features of the water surface. The shrill noise was don Juan yelling, "Heyyyy!" close to my ear. He told me to pay attention to his voice and go back into the fog and wait there until he called me. I said, "O.K.," in English and heard the cackling noise of his laughter.

"Please, don't talk," he said. "Don't give me any more O.K.s."

I could hear him very well. The sound of his voice was melodious and above all friendly. I knew that without thinking; it was a conviction that struck me and then passed.

Don Juan's voice ordered me to focus all my attention on the fog but not abandon myself to it. He said repeatedly that a warrior did not abandon himself to anything, not even to his death. I became immersed in the mist again and noticed that it was not fog at all, or at least it was not what I conceive fog to be like. The foglike phenomenon was composed of tiny bubbles, round objects that came into my field of "vision" and moved out of it with a floating quality. I watched their movement for a while, then a loud, distant noise jolted my attention and I lost my capacity to focus and could no longer perceive the tiny bubbles. All I was aware of then was a green, amorphous, foglike glow. I heard the loud noise again and the jolt it gave dispelled the fog at once and I found myself looking at the water of the irrigation ditch. Then I heard it again much closer; it was don Juan's voice. He was telling me to pay attention to him, because his voice was my only guide. He ordered me to look at the bank of the stream and at the vegetation directly in front of me. I saw some reeds and a space which was clear of reeds. It was a small cove on the bank, a place where don Juan steps across to plunge his bucket and fill it with water. After a few moments don

Juan ordered me to return to the fog and asked me again to pay attention to his voice, because he was going to guide me so I could learn how to move; he said that once I saw the bubbles I should board one of them and let it carry me.

I obeyed him and was at once surrounded by the green mist, and then I saw the tiny bubbles. I heard don Juan's voice again as a very strange and frightening rumble. Immediately upon hearing it I began losing my capacity to perceive the bubbles.

"Mount one of those bubbles," I heard him saying.

I struggled to maintain my perception of the green bubbles and still hear his voice. I don't know how long I fought to do that, when suddenly I was aware that I could listen to him and still keep sight of the bubbles, which kept on passing through, floating slowly out of my field of perception. Don Juan's voice kept on urging me to follow one of them and mount it.

I wondered how I was supposed to do that and automatically I voiced the word, "How." I felt that the word was very deep inside me and as it came out it carried me to the surface. The word was like a buoy that emerged out of my depth. I heard myself saying, "How," and I sounded like a dog howling. Don Juan howled back, also like a dog, and then he made some coyote sounds, and laughed. I thought it was very funny and I actually laughed.

Don Juan told me very calmly to let myself become affixed to a bubble by following it.

"Go back again," he said. "Go into the fog! Into the fog!"

I went back and noticed that the movement of the bubbles had slowed down and they had become as large as basketballs. In fact they were so large and slow that I could examine any one of them in great detail. They were not really bubbles, not like a soap bubble, nor like a balloon, nor any spherical container. They were not containers, yet they were contained. Nor were they round, although when I first perceived them I could have sworn they were round and the image that came to my mind was "bubbles." I viewed them as if I were looking through a window; that is, the frame of the window did not allow me to follow them but only permitted me to view them coming into and going out of my field of perception.

When I ceased to view them as bubbles, however, I was capable of following them; in the act of following them I became affixed to one of them and I floated with it. I truly felt I was moving. In fact I *was* the bubble, or that thing which resembled a bubble.

Then I heard the shrill sound of don Juan's voice. It jolted me and I lost my feeling of being "it." The sound was extremely frightening; it was a remote voice, very metallic, as if he were talking through a loud-speaker. I made out some of the words.

"Look at the banks," he said.

I saw a very large body of water. The water was rushing. I could hear the noise it made.

"Look at the banks," don Juan ordered me again.

I saw a concrete wall.

The sound of the water became terribly loud; the sound engulfed me. Then it ceased instantaneously, as if it had been cut off. I had the sensation of blackness, of sleep.

I became aware that I was immersed in the irrigation ditch. Don Juan was splashing water in my face as he hummed. Then he submerged me in the ditch. He pulled my head up, over the surface, and let me rest it on the bank as he held me by the back of my shirt collar. I had a most pleasant sensation in my arms and legs. I stretched them. My eyes were tired and they itched; I lifted my right hand to rub them. It was a difficult movement. My arm seemed to be heavy. I could hardly lift it out of the water, but when I did, my arm came out covered with a most astonishing mass of green mist. I held my arm in front of my eyes. I could see its contour as a darker mass of green surrounded by a most intense greenish glow. I got to my feet in a hurry and stood in the middle of the stream and looked at my body; my chest, arms, and legs were green, deep green. The hue was so intense that it gave me the feeling of a viscous substance. I looked like a figurine don Juan had made for me years before out of a datura root.

Don Juan told me to come out. I noticed an urgency in his voice.

"I'm green," I said.

"Cut it out," he said imperatively. "You have no time. Get out of there. The water is about to trap you. Get out of it! Out! Out!"

I panicked and jumped out.

"This time you must tell me everything that took place," he said matter-of-factly, as soon as we sat facing each other inside his room.

He was not interested in the sequence of my experience; he wanted to know only what I had encountered when he told me to look at the bank. He was interested in details. I described the wall I had seen.

'Was the wall to your left or to your right?" he asked.

I told him that the wall had really been in front of me. But he insisted that it had to be either to the left or to the right.

"When you first saw it, where was it? Close your eyes and don't open them until you have remembered."

He stood up and turned my body while I had my eyes closed until he had me facing east, the same direction I had faced when I was sitting in front of the stream. He asked me in which direction I had moved.

I said I had moved onward, ahead, in front of me. He insisted that I should remember and concentrate on the time when I was still viewing the water as bubbles.

"Which way did they flow?" he asked.

Don Juan urged me to recall, and finally I had to admit that the bubbles had seemed to be moving to my right. Yet I was not as absolutely sure as he wanted me to be. Under his probing I began to realize that I was incapable of classifying my perception. The bubbles had moved to my right when I first viewed them, but when they became larger they flowed everywhere. Some of them seemed to be coming directly at me, others seemed to go in every possible direction. There were bubbles moving above and below me. In fact they were all around me. I recollected hearing their fizzing; thus I must have perceived them with my ears as well as with my eyes.

When the bubbles became so large that I was able to "mount" one of them, I "saw" them rubbing each other like balloons.

My excitement increased as I recollected the details of my perception. Don Juan, however, was completely uninterested. I told him that I had seen the bubbles fizzing. It was not a purely auditory or purely visual effect, but something undifferentiated, yet crystal clear; the bubbles rasped against each other. I did not see or hear their movement, I felt it; I was part of the sound and the motion.

As I recounted my experience I became deeply moved. I held his arm and shook it in an outburst of great agitation. I had realized that the bubbles had no outer limit; nonetheless, they were contained and their edges changed shape and were uneven and jagged. The bubbles merged and separated with great speed, yet their movement was not dazzling. Their movement was fast and at the same time slow.

Another thing I remembered, as I recounted my experience, was the quality of color that the bubbles seemed to possess. They were transparent and very bright and seemed almost green, although it was not a hue, as I am accustomed to perceiving hues.

"You're stalling," don Juan said. "Those things are not important. You're dwelling on the wrong items. The direction is the only important issue."

I could only remember that I had moved without any point of reference, but don Juan concluded that since the bubbles had flowed consistently to my right—south—at the beginning, the south was the direction with which I had to be concerned. He again urged me imperatively to recollect whether the wall was to my right or my left. I strained to remember.

When don Juan "called me" and I surfaced, so to speak, I think I had the wall to my left. I was very close to it and was able to distinguish the grooves and protuberances of the wooden armature or mold into which the concrete had been poured. Very thin strips of wood had been used and the pattern they had created was compact. The wall was very high. One end of it was visible to me, and I noticed that it did not have a corner but curved around.

He sat in silence for a moment, as if he were thinking how to decipher the meaning of my experience; he finally said that I had not accomplished a great deal, that I had fallen short of what he expected me to do.

"What was I supposed to do?"

He did not answer but made a puckering gesture with his lips.

"You did very well," he said. "Today you learned that a brujo uses the water to move."

"But did I *see?*"

He looked at me with a curious expression. He rolled his eyes and said that I had to go into the green mist a good many times until I could answer that question myself. He changed the direction of our conversation in a subtle way, saying I had not really learned how to move using the water, but I had learned that a brujo could do that, and he had deliberately told me to look at the bank of the stream so I could check my movement.

"You moved very fast," he said, "as fast as a man who knows how to perform this technique. I had a hard time keeping up with you."

I begged him to explain what had happened to me from the beginning. He laughed, shaking his head slowly as though in disbelief.

"You always insist on knowing things from the beginning," he said. "But there's no beginning; the beginning is only in your thought."

"I think the beginning was when I sat on the bank and smoked," I said.

"But before you smoked I had to figure out what to do with you," he said. "I would have to tell you what I did and I can't do that, because it would take me to still another point. So perhaps things would be clearer to you if you didn't think about beginnings."

"Then tell me what happened after I sat on the bank and smoked."

"I think you have told me that already," he said, laughing.

"Was anything I did of any importance, don Juan?"

He shrugged his shoulders.

"You followed my directions very well and had no problem getting into and out of the fog. Then you listened to my voice and returned to the surface every time I called you. That was the exercise. The rest was very easy. You simply let the fog carry you. You behaved as though you knew what to do. When you were very far away I called you again and made you look at the bank, so you would know how far you had gone. Then I pulled you back."

"You mean, don Juan, that I really traveled in the water?"

"You did. And very far too."

"How far?"

"You wouldn't believe it."

I tried to coax him into telling me, but he dropped the subject and said he had to leave for a while. I insisted that he should at least give me a hint.

"I don't like to be kept in the dark," I said.

"You keep yourself in the dark," he said. "Think about the wall you saw. Sit down here on your mat and remember every detail of it. Then perhaps you yourself may discover how far you went. All I know now is that you traveled very far. I know that because I had a terrible time pulling you back. If I had not been around, you might have wandered off and never returned, in which case all that would be left of you now would be your dead body on the side of the stream. Or perhaps you might have returned by yourself. With you I'm not sure. So judging by the effort it took me to bring you back, I'd say you were clearly in . . ."

He made a long pause; he stared at me in a friendly way.

"I would go as far as the mountains of central Mexico," he said. "I don't know how far you would go, perhaps as far as Los Angeles, or perhaps even as far as Brazil."

Don Juan returned the next day late in the afternoon.

In the meantime I had written down everything I could recollect about my perception. While I wrote, it occurred to me to follow the banks up and down the stream in each direction and corroborate whether I had actually seen a feature on either side that might have elicited in me the image of a wall. I conjectured that don Juan might have made me walk, in a state of stupor, and then might have made me focus my attention on some wall on the way. In the hours that elapsed between the time I first detected the fog and the time I got out of the ditch and went back to his house, I calculated that if he had made me walk, we could have walked, at the most, two and a half miles. So I followed the banks of the stream for about three miles in each direction, carefully observing every feature which might have been pertinent to my vision of the wall. The stream was, as far as I could tell, a plain canal used for irrigation. It was four to five feet wide throughout its length and I could not find any visible features in it that would have reminded me or forced the image of a concrete wall.

When don Juan arrived at his house in the late afternoon I accosted him and insisted on reading my account to him. He refused to listen and made me sit down. He sat facing me. He was not smiling. He seemed to be thinking, judging by the penetrating look in his eyes, which were fixed above the horizon.

"I think you must be aware by now," he said in a tone that was suddenly very severe, "that everything is mortally dangerous. The water is as deadly as the guardian. If you don't watch out the water will trap you. It nearly did that yesterday. But in order to be trapped a man has to be willing. There's your trouble. You're willing to abandon yourself."

I did not know what he was talking about. His attack on me had been so sudden that I was disoriented. I feebly asked him to explain himself. He reluctantly mentioned that he had gone to the water canyon and had "seen" the spirit of the water hole and had the profound conviction I had flubbed my chances to "see" the water.

"How?" I asked, truly baffled.

"The spirit is a force," he said, "and as such, it responds only to strength. You cannot indulge in its presence."

"When did I indulge?"

"Yesterday, when you became green in the water."

"I did not indulge. I thought it was a very important moment and I told you what was happening to me."

"Who are you to think or decide what is important? You know nothing about the forces you're tapping. The spirit of the water hole exists out there and could have helped you; in fact it was helping you until you flubbed it. Now I don't know what will be the outcome of your doings. You have succumbed to the force of the water-hole spirit and now it can take you any time."

"Was it wrong to look at myself turning green?"

"You abandoned yourself. You willed to abandon yourself. That was wrong. I have told you this already and I will repeat it again. You can survive in the world of a brujo only if you are a warrior. A warrior treats everything with respect and does not trample on anything unless he has to. You did not treat the water with respect yesterday. Usually you behave very well. However, yesterday you abandoned yourself to your death, like a goddamned fool. A warrior does not abandon himself to anything, not even to his death. A warrior is not a willing partner; a warrior is not available, and if he involves himself with something, you can be sure that he is aware of what he is doing."

I did not know what to say. Don Juan was almost angry. That disturbed me. Don Juan had rarely behaved in such a way with me. I told him that I truly had no idea I was doing something wrong. After some minutes of tense silence he took off his hat and smiled and told me that I had gained control over my indulging self. He stressed that I had to avoid water and keep it from touching the surface of my body for three or four months.

"I don't think I could go without taking a shower," I said.

Don Juan laughed until tears rolled down his cheeks.

"You can't go without a shower! At times you're so weak I think you're putting me on. But it is not a joke. At times you really have no control and the forces of your life take you freely."

I raised the point that it was humanly impossible to be controlled at all times. He maintained that for a warrior there was nothing out of control. I brought up the idea of accidents and said that what happened to me at the water canal could certainly be classed as an accident, since I neither meant it nor was I aware of my improper behavior. I talked about different people who had misfortunes that could be explained as accidents; I talked especially about Lucas, a very fine old Yaqui man who had suffered a serious injury when the truck he was driving overturned.

"It seems to me it is impossible to avoid accidents," I said. "No man can control everything around him."

"True," don Juan said cuttingly. "But not everything is an unavoidable accident. Lucas doesn't live like a warrior. If he did, he'd know that he is waiting and what he is waiting for; and he wouldn't have driven that truck while he was drunk. He crashed against the rock side of the road because he was drunk and mangled his body for nothing.

"Life for a warrior is an exercise in strategy," don Juan went on. "But you want to find the meaning of life. A warrior doesn't care about meanings. If Lucas lived like a warrior—and he had a chance to, as we all have a chance to—he would set his life strategically. Thus if he couldn't avoid an accident that crushed his ribs, he would have found means to offset that handicap, or avoid its consequences, or battle aganst them. If Lucas were a warrior he wouldn't be sitting in his dingy house dying of starvation. He would be battling to the end."

I posed an alternative to don Juan, using him as an example, and asked him what would be the outcome if he himself were to be involved in an accident that severed his legs.

"If I cannot help it, and lose my legs," he said, "I won't be able to be a man any more, so I will join that which is waiting for me out there."

He made a sweeping gesture with his hand to point all around him.

I argued that he had misunderstood me. I had meant to

point out that it was impossible for any single individual to foresee all the variables involved in his day-to-day actions.

"All I can say to you," don Juan said, "is that a warrior is never available; never is he standing on the road waiting to be clobbered. Thus he cuts to a minimum his chances of the unforeseen. What you call accidents are, most of the time, very easy to avoid, except for fools who are living helter-skelter."

"It is not possible to live strategically all the time," I said. "Imagine that someone is waiting for you with a powerful rifle with a telescopic sight; he could spot you accurately five hundred yards away. What would you do?"

Don Juan looked at me with an air of disbelief and then broke into laughter.

"What would you do?" I urged him.

"If someone is waiting for me with a rifle with a telescopic sight?" he said, obviously mocking me.

"If someone is hiding out of sight, waiting for you. You won't have a chance. You can't stop a bullet."

"No. I can't. But I still don't understand your point."

"My point is that all your strategy cannot be of any help in a situation like that."

"Oh, but it can. If someone is waiting for me with a powerful rifle with a telescopic sight I simply will not come around."

13

My next attempt at "seeing" took place on September 3, 1969. Don Juan made me smoke two bowls of the mixture. The immediate effects were identical to those I had experienced during previous attempts. I remember that when my body was thoroughly numb, don Juan held me by my right armpit and made me walk into the thick desert chaparral that grows for miles around his house. I cannot recollect what I or don Juan did after we entered the brush, nor can I recall how long we walked; at a certain moment I found I was sitting on top of a small hill. Don Juan was sitting on my left side, touching me. I could not feel him but I could see him with the corner of my eye. I had the feeling that he had been talking to me although I could not remember his words. Yet I felt I knew exactly what he had said, in spite of the fact that I could not bring it back into my clear memory. I had the sensation that his words were like the cars of a train which was moving away and his last word was like a square caboose. I knew what that last word was but I could not say it or think clearly about it. It was a state of half-wakefulness with a dreamlike image of a train of words.

Then very faintly I heard don Juan's voice talking to me.

"Now you must look at me," he said as he turned my head to face him. He repeated the statement three or four times.

I looked and detected right away the same glowing effect I had perceived twice before while looking at his face; it was a mesmerizing movement, an undulatory shift of light within contained areas. There were no definite boundaries to those areas, and yet the waving light never spilled over but moved within invisible limits.

I scanned the glowing object in front of me and immediately it started to lose its glow and the familiar features of don Juan's face emerged, or rather became superimposed on the fading glow. I must have then focused my gaze again; don Juan's features faded and the glow intensified. I had placed my attention on an area which must have been his left eye. I noticed that there the movement of the glow was not contained. I detected something perhaps resembling explosions of sparks. The explosions were rhythmical and actually sent out something like particles of light that flew out with apparent force toward me and then retreated as if they were rubber fibers.

Don Juan must have turned my head around. Suddenly I found myself looking at a plowed field.

"Now look ahead," I heard don Juan saying.

In front of me, perhaps two hundred yards away, was a large, long hill; its entire slope had been plowed. Horizontal furrows ran parallel to each other from the bottom to the very top of the hill. I noticed that in the plowed field there were quantities of small rocks and three huge boulders that interrupted the lineality of the furrows. There were some bushes right in front of me which prevented me from observing the details of a ravine or water canyon at the bottom of the hill. From where I was, the canyon appeared as a deep cut, with green vegetation markedly different from the barren hill. The greenness seemed to be trees that grew in the bottom of the canyon. I felt a breeze blowing in my eyes. I had a feeling of peace and profound quietness. There were no sounds of birds or insects.

Don Juan spoke to me again. It took me a moment to understand what he was saying.

"Do you see a man in that field?" he kept on asking.

I wanted to tell him that there was no man in that field, but I could not vocalize the words. Don Juan took my head in his hands from behind—I could see his fingers over my eyebrows and on my cheeks—and made me pan over the field, moving my head slowly from right to left and then in the opposite direction.

"Watch every detail. Your life may depend on it," I heard him saying over and over.

He made me pan four times over the 180-degree visual horizon in front of me. At one moment, when he had moved my head to face the extreme left, I thought I detected something moving in the field. I had a brief perception of movement with the corner of my right eye. He began to shift my head back to my right and I was capable of focusing my gaze on the plowed field. I saw a man walking alongside the furrows. He was a plain man dressed like a Mexican peasant; he wore sandals, a pair of light gray pants, a long-sleeved beige shirt, and a straw hat, and carried a light brown bag with a strap over his right shoulder.

Don Juan must have noticed that I had seen the man. He asked me repeatedly if the man was looking at me or if he was coming toward me. I wanted to tell him that the man was walking away and that his back was turned to me, but I could only say, "No." Don Juan said that if the man turned and came to me I should yell and he would turn my head away in order to protect me.

I had no sense of fear or apprehension or involvement. I coldly watched the scene. The man stopped walking at the middle of the field. He stood with his right foot on a ledge of a large round boulder, as if he were tying his sandal. Then he straightened up, pulled a string from his bag, and wrapped it around his left hand. He turned his back to me and, facing the top of the hill, began scanning the area in front of him. I thought he was scanning because of the way he moved his head, which he kept turning slowly to his right; I saw him in profile, and then he began to turn his whole body toward me until he was looking at me. He actually jerked his head, or moved it in such a way that I knew beyond a doubt that he had seen me. He extended his left arm in front of him, pointing to the ground, and holding his arm in that position he began to walk toward me.

"He's coming!" I yelled without any difficulty.

Don Juan must have turned my head around, for next I was looking at the chaparral. He told me not to gaze but look "lightly" at things and scan over them. He said that he was going to stand a short distance in front of me and then walk toward me, and that I should gaze at him until I saw his glow.

I saw don Juan moving to a spot perhaps twenty yards away. He walked with such incredible speed and agility that I could hardly believe it was don Juan. He turned around and faced me and ordered me to gaze at him.

His face was glowing; it looked like a blotch of light. The light seemed to spill over his chest almost to the middle of his body. It was as if I were looking at a light through my half-closed eyelids. The glow seemed to expand and recede. He must have begun to walk toward me because the light became more intense and more discernible.

He said something to me. I struggled to understand and

lost my view of the glow, and then I saw don Juan as I see him in everyday life; he was a couple of feet away from me. He sat down facing me.

As I pinpointed my attention on his face I began to perceive a vague glow. Then it was as if his face were crisscrossed by thin beams of light. Don Juan's face looked as if someone were shining tiny mirrors on it; as the light became more intense the face lost its contours and was again an amorphous glowing object. I perceived once more the effect of pulsating explosions of light emanating from an area which must have been his left eye. I did not focus my attention on it, but deliberately gazed at an adjacent area which I surmised to be his right eye. I caught at once the sight of a clear, transparent pool of light. It was a liquid light.

I noticed that perceiving was more than sighting; it was feeling. The pool of dark, liquid light had an extraordinary depth. It was "friendly," "kind." The light that emanated from it did not explode but whirled slowly inward, creating exquisite reflections. The glow had a very lovely and delicate way of touching me, of soothing me, which gave me a sensation of exquisiteness.

I saw a symmetrical ring of brilliant dashes of light that expanded rhythmically on the vertical plain of the glowing area. The ring expanded to cover nearly all the glowing surface and then contracted to a point of light in the middle of the brilliant pool. I saw the ring expanding and contracting several times. Then I deliberately moved back without losing my gaze and was capable of seeing both eyes. I distinguished the rhythm of both types of light explosions. The left eye sent out dashes of light that actually protruded out of the vertical plain, while the right eye sent out dashes that radiated without protruding. The rhythm of the two eyes was alternating, the light of the left eye exploded outward while the radiating light beams of the right eye contracted and whirled inward. Then the light of the right eye extended to cover the whole glowing surface while the exploding light of the left eye receded.

Don Juan must have turned me around once more, for

I was again looking at the plowed field. I heard him telling me to watch the man.

The man was standing by the boulder looking at me. I could not distinguish his features; his hat covered most of his face. After a moment he tucked his bag under his right arm and began to walk away toward my right. He walked almost to the end of the plowed area, changed direction, and took a few steps toward the gully. Then I lost control of my focusing and he vanished and so did the total scenery. The image of the desert shrubs became super-imposed on it.

I do not recollect how I returned to don Juan's house, nor do I remember what he did to me to "bring me back." When I woke up I was lying on my straw mat in don Juan's room. He came to my side and helped me up. I was dizzy; my stomach was upset. Don Juan in a very quick and efficient manner dragged me to the shrubs at the side of his house. I got sick and he laughed.

Afterwards I felt better. I looked at my watch; it was eleven P.M. I went back to sleep and by one o'clock the next afternoon I thought I was myself again.

Don Juan kept asking me how I felt. I had the sensation of being absent-minded. I could not really concentrate. I walked around the house for a while under don Juan's close scrutiny. He followed me around. I felt there was nothing to do and I went back to sleep. I woke up in the late afternoon feeling much better. I found a great many mashed leaves around me. In fact when I woke up I was lying on my stomach on top of a pile of leaves. Their scent was very strong. I remember becoming aware of the scent before I fully woke up.

I wandered to the back and found don Juan sitting by the irrigation ditch. When he saw me approaching he made frantic gestures to make me stop and go back into the house.

"Run inside!" he yelled.

I ran into the house and he joined me a while later.

"Don't ever come after me," he said. "If you want to see me wait for me here."

I apologized. He told me not to waste myself in silly

apologies which did not have the power to cancel my acts. He said that he had had a very difficult time bringing me back and that he had been interceding for me at the water.

"We have to take a chance now and wash you in the water," he said.

I assured him I felt fine. He gazed into my eyes for a long time.

"Come with me," he said. "I'm going to put you in the water."

"I'm fine," I said. "Look, I'm taking notes."

He pulled me up from my mat with considerable force.

"Don't indulge!" he said. "In no time at all you will fall asleep again. Maybe I won't be able to wake you up this time."

We ran to the back of his house. Before we reached the water he told me in a most dramatic tone to shut my eyes tight and not open them until he said to. He told me that if I gazed at the water even for an instant I might die. He led me by the hand and dunked me into the irrigation ditch head first.

I kept my eyes shut as he went on submerging and pulling me out of the water for hours. The change I experienced was remarkable. Whatever was wrong with me before I entered the water was so subtle that I did not really notice it until I compared it with the feeling of well-being and alertness I had while don Juan kept me in the irrigation canal.

Water got into my nose and I began to sneeze. Don Juan pulled me out and led me, with my eyes still closed, into the house. He made me change my clothes and then guided me into his room, had me sit down on my mat, arranged the direction of my body, and then told me to open my eyes. I opened them and what I saw caused me to jump back and grab onto his leg. I experienced a tremendously confusing moment. Don Juan rapped me with his knuckles on the very top of my head. It was a quick blow which was not hard or painful but somehow shocking.

"What is the matter with you? What did you see?" he asked.

Upon opening my eyes I had seen the same scene I had watched before. I had seen the same man. This time, however, he was almost touching me. I saw his face. There was an air of familiarity about it. I almost knew who he was. The scene vanished when don Juan hit me on the head.

I looked up at don Juan. He had his hand ready to hit me again. He laughed and asked if I would like to get another blow. I let go of his leg and relaxed on my mat. He ordered me to look straight ahead and not to turn around for any reason in the direction of the water at the back of his house.

I then noticed for the first time that it was pitch black in the room. For a moment I was not sure whether I had my eyes open. I touched them with my hands to make sure. I called don Juan loudly and told him something was wrong with my eyes; I could not see at all, while a moment before I had seen him ready to hit me. I heard his laughter over my head to my right, and then he lit his kerosene lantern. My eyes adapted to the light in a matter of seconds. Everything was as it always had been: the wattle-and-daub walls of the room and the strangely contorted, dry medicinal roots hanging on them; the bundles of herbs; the thatched roof; the kerosene lantern hanging from a beam. I had seen the room hundreds of times, yet this time there was something unique about it and about myself. This was the first time I did not believe in the final "reality" of my perception. I had been edging toward that feeling and I had perhaps intellectualized it at various times, but never had I been at the brink of a serious doubt. This time, however, I did not believe the room was "real," and for a moment I had the strange sensation that it was a scene which would vanish if don Juan rapped me on top of my head with his knuckles.

I began to shiver without being cold. Nervous spasms ran down my spine. My head felt heavy, especially in the area right above my neck.

I complained that I did not feel well and told him what

I had seen. He laughed at me, saying that to succumb to
fright was a miserable indulgence.

"You're frightened without being afraid," he said. "You
saw the ally staring at you, big deal. Wait until you have
him face to face before you shit in your pants."

He told me to get up and walk to my car without turning around in the direction of the water, and to wait for
him while he got a rope and a shovel. He made me drive
to a place where we had found a tree stump. We proceeded
to dig it out in the darkness. I worked terribly hard for
hours. We did not get the stump out but I felt much better.
We went back to his house and ate and things were again
perfectly "real" and commonplace.

"What happened to me?" I asked. "What did I do yesterday?"

"You smoked me and then you smoked an ally," he
said.

"I beg your pardon?"

Don Juan laughed and said that next I was going to demand that he start telling me everything from the beginning.

"You smoked me," he repeated. "You gazed into my
face, into my eyes. You saw the lights that mark a man's
face. I am a sorcerer, you saw that in my eyes. You did
not know that, though, because this is the first time you've
done it. The eyes of men are not all alike. You will soon
find that out. Then you smoked an ally."

"Do you mean the man in the field?"

"That was not a man, that was an ally beckoning you."

"Where did we go? Where were we when I saw that
man, I mean that ally?"

Don Juan made a gesture with his chin to point out an
area in front of his house and said that he had taken me
to the top of a small hill. I said that the scenery I had
viewed had nothing to do with the desert chaparral around
his house and he replied that the ally that had "beckoned"
me was not from the surroundings.

"Where is it from?"

"I'll take you there very soon."

"What is the meaning of my vision?"

"You were learning to *see*, that was all; but now you are about to lose your pants because you indulge; you have abandoned yourself to your fright. Maybe you should describe everything you saw."

When I started to describe the way his own face had appeared to me, he made me stop and said that it was of no importance whatsoever. I told him that I had almost *seen* him as a "luminous egg." He said that "almost" was not enough and that *seeing* was going to take me a great deal of time and work.

He was interested in the scene of the plowed field and in every detail I could remember about the man.

"That ally was beckoning you," he said. "I made you move your head when he came to you not because he was endangering you but because it is better to wait. You are not in a hurry. A warrior is never idle and never in a hurry. To meet an ally without being prepared is like attacking a lion with your farts."

I liked the metaphor. We had a delightful moment of laughter.

"What would've happened if you hadn't moved my head?"

"You would've had to move your head yourself."

"And if I didn't?"

"The ally would have come to you and scared you stiff. If you had been alone he might have killed you. It is not advisable for you to be alone in the mountains or the desert until you can defend yourself. An ally might catch you alone there and make mincemeat out of you."

"What was the meaning of the acts he performed?"

"By looking at you he meant he welcomes you. He showed you that you need a spirit catcher and a pouch, but not from this area; his bag was from another part of the country. You have three stumbling blocks in your way that make you stop; those were the boulders. And you definitely are going to get your best powers in water canyons and gullies; the ally pointed out the gully to you. The rest of the scene was meant to help you locate the exact place to find him. I know now where the place is. I will take you there very soon."

"Do you mean that the scenery I saw really exists?"

"Of course."

"Where?"

"I cannot tell you that."

"How would I find that area?"

"I cannot tell you that either, and not because I don't want to but because I simply don't know how to tell you."

I wanted to know the meaning of seeing the same scene while I was in his room. Don Juan laughed and imitated me holding onto his leg.

"That was a reaffirmation that the ally wants you," he said. "He made sure you or I knew that he was welcoming you."

"What about the face I saw?"

"It is a familiar face to you because you know him. You have seen it before. Maybe it is the face of your death. You got frightened but that was your carelessness. He was waiting for you and when he showed up you succumbed to fright. Fortunately I was there to hit you or he would've turned against you, which would have been only proper. To meet an ally a man must be a spotless warrior or the ally may turn against him and destroy him."

Don Juan dissuaded me from going back to Los Angeles the next morning. Apparently he thought I still had not totally recovered. He insisted that I sit inside his room facing the southeast, in order to preserve my strength. He sat to my left, handed me my notebook, and said that this time I had him pinned down; he not only had to stay with me, he also had to talk to me.

"I have to take you to the water again in the twilight," he said. "You're not solid yet and you shouldn't be alone today. I'll keep you company all morning; in the afternoon you'll be in better shape."

His concern made me feel very apprehensive.

"What's wrong with me?" I asked.

"You've tapped an ally."

"What do you mean by that?"

"We must not talk about allies today. Let us talk about anything else."

I really did not want to talk at all. I had begun to feel anxious and restless. Don Juan apparently found the situation utterly ludicrous; he laughed till the tears came.

"Don't tell me that at a time when you should talk you are not going to find anything to say," he said, his eyes shining with a mischievous glint.

His mood was very soothing to me.

There was only one topic that interested me at that moment: the ally. His face was so familiar; it was not as if I knew him or as if I had seen him before. It was something else. Every time I began to think about his face my mind experienced a bombardment of other thoughts, as if some part of myself knew the secret but did not allow the rest of me to come close to it. The sensation of the ally's face being familiar was so eerie that it had forced me into a state of morbid melancholy. Don Juan had said that it might have been the face of my death. I think that statement had clinched me. I wanted desperately to ask about it and I had the clear sensation that don Juan was holding me back. I took a couple of deep breaths and blurted out a question.

"What is death, don Juan?"

"I don't know," he said, smiling.

"I mean, how would you describe death? I want your opinions. I think everybody has definite opinions about death."

"I don't know what you're talking about."

I had the *Tibetan Book of the Dead* in the trunk of my car. It occurred to me to use it as a topic of conversation, since it dealt with death. I said I was going to read it to him and began to get up. He made me sit down and went out and got the book himself.

"The morning is a bad time for sorcerers," he said as an explanation for my having to stay put. "You're too weak to leave my room. Inside here you are protected. If you were to wander off now, chances are that you would find a terrible disaster. An ally could kill you on the road or in the bush, and later on when they found your body they would say that you had either died mysteriously or had an accident."

I was in no position or mood to question his decisions, so I stayed put nearly all morning reading and explaining some parts of the book to him. He listened attentively and did not interrupt me at all. Twice I had to stop for short periods of time while he brought some water and food, but as soon as he was free again he urged me to continue reading. He seemed to be very interested.

When I finished he looked at me.

"I don't understand why those people talk about death as if death were like life," he said softly.

"Maybe that's the way they understand it. Do you think the Tibetans *see?*"

"Hardly. When a man learns to *see,* not a single thing he knows prevails. Not a single one. If the Tibetans could *see* they could tell right away that not a single thing is any longer the same. Once we *see,* nothing is known; nothing remains as we used to know it when we didn't *see.*"

"Perhaps, don Juan, *seeing* is not the same for everyone."

"True. It's not the same. Still, that does not mean that the meanings of life prevail. When one learns to *see,* not a single thing is the same."

"Tibetans obviously think that death is like life. What do you think death is like, yourself?" I asked.

"I don't think death is like anything and I think the Tibetans must be talking about something else. At any rate, what they're talking about is not death."

"What do you think they're talking about?"

"Maybe you can tell me that. You're the one who reads."

I tried to say something else but he began to laugh.

"Perhaps the Tibetans really *see,*" don Juan went on, "in which case they must have realized that what they *see* makes no sense at all and they wrote that bunch of crap because it doesn't make any difference to them; in which case what they wrote is not crap at all."

"I really don't care about what the Tibetans have to say," I said, "but I certainly care about what you have to say. I would like to hear what you think about death."

He stared at me for an instant and then giggled. He

opened his eyes and raised his eyebrows in a comical gesture of surprise.

"Death is a whorl," he said. "Death is the face of the ally; death is a shiny cloud over the horizon; death is the whisper of Mescalito in your ears; death is the toothless mouth of the guardian; death is Genaro sitting on his head; death is me talking; death is you and your writing pad; death is nothing. Nothing! It is here yet it isn't here at all."

Don Juan laughed with great delight. His laughter was like a song, it had a sort of dancing rhythm.

"I make no sense, huh?" don Juan said. "I cannot tell you what death is like. But perhaps I could tell you about your own death. There is no way of knowing what it will be like for sure; however, I could tell you what it may be like."

I became frightened at that point and argued that I only wanted to know what death appeared to be like to him; I emphasized that I was interested in his opinions about death in a general sense, but did not care to know about the particulars of anybody's personal death, especially my own.

"I can't talk about death except in personal terms," he said. "You wanted me to tell you about death. All right! Then don't be afraid of hearing about your own death."

I admitted that I was too nervous to talk about it. I said that I wanted to talk about death in general terms, as he himself had done when he told me that at the time of his son Eulalio's death, life and death mixed like a fog of crystals.

'I told you that my son's life expanded at the time of his personal death," he said. "I was not talking about death in general but about my son's death. Death, whatever it is, made his life expand."

I definitely wanted to steer the conversation out of the realm of particulars, and mentioned that I had been reading accounts of people who had died for several minutes and had been revived through medical techniques. In all the cases I had read, the persons involved had made statements, upon reviving, that they could not recollect anything at all; that dying was simply a sensation of blacking out.

"That's perfectly understandable," he said. "Death has two stages. The first is a blackout. It is a meaningless stage, very similar to the first effect of Mescalito, in which one experiences a lightness that makes one feel happy, complete, and that everything in the world is at ease. But that is only a shallow state; it soon vanishes and one enters a new realm, a realm of harshness and power. That second stage is the real encounter with Mescalito. Death is very much like this. The first stage is a shallow blackout. The second, however, is the real stage where one meets with death; it is a brief moment, after the first blackout, when we find that we are, somehow, ourselves again. It is then that death smashes against us with quiet fury and power until it dissolves our lives into nothing."

"How can you be sure that you are talking about death?"

"I have my ally. The little smoke has shown me my unmistakable death with great clarity. This is why I can only talk about personal death."

Don Juan's words caused me a profound apprehension and a dramatic ambivalence. I had a feeling he was going to describe the overt, commonplace details of my death and tell me how or when I was going to die. The mere thought of knowing that made me despair and at the same time provoked my curiosity. I could have asked him to describe his own death, of course, but I felt that such a request would be rather rude and I ruled it out automatically.

Don Juan seemed to be enjoying my conflict. His body convulsed with laughter.

"Do you want to know what your death may be like?" he asked me with childlike delight in his face.

I found his mischievous pleasure in teasing me rather comforting. It almost took the edge off my apprehension.

"O.K., tell me," I said, and my voice cracked.

He had a formidable explosion of laughter. He held his stomach and rolled on his side and mockingly repeated, " 'O.K., tell me,' " with a crack in his voice. Then he straightened out and sat down, assuming a feigned stiffness, and in a tremulous voice he said, "The second stage of your death may very well be as follows."

His eyes examined me with apparently genuine curiosity. I laughed. I clearly realized that his making fun was the only device that could dull the edge of the idea of one's death.

"You drive a great deal," he went on saying, "so you may find yourself, at a given moment, behind the wheel again. It will be a very fast sensation that won't give you time to think. Suddenly, let's say, you would find yourself driving, as you have done thousands of times. But before you could wonder about yourself, you would notice a strange formation in front of your windshield. If you looked closer you'd realize that it is a cloud that looks like a shiny whorl. It would resemble, let's say, a face, right in the middle of the sky in front of you. As you watched it, you would see it moving backward until it was only a brilliant point in the distance, and then you would notice that it began moving toward you again; it would pick up speed and in a blink of an eye it would smash against the windshield of your car. You are strong; I'm sure it would take death a couple of whams to get you.

"By then you would know where you were and what was happening to you; the face would recede again to a position on the horizon, would pick up speed and smash against you. The face would enter inside you and then you'd know—it was the ally's face all the time, or it was me talking, or you writing. Death was nothing all the time. Nothing. It was a little dot lost in the sheets of your notebook. And yet it would enter inside you with uncontrollable force and would make you expand; it would make you flat and extend you over the sky and the earth and beyond. And you would be like a fog of tiny crystals moving, moving away."

I was very taken by his description of my death. I had expected to hear something so different. I could not say anything for a long time.

"Death enters through the belly," he continued. "Right through the gap of the will. That area is the most important and sensitive part of man. It is the area of the will and also the area through which all of us die. I know it because my ally has guided me to that stage. A sorcerer tunes his will by letting his death overtake him, and when he is flat and begins to expand, his impeccable will takes over and assembles the fog into one person again."

Don Juan made a strange gesture. He opened his hands like two fans, lifted them to the level of his elbows, turned them until his thumbs were touching his sides, and then brought them slowly together at the center of his body over his navel. He kept them there for a moment. His arms shivered with the strain. Then he brought them up until the tips of his middle fingers touched his forehead, and then pulled them down in the same position to the center of his body.

It was a formidable gesture. Don Juan had performed it with such force and beauty that I was spellbound.

"It is his will which assembles a sorcerer," he said, "but as his old age makes him feeble his will wanes and a moment unavoidably comes when he is no longer capable of commanding his will. He then has nothing with which to oppose the silent force of his death, and his life becomes like the lives of all his fellow men, an expanding fog moving beyond its limits."

Don Juan stared at me and stood up. I was shivering.

"You can go to the bushes now," he said. "It is afternoon."

I needed to go but I did not dare. I felt perhaps more jumpy than afraid. However, I was no longer apprehensive about the ally.

Don Juan said that it did not matter how I felt as long as I was "solid." He assured me I was in perfect shape and could safely go into the bushes as long as I did not get close to the water.

"That is another matter," he said. "I need to wash you once more, so stay away from the water."

Later on he wanted me to drive him to the nearby town. I mentioned that driving would be a welcome change for me because I was still shaky; the idea that a sorcerer actually played with his death was quite gruesome to me.

"To be a sorcerer is a terrible burden," he said in a reassuring tone. "I've told you that it is much better to learn to *see*. A man who *sees* is everything; in comparison, the sorcerer is a sad fellow."

"What is sorcery, don Juan?"

He looked at me for a long time as he shook his head almost imperceptibly.

"Sorcery is to apply one's will to a key joint," he said. "Sorcery is interference. A sorcerer searches and finds the key joint of anything he wants to affect and then he applies his will to it. A sorcerer doesn't have to *see* to be a sorcerer, all he has to know is how to use his will."

I asked him to explain what he meant by a key joint. He thought for a while and then he said that he knew what my car was.

"It's obviously a machine," I said.

"I mean your car is the spark plugs. That's its key joint for me. I can apply my will to it and your car won't work."

Don Juan got into my car and sat down. He beckoned me to do likewise as he made himself comfortable on the seat.

"Watch what I do," he said. "I'm a crow, so first I'll make my feathers loose."

He shivered his entire body. His movement reminded me of a sparrow wetting its feathers in a puddle. He lowered his head like a bird dipping its beak into the water.

"That feels really good," he said, and began to laugh. His laughter was strange. It had a very peculiar mesmerizing effect on me. I recollected having heard him laugh in that manner many times before. Perhaps the reason I had never become overtly aware of it was that he had never laughed like that long enough in my presence.

"A crow loosens its neck next," he said, and began twisting his neck and rubbing his cheeks on his shoulders. "Then he looks at the world with one eye and then with the other."

His head shook as he allegedly shifted his view of the world from one eye to the other. The pitch of his laughter became higher. I had the absurd feeling that he was going to turn into a crow in front of my eyes. I wanted to laugh it off but I was almost paralyzed. I actually felt some kind of enveloping force around me. I was not afraid nor was I dizzy or sleepy. My faculties were unimpaired, to the best of my judgment.

"Turn on your car now," don Juan said.

I turned on the starter and automatically stepped on the gas pedal. The starter began to grind without igniting the engine. Don Juan's laughter was a soft, rhythmical cackle. I tried it again; and again. I spent perhaps ten minutes grinding the starter of my car. Don Juan cackled all that time. Then I gave up and sat there with a heavy head.

He stopped laughing and scrutinized me and I "knew" then that his laughter had forced me into a sort of hypnotic trance. Although I had been thoroughly aware of what was taking place, I felt I was not myself. During the time I could not start my car I was very docile, almost numb. It was as if don Juan was not only doing something to my car but also to me. When he stopped cackling I was convinced the spell was over, and impetuously I turned on the starter again. I had the certainty don Juan had only mesmerized me with his laughter and made me believe I could not start my car. With the corner of my eye I saw him looking curiously at me as I ground the motor and pumped the gas furiously.

Don Juan patted me gently and said that fury would make me "solid" and perhaps I would not need to be washed in the water again. The more furious I could get, the quicker I could recover from my encounter with the ally.

"Don't be embarrassed," I heard don Juan saying. "Kick the car."

His natural everyday laughter exploded, and I felt ridiculous and laughed sheepishly.

After a while don Juan said he had released the car. It started!

14

September 28, 1969

There was something eerie about don Juan's house. For a
moment I thought he was hiding somewhere around the
place to scare me. I called out to him and then gathered
enough nerve to walk inside. Don Juan was not there. I
put the two bags of groceries I had brought on a pile of
firewood and sat down to wait for him, as I had done
dozens of times before. But for the first time in my years
of associating with don Juan I was afraid to stay alone in
his house. I felt a presence, as if someone invisible was
there with me. I remembered then that years before I had
had the same vague feeling that something unknown was
prowling around me when I was alone. I jumped to my
feet and ran out of the house.

I had come to see don Juan to tell him that the cumu-
lative effect of the task of "seeing" was taking its toll on
me. I had begun to feel uneasy; vaguely apprehensive
without any overt reason; tired without being fatigued.
Then my reaction at being alone in don Juan's house
brought back the total memory of how my fear had built
up in the past.

The fear traced back to years before, when don Juan
had forced the very strange confrontation between a sorceress, a woman he called "la Catalina," and me. It began
on November 23, 1961, when I found him in his house
with a dislocated ankle. He explained that he had an
enemy, a sorceress who could turn into a blackbird and
who had attempted to kill him.

"As soon as I can walk I'm going to show you who the woman is," don Juan said. "You must know who she is."

"Why does she want to kill you?"

He shrugged his shoulders impatiently and refused to say anything else.

I came back to see him ten days later and found him perfectly well. He rotated his ankle to demonstrate to me that it was fine and attributed his prompt recovery to the nature of the cast he himself had made.

"It's good you're here," he said. "Today I'm going to take you on a little journey."

He then directed me to drive to a desolate area. We stopped there; don Juan stretched his legs and made himself comfortable on the seat, as if he were going to take a nap. He told me to relax and remain very quiet; he said we had to be as inconspicuous as possible until nightfall because the late afternoon was a very dangerous time for the business we were pursuing.

"What kind of business are we pursuing?" I asked.

"We are here to stake out la Catalina," he said.

When it was fairly dark we slid out of the car and walked very slowly and noiselessly into the desert chaparral.

From the place where we stopped I could distinguish the black silhouette of the hills on both sides. We were in a flat, fairly wide canyon. Don Juan gave me detailed instructions on how to stay merged with the chaparral and taught me a way to sit "in vigil," as he called it. He told me to tuck my right leg under my left thigh and keep my left leg in a squat position. He explained that the tucked leg was used as a spring in order to stand up with great speed, if it were necessary. He then told me to sit facing the west, because that was the direction of the woman's house. He sat next to me, to my right, and told me in a whisper to keep my eyes focused on the ground, searching, or rather, waiting, for a sort of wind wave that would make a ripple in the bushes. Whenever the ripple touched the bushes on which I had focused my gaze, I was supposed to look up and see the sorceress in all her "magnificent evil splendor." Don Juan actually used those words.

When I asked him to explain what he meant, he said that if I detected a ripple I simply had to look up and see for myself, because "a sorcerer in flight" was such a unique sight that it defied explanations.

There was a fairly steady wind and I thought I detected a ripple in the bushes many times. I looked up each time, prepared to have a transcendental experience, but I did not see anything. Every time the wind blew the bushes don Juan would kick the ground vigorously, whirling around, moving his arms as if they were whips. The strength of his movements was extraordinary.

After a few failures to see the sorceress "in flight" I was sure I was not going to witness any transcendental event, yet don Juan's display of "power" was so exquisite that I did not mind spending the night there.

At daybreak don Juan sat down by me. He seemed to be totally exhausted. He could hardly move. He lay down on his back and mumbled that he had failed to "pierce the woman." I was very intrigued by that statement; he repeated it several times and each time his tone became more downhearted, more desperate. I began to experience an unusual anxiety. I found it very easy to project my feelings into don Juan's mood.

Don Juan did not mention anything about the incident or the woman for several months. I thought he had either forgotten or resolved the whole affair. One day, however, I found him in a very agitated mood, and in a manner that was completely incongruous with his natural calmness he told me that the "blackbird" had stood in front of him the night before, almost touching him, and that he had not even awakened. The woman's artfulness was so great that he had not felt her presence at all. He said his good fortune was to wake up in the nick of time to stage a horrendous fight for his life. Don Juan's tone of voice was moving, almost pathetic. I felt an overwhelming surge of compassion and concern.

In a somber and dramatic tone he reaffirmed that he had no way to stop her and that the next time she came near him was going to be his last day on earth. I became despondent and was nearly in tears. Don Juan seemed to notice my profound concern and laughed, I thought, bravely. He patted me on the back and said that I should not worry, that he was not altogether lost yet, because he had one last card, a trump card.

"A warrior lives strategically," he said, smiling. "A warrior never carries loads he cannot handle."

Don Juan's smile had the power to dispel the ominous clouds of doom. I suddenly felt elated and we both laughed. He patted my head.

"You know, of all the things on this earth, you are my last card," he said abruptly, looking straight into my eyes.

"What?"

"You are my trump card in my fight against that witch."

I did not understand what he meant and he explained that the woman did not know me and that if I played my hand as he would direct me, I had a better than good chance to "pierce her."

"What do you mean by 'pierce her'?"

"You cannot kill her but you must pierce her like a balloon. If you do that she'll leave me alone. But don't think about it now. I'll tell you what to do when the time comes."

Months went by. I had forgotten the incident and was caught by surprise when I arrived at his house one day; don Juan came out running and did not let me get out of my car.

"You must leave immediately," he whispered with appalling urgency. "Listen carefully. Buy a shotgun, or get one in any way you can; don't bring me your own gun, do you understand? Get any gun, except your own, and bring it here right away."

"Why do you want a shotgun?"

"Go now!"

I returned with a shotgun. I had not had enough money to buy one but a friend of mine had given me his old gun. Don Juan did not look at it; he explained, laughing, that he had been abrupt with me because the blackbird was on the roof of the house and he did not want her to see me.

"Finding the blackbird on the roof gave me the idea that you could bring a gun and pierce her with it," don

Juan said emphatically. "I don't want anything to happen to you, so I suggested that you buy the gun or that you get one in any other way. You see, you have to destroy the gun after completing the task."

"What kind of task are you talking about?"

"You must attempt to pierce the woman with your shotgun."

He made me clean the gun by rubbing it with the fresh leaves and stems of a peculiarly scented plant. He himself rubbed two shells and placed them inside the barrels. Then he said I was to hide in front of his house and wait until the blackbird landed on the roof and then, after taking careful aim, I was supposed to let go with both barrels. The effect of the surprise, more than the pellets, would pierce the woman, and if I were powerful and determined I could force her to leave him alone. Thus my aim had to be impeccable and so did my determination to pierce her.

"You must scream at the moment you shoot," he said. "It must be a potent and piercing yell."

He then piled bundles of bamboo and fire sticks about ten feet away from the *ramada* of his house. He made me lean against the piles. The position was quite comfortable. I was sort of half-seated; my back was well propped and I had a good view of the roof.

He said it was too early for the witch to be out, and that we had until dusk to do all the preparations; he would then pretend he was locking himself inside the house, in order to attract her and elicit another attack on his person. He told me to relax and find a comfortable position that I could shoot from without moving. He made me aim at the roof a couple of times and concluded that the act of lifting the gun to my shoulder and taking aim was too slow and cumbersome. He then built a prop for the gun. He made two deep holes with a pointed iron bar, planted two forked sticks in them, and tied a long pole in between the forks. The structure gave me a shooting support and allowed me to keep the gun aimed at the roof.

Don Juan looked at the sky and said it was time for him to go into the house. He got up and calmly went inside, giving me the final admonition that my endeavor was not a joke and that I had to hit the bird with the first shot.

After don Juan left I had a few more minutes of twilight and then it became quite dark. It seemed as if darkness had been waiting until I was alone and suddenly it descended on me. I tried to focus my eyes on the roof, which was silhouetted against the sky; for a while there was enough light on the horizon so the line of the roof was still visible, but then the sky became black and I could hardly see the house. I kept my eyes focused on the roof for hours without noticing anything at all. I saw a couple of owls flying by toward the north; the span of their wings was quite remarkable and they could not be mistaken for blackbirds. At a given moment, however, I distinctly noticed the black shape of a small bird landing on the roof. It was definitely a bird! My heart began pounding hard; I felt a buzzing in my ears. I aimed in the dark and pulled both triggers. There was quite a loud explosion. I felt a strong recoil of the gun butt on my shoulder and at the same time I heard a most piercing and horrendous human shriek. It was loud and eerie and seemed to have come from the roof. I had a moment of total confusion. I then remembered that don Juan had admonished me to yell as I shot and I had forgotten to do so. I was thinking of reloading my gun when don Juan opened the door and came out running. He had his kerosene lantern with him. He appeared to be quite nervous.

"I think you got her," he said. "We must find the dead bird now."

He brought a ladder and made me climb up and look on the *ramada,* but I could not find anything there. He climbed up and looked himself for a while, with equally negative results.

"Perhaps you have blasted the bird to bits," don Juan said, "in which case we must find at least a feather."

We began looking around the *ramada* first and then around the house. We looked with the light of the lantern until morning. Then we started looking again all over the area we had covered during the night. Around 11:00 A.M. don Juan called off our search. He sat down dejected, smiled sheepishly at me, and said that I had failed to stop his enemy and that now, more than ever before, his life was not worth a hoot because the woman was doubtlessly irked, itching to take revenge.

"You're safe, though," don Juan said reassuringly. "The woman doesn't know you."

As I was walking to my car to return home, I asked him if I had to destroy the shotgun. He said the gun had done nothing and I should give it back to its owner. I noticed a profound look of despair in don Juan's eyes. I felt so moved by it that I was about to weep.

"What can I do to help you?" I asked.

"There's nothing you can do," don Juan said.

We remained silent for a moment. I wanted to leave right away. I felt an oppressive anguish. I was ill at ease.

"Would you really try to help me?" don Juan asked in a childlike tone.

I told him again that my total person was at his disposal, that my affection for him was so profound I would undertake any kind of action to help him.

Don Juan smiled and asked again if I really meant that, and I vehemently reaffirmed my desire to help him.

"If you really mean it," he said, "I may have one more chance."

He seemed to be delighted. He smiled broadly and clapped his hands several times, the way he always does when he wants to express a feeling of pleasure. This change of mood was so remarkable that it also involved me. I suddenly felt that the oppressive mood, the anguish, had been vanquished and life was inexplicably exciting again. Don Juan sat down and I did likewise. He looked at me for a long moment and then proceeded to tell me in a very calm and deliberate manner that I was in fact the only person who could help him at that moment, and thus he was going to ask me to do something very dangerous and very special.

He paused for a moment as if he wanted a reaffirmation on my part, and I again reiterated my firm desire to do anything for him.

"I'm going to give you a weapon to pierce her," he said.

He took a long object from his pouch and handed it to me. I took it and then examined it. I almost dropped it.

"It is a wild boar," he went on. "You must pierce her with it."

The object I was holding was a dry foreleg of a wild boar. The skin was ugly and the bristles were revolting to the touch. The hoof was intact and its two halves were spread out, as if the leg were stretched. It was an awful-looking thing. It made me feel almost sick to my stomach. He quickly took it back.

"You must ram the wild boar right into her navel," don Juan said.

"What?" I said in a feeble voice.

"You must hold the wild boar in your left hand and stab her with it. She is a sorceress and the wild boar will enter her belly and no one in this world, except another sorcerer, will see it stuck in there. This is not an ordinary battle but an affair of sorcerers. The danger you will run is that if you fail to pierce her she might strike you dead on the spot, or her companions and relatives will shoot you or knife you. You may, on the other hand, get out without a scratch.

"If you succeed she will have a hellish time with the wild boar in her body and she will leave me alone."

An oppressive anguish enveloped me again. I had a profound affection for don Juan. I admired him. At the time of this startling request, I had already learned to regard his way of life and his knowledge as a paramount accomplishment. How could anyone let a man like that die? And yet how could anyone deliberately risk his life? I became so immersed in my deliberations I did not notice that don Juan had stood up and was standing by me until he patted me on the shoulder. I looked up; he was smiling benevolently.

"Whenever you feel that you really want to help me, you should return," he said, "but not until then. If you come back I know what we will have to do. Go now! If you don't want to return I'll understand that too."

I automatically stood up, got into my car, and drove away. Don Juan had actually let me off the hook. I could have left and never returned, but somehow the thought of being free to leave did not soothe me. I drove a while longer and then impulsively turned around and drove back to don Juan's house.

He was still sitting underneath his *ramada* and did not seem surprised to see me.

"Sit down," he said. "The clouds in the west are beautiful. It will be dark shortly. Sit quietly and let the twilight fill you. Do whatever you want now, but when I tell you, look straight at those shiny clouds and ask the twilight to give you power and calmness."

I sat facing the western clouds for a couple of hours. Don Juan went into the house and stayed inside. When it was getting dark he returned.

"The twilight has come," he said. "Stand up! Don't close your eyes, but look straight at the clouds; put your arms up with your hands open and your fingers extended and trot in place."

I followed his instructions; I lifted my arms over my head and began trotting. Don Juan came to my side and corrected my movements. He placed the leg of the wild boar against the palm of my left hand and made me hold it with my thumb. He then pulled my arms down until they pointed to the orange and dark gray clouds over the horizon, toward the west. He extended my fingers like fans and told me not to curl them over the palms of my hands. It was of crucial importance that I keep my fingers spread because if I closed them I would not be asking the twilight for power and calm, but would be menacing it. He also corrected my trotting. He said it should be peaceful and uniform, as if I were actually running toward the twilight with my extended arms.

I could not fall asleep during that night. It was as if, instead of calming me, the twilight had agitated me into a frenzy.

"I still have so many things pending in my life," I said. "So many things unresolved."

Don Juan chuckled softly.

"Nothing is pending in the world," he said. "Nothing is finished, yet nothing is unresolved. Go to sleep."

Don Juan's words were strangely soothing.

Around ten o'clock the next morning, don Juan gave me something to eat and then we were on our way. He whispered that we were going to approach the woman around noon, or before noon if possible. He said that the ideal time would have been the early hours of the day, because a witch is always less powerful or less aware in the morning, but she would never leave the protection of her house at those hours. I did not ask any questions. He directed me to the highway and at a certain point he told me to stop and park on the side of the road. He said we had to wait there.

I looked at my watch; it was five minutes to eleven. I yawned repeatedly. I was actually sleepy; my mind wandered around aimlessly.

Suddenly don Juan straightened up and nudged me. I jumped up in my seat.

"There she is!" he said.

I saw a woman walking toward the highway on the edge of a cultivated field. She was carrying a basket looped in her right arm. It was not until then that I noticed we were parked near a crossroads. There were two narrow trails which ran parallel to both sides of the highway and another wider and more trafficked trail that ran perpendicular to the highway; obviously people who used that trail had to walk across the paved road.

When the woman was still on the dirt road don Juan told me to get out of the car.

"Do it now," he said firmly.

I obeyed him. The woman was almost on the highway. I ran and overtook her. I was so close to her that I felt her clothes on my face. I took the wild boar hoof from under my shirt and thrust it at her. I did not feel any resistance to the blunt object I had in my hand. I saw a fleeting shadow in front of me, like a drape; my head turned to my right and I saw the woman standing fifty feet away on the opposite side of the road. She was a fairly young, dark woman with a strong, stocky body. She was smiling at me. Her teeth were white and big and her smile was placid. She had closed her eyes halfway, as if to protect them from the wind. She was still holding her basket, looped over her right arm.

I then had a moment of unique confusion. I turned around to look at don Juan. He was making frantic gestures to call me back. I ran back. There were three or four men coming in a hurry toward me. I got into the car and sped away in the opposite direction.

I tried to ask don Juan what had happened but I could not talk; my ears were bursting with an overwhelming pressure; I felt that I was choking. He seemed to be pleased and began to laugh. It was as if my failure did not concern him. I had my hands so tight around the steering wheel that I could not move them; they were frozen; my arms were rigid and so were my legs. In fact I could not take my foot off the gas pedal.

Don Juan patted me on the back and told me to relax. Little by little the pressure in my ears diminished.

"What happened back there?" I finally asked.

He giggled like a child without answering. Then he asked me if I had noticed the way the woman got out of the way. He praised her excellent speed. Don Juan's talk seemed so incongruous that I could not really follow him. He praised the woman! He said her power was impeccable and she was a relentless enemy.

I asked don Juan if he did not mind my failure. I was truly surprised and annoyed at his change of mood. He seemed to be actually glad.

He told me to stop. I parked alongside the road. He put his hand on my shoulder and looked piercingly into my eyes.

"Whatever I have done to you today was a trick," he said bluntly. "The rule is that a man of knowledge has to trap his apprentice. Today I have trapped you and I have tricked you into learning."

I was dumfounded. I could not arrange my thoughts. Don Juan explained that the whole involvement with the woman was a trap; that she had never been a threat to him; and that his job was to put me in touch with her, under specific conditions of abandon and power I had experienced when I tried to pierce her. He commended my resolution and called it an act of power which demonstrated to the woman that I was capable of great exertion. Don Juan said that even though I was not aware of it, all I did was to show off in front of her.

"You could never touch her," he said, "but you showed your claws to her. She knows now that you're not afraid. You have challenged her. I used her to trick you because she's powerful and relentless and never forgets. Men are usually too busy to be relentless enemies."

I felt a terrible anger. I told him that one should not play with a person's innermost feelings and loyalties.

Don Juan laughed until tears rolled down his cheeks, and I hated him. I had an overwhelming desire to punch him and leave; there was, however, such a strange rhythm in his laughter that it kept me almost paralyzed.

"Don't be so angry," don Juan said soothingly.

Then he said that his acts had never been a farce, that he also had thrown his life away a long time before when his own benefactor tricked him, just as he had tricked me. Don Juan said that his benefactor was a cruel man who did not think about him the way he, don Juan, thought about me. He added very sternly that the woman had tested her strength against him and had really tried to kill him.

"Now she knows that I was playing with her," he said, laughing, "and she'll hate *you* for it. She can't do anything to me, but she will take it out on you. She doesn't know yet how much power you have, so she will come to test you, little by little. Now you have no choice but to learn in order to defend yourself, or you will fall prey to that lady. She is no trick."

Don Juan reminded me of the way she had flown away.

"Don't be angry," he said. "It was not an ordinary trick. It was the rule."

There was something about the way the woman moved away from me that was truly maddening. I had witnessed it myself: she had jumped the width of the highway in a flick of an eyelash. I had no way to get out of that certainty. From that moment on I focused all my attention on that incident and little by little I accumulated "proof" that she was actually following me. The final outcome was that

I had to withdraw from the apprenticeship under the pressure of my irrational fear.

I came back to don Juan's house hours later, in the early afternoon. He was apparently waiting for me. He came up to me as I got out of my car and examined me with curious eyes, walking around me a couple of times.

"Why the nervousness?" he asked before I had time to say anything.

I explained that something had scared me off that morning and that I had begun to feel something prowling around me, as in the past. Don Juan sat down and seemed to be engulfed in thoughts. His face had an unusually serious expression. He seemed to be tired. I sat by him and arranged my notes.

After a very long pause his face brightened up and he smiled.

"What you felt this morning was the spirit of the water hole," he said. "I've told you that you must be prepared for unexpected encounters with those forces. I thought you understood."

I could not answer.

"I did."

"Then why the fear?"

"That spirit is on your trail," he said. "It already tapped you in the water. I assure you it will tap you again and probably you won't be prepared and that encounter will be your end."

Don Juan's words made me feel genuinely concerned. My feelings were strange, however; I was concerned but not afraid. Whatever was happening to me had not been able to elicit my old feelings of blind fear.

"What should I do?" I asked.

"You forget too easily," he said. "The path of knowledge is a forced one. In order to learn we must be spurred. In the path of knowledge we are always fighting something, avoiding something, prepared for something; and that something is always inexplicable, greater, more powerful than us. The inexplicable forces will come to you. Now it is the spirit of the water hole, later on it'll be your own ally, so there is nothing you can do now but to prepare yourself for the struggle. Years ago la Catalina spurred you, she was only a sorceress, though, and that was a beginner's trick.

"The world is indeed full of frightening things and we are helpless creatures surrounded by forces that are inexplicable and unbending. The average man, in ignorance, believes that those forces can be explained or changed; he doesn't really know how to do that, but he expects that the actions of mankind will explain them or change them sooner or later. The sorcerer, on the other hand, does not think of explaining or changing them; instead, he learns to use such forces by redirecting himself and adapting to their direction. That's his trick. There is very little to sorcery once you find out its trick. A sorcerer is only slightly better off than the average man. Sorcery does not help him to live a better life; in fact I should say that sorcery hinders him; it makes his life cumbersome, precarious. By opening himself to knowledge a sorcerer becomes more vulnerable than the average man. On the one hand his fellow men hate him and fear him and will strive to end his life; on the other hand the inexplicable and unbending forces that surround every one of us, by right of our being alive, are for a sorcerer a source of even greater danger. To be pierced by a fellow man is indeed painful, but nothing in comparison to being touched by an ally. A sorcerer, by opening himself to knowledge, falls prey to such forces and has only one means of balancing himself, his will; thus he must feel and act like a warrior. I will repeat this once more: Only as a warrior can one survive the path of knowledge. What helps a sorcerer live a better life is the strength of being a warrior.

"It is my commitment to teach you to *see*. Not because I personally want to do so but because you were chosen; you were pointed out to me by Mescalito. I am compelled by my personal desire, however, to teach you to feel and act like a warrior. I personally believe that to be a warrior is more suitable than anything else. Therefore I have endeavored to show you those forces as a sorcerer perceives them, because only under their terrifying impact can one become a warrior. To *see* without first being a warrior would make you weak; it would give you a false meekness, a desire to retreat; your body would decay because you would become indifferent. It is my personal commitment to make you a warrior so you won't crumble.

"I have heard you say time and time again that you are always prepared to die. I don't regard that feeling as necessary. I think it is a useless indulgence. A warrior should be prepared only to battle. I have also heard you say that your parents injured your spirit. I think the spirit of man is something that can be injured very easily, although not by the same acts you yourself call injurious. I believe that your parents did injure you by making you indulgent and soft and given to dwelling.

"The spirit of a warrior is not geared to indulging and complaining, nor is it geared to winning or losing. The spirit of a warrior is geared only to struggle, and every struggle is a warrior's last battle on earth. Thus the outcome matters very little to him. In his last battle on earth a warrior lets his spirit flow free and clear. And as he wages his battle, knowing that his will is impeccable, a warrior laughs and laughs."

I finished writing and looked up. Don Juan was staring at me. He shook his head from side to side and smiled.

"You really write everything?" he asked in an incredulous tone. "Genaro says that he can never be serious with you because you're always writing. He's right; how can anyone be serious if you're always writing?"

He chuckled and I tried to defend my position.

"It doesn't matter," he said, "If you ever learn to *see,* I suppose you must do it your own weird way."

He stood up and looked at the sky. It was around noon. He said there was still time to start on a hunting trip to a place in the mountains.

"What are we going to hunt?" I asked.

"A special animal, either a deer or a wild boar or even a mountain lion."

He paused for a moment and then added, "Even an eagle."

I stood up and followed him to my car. He said that this

time we were going only to observe and to find out what animal we had to hunt. He was about to get in my car when he seemed to remember something. He smiled and said that the journey had to be postponed until I had learned something without which our hunting would be impossible.

We went back and sat down again underneath his *ramada*. There were so many things I wanted to ask, but he did not give me time to say anything before he spoke again.

"This brings us to the last point you must know about a warrior," he said. "A warrior selects the items that make his world.

"The other day when you saw the ally and I had to wash you twice, do you know what was wrong with you?"

"No."

"You had lost your shields."

"What shields? What are you talking about?"

"I said that a warrior selects the items that make his world. He selects deliberately, for every item he chooses is a shield that protects him from the onslaughts of the forces he is striving to use. A warrior would use his shields to protect himself from his ally, for instance.

"An average man who is equally surrounded by those inexplicable forces is oblivious to them because he has other kinds of special shields to protect himself."

He paused and looked at me with a question in his eyes. I had not understood what he meant.

"What are those shields?" I insisted.

"What people do," he repeated.

"What do they do?"

"Well, look around. People are busy doing that which people do. Those are their shields. Whenever a sorcerer has an encounter with any of those inexplicable and unbending forces we have talked about, his gap opens, making him more susceptible to his death than he ordinarily is; I've told you that we die through that gap, therefore if it is open one should have his will ready to fill it; that is, if one is a warrior. If one is not a warrior, like yourself, then one has no other recourse but to use the activities of daily life to take one's mind away from the fright of the encounter and thus to allow one's gap to close. You got angry with me that day when you met the ally. I made you angry when I stopped your car and I made you cold when I dumped you into the water. Having your clothes on made you even colder. Being angry and cold helped you close your gap and you were protected. At this time in your life, however, you can no longer use those shields as effectively as an average man. You know too much about those forces and now you are finally at the brink of feeling and acting as a warrior. Your old shields are no longer safe."

"What am I supposed to do?"

"Act like a warrior and select the items of your world. You cannot surround yourself with things helter-skelter any longer. I tell you this in a most serious vein. Now for the first time you are not safe in your old way of life."

"What do you mean by selecting the items of my world?"

"A warrior encounters those inexplicable and unbending forces because he is deliberately seeking them, thus he is always prepared for the encounter. You, on the other hand, are never prepared for it. In fact if those forces come to you they will take you by surprise; the fright will open your gap and your life will irresistibly escape through it. The first thing you must do, then, is be prepared. Think that the ally is going to pop in front of your eyes any minute and you must be ready for him. To meet an ally is no party or Sunday picnic and a warrior takes the responsibility of protecting his life. Then if any of those forces tap you and open your gap, you must deliberately strive to close it by yourself. For that purpose you must have a selected number of things that give you great peace and pleasure, things which you can deliberately use to take your thoughts from your fright and close your gap and make you solid."

"What kind of things?"

"Years ago I told you that in his day-to-day life a warrior chooses to follow the path with heart. It is the consistent choice of the path with heart which makes a warrior

different from the average man. He knows that a path has
heart when he is one with it, when he experiences a great
peace and pleasure traversing its length. The things a warrior selects to make his shields are the items of a path
with heart."

"But you said I'm not a warrior, so how can I choose a
path with heart?"

"This is your turning point. Let's say that before you
did not really need to live like a warrior. Now it is different, now you must surround yourself with the items of a
path with heart and you must refuse the rest, or you will
perish in the next encounter. I may add that you don't
need to ask for the encounter any longer. An ally can now
come to you in your sleep; while you are talking to your
friends; while you are writing."

"For years I have truly tried to live in accordance with
your teachings," I said. "Obviously I have not done well.
How can I do better now?"

"You think and talk too much. You must stop talking to
yourself."

"What do you mean?"

"You talk to yourself too much. You're not unique
at that. Every one of us does that. We carry on an internal talk. Think about it. Whenever you are alone, what
do you do?"

"I talk to myself."

"What do you talk to yourself about?"

"I don't know; anything, I suppose."

"I'll tell you what we talk to ourselves about. We talk
about our world. In fact we maintain our world with our
internal talk."

"How do we do that?"

"Whenever we finish talking to ourselves the world is
always as it should be. We renew it, we kindle it with life,
we uphold it with our internal talk. Not only that, but we
also choose our paths as we talk to ourselves. Thus we
repeat the same choices over and over until the day we
die, because we keep on repeating the same internal talk
over and over until the day we die.

"A warrior is aware of this and strives to stop his talking. This is the last point you have to know if you want to live like a warrior."

"How can I stop talking to myself?"

"First of all you must use your ears to take some of the burden from your eyes. We have been using our eyes to judge the world since the time we were born. We talk to others and to ourselves mainly about what we see. A warrior is aware of that and listens to the world; he listens to the sounds of the world."

I put my notes away. Don Juan laughed and said that he did not mean I should force the issue, that listening to the sounds of the world had to be done harmoniously and with great patience.

"A warrior is aware that the world will change as soon as he stops talking to himself," he said, "and he must be prepared for that monumental jolt."

"What do you mean, don Juan?"

"The world is such-and-such or so-and-so only because we tell ourselves that that is the way it is. If we stop telling ourselves that the world is so-and-so, the world will stop being so-and-so. At this moment I don't think you're ready for such a momentous blow, therefore you must start slowly to undo the world."

"I really do not understand you!"

"Your problem is that you confuse the world with what people do. Again you're not unique at that. Every one of us does that. The things people do are the shields against the forces that surround us; what we do as people gives us comfort and makes us feel safe; what people do is rightfully very important, but only as a shield. We never learn that the things we do as people are only shields and we let them dominate and topple our lives. In fact I could say that for mankind, what people do is greater and more important than the world itself."

"What do you call the world?"

"The world is all that is encased here," he said, and stomped the ground. "Life, death, people, the allies, and everything else that surrounds us. The world is incomprehensible. We won't ever understand it; we won't ever unravel its secrets. Thus we must treat it as it is, a sheer mystery!

"An average man doesn't do this, though. The world is never a mystery for him, and when he arrives at old age he is convinced he has nothing more to live for. An old man has not exhausted the world. He has exhausted only what people do. But in his stupid confusion he believes that the world has no more mysteries for him. What a wretched price to pay for our shields!

"A warrior is aware of this confusion and learns to treat things properly. The things that people do cannot under any conditions be more important than the world. And thus a warrior treats the world as an endless mystery and what people do as an endless folly."

15

I began the exercise of listening to the "sounds of the world" and kept at it for two months, as don Juan had specified. It was excruciating at first to listen and not look, but even more excruciating was not to talk to myself. By the end of the two months I was capable of shutting off my internal dialogue for short periods of time and I was also capable of paying attention to sounds.

I arrived at don Juan's house at 9:00 A.M. on November 10, 1969.

"We should start that trip right now," he said upon my arrival at his house.

I rested for an hour and then we drove toward the low slopes of the mountains to the east. We left my car in the care of one of his friends who lived in that area while we hiked into the mountains. Don Juan had put some crackers and sweet rolls in a knapsack for me. There were enough provisions for a day or two. I had asked don Juan if we needed more. He shook his head negatively.

We walked the entire morning. It was a rather warm day. I carried one canteen of water, most of which I drank myself. Don Juan drank only twice. When there was no more water he assured me it was all right to drink from the streams we found on our way. He laughed at my reluctance. After a short while my thirst made me overcome my fears.

In the early afternoon we stopped in a small valley at the bottom of some lush green hills. Behind the hills, toward the east, the high mountains were silhouetted against a cloudy sky.

"You can think, you can write about what we say or about what you perceive, but nothing about where we are," he said.

We rested for a while and then he took a bundle from inside his shirt. He untied it and showed me his pipe. He filled its bowl with smoking mixture, lighted a match and kindled a small dry twig, placed the burning twig inside the bowl, and told me to smoke. Without a piece of charcoal inside the bowl it was difficult to light the pipe; we had to keep kindling twigs until the mixture caught on fire.

When I had finished smoking he said that we were there so I could find out the kind of game I was supposed to hunt. He carefully repeated three or four times that the most important aspect of my endeavor was to find some holes. He emphasized the word "holes" and said that inside them a sorcerer could find all sorts of messages and directions.

I wanted to ask what kind of holes they were; don Juan seemed to have guessed my question and said that they were impossible to describe and were in the realm of "seeing." He repeated at various times that I should focus all my attention on listening to sounds and do my best to find the holes between the sounds. He said that he was going to play his spirit catcher four times. I was supposed to use those eerie calls as a guide to the ally that had welcomed me; that ally would then give me the message I was seeking. Don Juan told me I should stay in complete alertness,

since he had no idea how the ally would manifest himself
to me.

I listened attentively. I was sitting with my back against
the rock side of the hill. I experienced a mild numbness.
Don Juan warned me against closing my eyes. I began to
listen and I could distinguish the whistling of birds, the
wind rustling the leaves, the buzzing of insects. As I placed
my individual attention on those sounds, I could actually
make out four different types of bird whistlings. I could
distinguish the speeds of the wind, in terms of slow or fast;
I could also hear the different rustlings of three types of
leaves. The buzzings of insects were dazzling. There were
so many that I could not count them or correctly differen-
tiate them.

I was immersed in a strange world of sound, as I had
never been in my life. I began to slide to my right. Don
Juan made a motion to stop me but I caught myself before
he did. I straightened up and sat erect again. Don Juan
moved my body until he had propped me on a crevice in
the rock wall. He swept the small rocks from under my
legs and placed the back of my head against the rock.

He told me imperatively to look at the mountains to the
southeast. I fixed my gaze in the distance but he corrected
me and said I should not gaze but look, sort of scanning,
at the hills in front of me and at the vegetation on them.
He repeated over and over that I should concentrate all
my attention on my hearing.

Sounds began to be prominent again. It was not so
much that I wanted to hear them; rather, they had a way
of forcing me to concentrate on them. The wind rustled
the leaves. The wind came high above the trees and then
it dropped into the valley where we were. Upon dropping,
it touched the leaves of the tall trees first; they made a
peculiar sound which I fancied to be a sort of rich, raspy,
lush sound. Then the wind hit the bushes and their leaves
sounded like a crowd of small things; it was an almost
melodious sound, very engulfing and quite demanding; it
seemed capable of drowning everything else. I found it
displeasing. I felt embarrassed because it occurred to me
that I was like the rustle of the bushes, nagging and

demanding. The sound was so akin to me that I hated it. Then I heard the wind rolling on the ground. It was not a rustling sound but more of a whistle, almost a beep or a flat buzz. Listening to the sounds the wind was making, I realized that all three of them happened at once. I was wondering how I had been capable of isolating each of them, when I again became aware of the whistling of birds and the buzzing of insects. At one moment there were only the sounds of the wind and the next moment a gigantic flow of other sounds emerged at once into my field of awareness. Logically, all the existing sounds must have been continually emitted during the time I was hearing only the wind.

I could not count all the whistles of birds or buzzings of insects, yet I was convinced I was listening to each separate sound as it was produced. Together they created a most extraordinary order. I cannot call it any other thing but "order." It was an order of sounds that had a pattern; that is, every sound happened in sequence.

Then I heard a unique prolonged wail. It made me shiver. Every other noise ceased for an instant, and the valley was dead still as the reverberation of the wail reached the valley's outer limits; then the noises began again. I picked up their pattern immediately. After a moment of attentive listening I thought I understood don Juan's recommendation to watch for the holes between the sounds. The pattern of noises had spaces in between sounds! For example, specific whistles of birds were timed and had pauses in between them, and so had all the other sounds I was perceiving. The rustling of leaves was like a binding glue that made them into a homogeneous buzz. The fact of the matter was that the timing of each sound was a unit in the overall pattern of sounds. Thus the spaces or pauses in between sounds were, if I paid attention to them, holes in a structure.

I heard again the piercing wail of don Juan's spirit catcher. It did not jolt me, but the sounds again ceased for an instant and I perceived such a cessation as a hole, a very large hole. At that precise moment I shifted my attention from hearing to looking. I was looking at a cluster of low hills with lush green vegetation. The silhouette of the hills was arranged in such a way that from the place where I was looking there seemed to be a hole on the side of one of the hills. It was a space in between two hills and through it I could see the deep, dark, gray hue of the mountains in the distance. For a moment I did not know what it was. It was as if the hole I was looking at was the "hole" in the sound. Then the noises began again but the visual image of the huge hole remained. A short while later I became even more keenly aware of the pattern of sounds and their order and the arrangement of their pauses. My mind was capable of distinguishing and discriminating among an enormous number of individual sounds. I could actually keep track of all the sounds, thus each pause between sounds was a definite hole. At a given moment the pauses became crystallized in my mind and formed a sort of solid grid, a structure. I was not seeing or hearing it. I was feeling it with some unknown part of myself.

Don Juan played his string once again; the sounds ceased as they had done before, creating a huge hole in the sound structure. This time, however, that big pause blended with the hole in the hills I was looking at; they became superimposed on each other. The effect of perceiving two holes lasted for such a long time that I was capable of seeing-hearing their contours as they fit one another. Then the other sounds began again and their structure of pauses became an extraordinary, almost visual perception. I began seeing the sounds as they created patterns and then all those patterns became superimposed on the environment in the same way I had perceived the two big holes becoming superimposed. I was not looking or hearing as I was accustomed to doing. I was doing something which was entirely different but combined features of both. For some reason my attention was focused on the large hole in the hills. I felt I was hearing it and at the same time looking at it. There was something of a lure about it. It dominated my field of perception and every single sound pattern which coincided with a feature of the environment was hinged on that hole.

I heard once more the eerie wail of don Juan's spirit

catcher; all other sounds stopped; the two large holes seemed to light up and next I was looking again at the plowed field; the ally was standing there as I had seen him before. The light of the total scene became very clear. I could see him plainly, as if he were fifty yards away. I could not see his face; his hat covered it. Then he began to come toward me, lifting up his head slowly as he walked; I could almost see his face and that terrified me. I knew I had to stop him without delay. I had a strange surge in my body; I felt an outflow of "power." I wanted to move my head to the side to stop the vision but I could not do it. At that crucial instant a thought came to my mind. I knew what don Juan meant when he spoke of the items of a "path with heart" being the shields. There was something I wanted to do in my life, something very consuming and intriguing, something that filled me with great peace and joy. I knew the ally could not overcome me. I moved my head away without any trouble before I could see his entire face.

I began hearing all the other sounds; they suddenly became very loud and shrill, as if they were actually angry with me. They lost their patterns and turned into an amorphous conglomerate of sharp, painful shrieks. My ears began to buzz under their pressure. I felt that my head was about to explode. I stood up and put the palms of my hands to my ears.

Don Juan helped me walk to a very small stream, made me take off my clothes, and rolled me in the water. He made me lie on the almost dry bed of the stream and then gathered water in his hat and splashed me with it.

The pressure in my ears subsided very rapidly and it took only a few minutes to "wash" me. Don Juan looked at me, shook his head in approval, and said I had made myself "solid" in no time at all.

I put on my clothes and he took me back to the place where I had been sitting. I felt extremely vigorous, buoyant, and clearheaded.

He wanted to know all the details of my vision. He said that the "holes" in the sounds were used by sorcerers to find out specific things. A sorcerer's ally would reveal complicated affairs through the holes in the sounds. He refused to be more specific about the "holes" and sloughed off my questions, saying that since I did not have an ally such information would only be harmful to me.

"Everything is meaningful for a sorcerer," he said. "The sounds have holes in them and so does everything around you. Ordinarily a man does not have the speed to catch the holes, and thus he goes through life without protection. The worms, the birds, the trees, all of them can tell us unimaginable things if only one could have the speed to grasp their message. The smoke can give us that grasping speed. But we must be on good terms with all the living things of this world. This is the reason why we must talk to plants we are about to kill and apologize for hurting them; the same thing must be done with the animals we are going to hunt. We should take only enough for our needs, otherwise the plants and the animals and the worms we have killed would turn against us and cause us disease and misfortune. A warrior is aware of this and strives to appease them, so when he peers through the holes, the trees and birds and the worms give him truthful messages.

"But all this is not important now. What is important is that you saw the ally. That is your game! I've told you that we were going to hunt for something. I thought it was going to be an animal. I figured that you were going to see the animal we had to hunt. I myself saw a wild boar; my spirit catcher is a wild boar."

"Do you mean your spirit catcher is made out of a wild boar?"

"No! Nothing in the life of a sorcerer is made out of anything else. If something is anything at all, it is the thing itself. If you knew wild boars you would realize my spirit catcher is one."

"Why did we come here to hunt?"

"The ally showed you a spirit catcher that he got from his pouch. You need to have one if you are going to call him."

"What is a spirit catcher?"

"It is a fiber. With it I can call the allies, or my own

ally, or I can call the spirits of water holes, the spirits of rivers, the spirits of mountains. Mine is a wild boar and cries like a wild boar. I used it twice around you to call the spirit of the water hole to help you. The spirit came to you as the ally came to you today. You could not see it, though, because you did not have the speed; however, that day I took you to the water canyon and put you on a rock, you knew the spirit was almost on top of you without actually seeing it. Those spirits are helpers. They are hard to handle and sort of dangerous. One needs an impeccable will to hold them at bay."

"What do they look like?"

"They are different for every man and so are the allies. For you an ally would apparently look like a man you once knew, or like a man you will always be about to know; that's the bent of your nature. You are given to mysteries and secrets. I'm not like you, so an ally for me is something very precise.

"The spirits of water holes are proper to specific places. The one I called to help you is one I have known myself. It has helped me many times. Its abode is that canyon. At the time I called it to help you, you were not strong and the spirit took you hard. That was not its intention—they have none—but you were lying there very weak, weaker than I suspected. Later on the spirit nearly lured you to your death; in the water at the irrigation canal you were phosphorescent. The spirit took you by surprise and you nearly succumbed. Once a spirit does that, it always comes back for its prey. I'm sure it will come back for you. Unfortunately, you need the water to become solid again when you use the little smoke; that puts you at a terrible disadvantage. If you don't use the water you will probably die, but if you do use it, the spirit will take you."

"Can I use water at another place?"

"It doesn't make any difference. The spirit of the water hole around my house can follow you anywhere, unless you have a spirit catcher. That is why the ally showed it to you. He told you that you need one. He wrapped it around his left hand and came to you after pointing out the water canyon. Today he again wanted to show you the spirit catcher, as he did the first time you met him. It was wise of you to stop; the ally was going too fast for your strength and a direct jolt with him would be very injurious to you."

"How can I get a spirit catcher now?"

"Apparently the ally is going to give you one himself."

"How?"

"I don't know. You will have to go to him. He has already told you where to look for it."

"Where?"

"Up there, on those hills where you saw the hole."

"Would I be looking for the ally himself?"

"No. But he is already welcoming you. The little smoke has opened your way to him. Then, later on, you will meet him face to face, but that will happen only after you know him very well."

16

We arrived in the same valley in the late afternoon of December 15, 1969. Don Juan mentioned repeatedly as we moved through the shrubs that directions or points of orientation were of crucial importance in the endeavor I was going to undertake.

"You must determine the right direction immediately upon arriving at the top of a hill," don Juan said. "As soon as you are on the top, face that direction." He pointed to the southeast. "That is your good direction and you should always face it, especially when you're in trouble. Remember that."

We stopped at the bottom of the hills where I had perceived the hole. He pointed at a specific place where I had to sit down; he sat next to me and in a very quiet voice gave me detailed instructions. He said that as soon as I reached the hilltop I had to extend my right arm in front of me with the palm of my hand down and my fingers stretched like a fan, except the thumb, which had to be tucked against the palm. Next I had to turn my head to the north and fold my arm over my chest, pointing my hand also toward the north; then I had to dance, putting my left foot behind the right one, beating the ground with the tip of my left toes. He said that when I felt a warmth coming up my left leg I had to begin sweeping my arm slowly from north to south and then to the north again.

"The spot over which the palm of your hand feels warm as you sweep your arm is the place where you must sit, and it is also the direction in which you must look," he said. "If the spot is toward the east, or if it is in that direction"—he pointed to the southeast again—"the results will be excellent. If the spot where your hand gets warm is toward the north, you will take a bad beating but you may turn the tide in your favor. If the spot is toward the south you will have a hard fight.

"You will need to sweep your arm up to four times at first, but as you become more familiar with the movement you will need only one single sweep to know whether or not your hand is going to get warm.

"Once you establish a spot where your hand gets warm, sit there; that is your first point. If you are facing the south or the north, you have to make up your mind whether you feel strong enough to stay. If you have doubts about yourself, get up and leave. There is no need to stay if you are not confident. If you decide to stick around, clean an area big enough to build a fire about five feet away from your first point. The fire must be in a straight line in the direction you are looking. The area where you build the fire is your second point. Then gather all the twigs you can in between those two points and make a fire. Sit on your first point and look at the fire. Sooner or later the spirit will come and you will see it.

"If your hand does not get warm at all after four sweeping movements, sweep your arm slowly from north to south and then turn around and sweep it to the west. If your hand gets warm on any place toward the west, drop everything and run. Run downhill toward the flat area, and no matter what you hear or feel behind you, don't turn around. As soon as you get to the flat area, no matter how frightened you are, don't keep on running, drop to the ground, take off your jacket, bunch it around your navel, and curl up like a ball, tucking your knees against your stomach. You must also cover your eyes with your hands, and your arms have to remain tight against your thighs. You must stay in that position until morning. If you follow these simple steps no harm will ever come to you.

"In case you cannot get to the flat area in time, drop to the ground right where you are. You will have a horrid time there. You will be harassed, but if you keep calm and don't move or look you will come out of it without a single scratch.

"Now if your hand does not get warm at all while you sweep it to the west, face the east again and run in an easterly direction until you are out of breath. Stop there and repeat the same maneuvers. You must keep on running toward the east, repeating these movements, until your hand gets warm."

After giving me these instructions he made me repeat them until I had memorized them. Then we sat in silence for a long time. I attempted to revive the conversation a couple of times, but he forced me into silence each time by an imperative gesture.

It was getting dark when don Juan got up and without a word began climbing the hill. I followed him. At the top of the hill I performed all the movements he had prescribed. Don Juan stood by, a short distance away, and kept a sharp look on me. I was very careful and deliberately slow. I tried to feel any perceivable change of temperature, but I could not detect whether or not the palm of my hand became warm. By that time it was fairly dark, yet I was still capable of running in an easterly direction without stumbling on the shrubs. I stopped running when I was out of breath, which was not too far from my point of departure. I was extremely tired and tense. My forearms ached and so did my calves.

I repeated there all the required motions and again had the same negative results. I ran in the dark two more times, and then, while I was sweeping my arm for the third time, my hand became warm over a point toward the east. It was such a definite change of temperature that it startled me. I sat down and waited for don Juan. I told him I had detected a change in temperature in my hand. He told me to proceed, and I picked all the dry brush I could find and started a fire. He sat to my left a couple of feet away.

The fire drew strange, dancing silhouettes. At times the flames became iridescent; they grew bluish and then brilliantly white. I explained that unusual play of colors by assuming that it was produced by some chemical property of the specific dry twigs and branches I had collected. Another very unusual feature of the fire was the sparks. The new twigs I kept adding created extremely big sparks. I thought they were like tennis balls that seemed to explode in midair.

I stared at the fire fixedly, the way I believed don Juan had recommended, and I became dizzy. He handed me his water gourd and signaled me to drink. The water relaxed me and gave me a delightful feeling of freshness.

Don Juan leaned over and whispered in my ear that I did not have to stare at the flames, that I should only watch in the direction of the fire. I became very cold and clammy after watching for almost an hour. At a moment when I was about to lean over and pick up a twig, something like a moth or a spot in my retina swept across from right to left between myself and the fire. I immediately recoiled. I looked at don Juan and he signaled me with a movement of his chin to look back at the flames. A moment later the same shadow swept across in the opposite direction.

Don Juan got up hurriedly and began piling loose dirt on top of the burning twigs until he had completely extinguished the flames. He executed the maneuver of putting out the fire with tremendous speed. By the time I moved to help him he had finished. He stomped on the dirt on top of the smoldering twigs and then he nearly dragged me downhill and out of the valley. He walked very fast without turning his head back and did not allow me to talk at all.

When we got to my car hours later I asked him what was the thing I had seen. He shook his head imperatively and we drove in complete silence.

He went directly inside when we arrived at his house in the early morning, and he again hushed me up when I tried to talk.

Don Juan was sitting outside, behind his house. He seemed to have been waiting for me to wake up, because he started talking as I came out of the house. He said that the shadow I had seen the night before was a spirit, a force that belonged to the particular place where I had seen it. He spoke of that specific being as a useless one.

"It only exists there," he said. "It has no secrets of power, so there was no point in remaining there. You would have seen only a fast, passing shadow going back and forth all night. There are other types of beings, however, that can give you secrets of power, if you are fortunate enough to find them."

We ate some breakfast then and did not talk for quite a while. After eating we sat in front of his house.

"There are three kinds of beings," he said suddenly, "those that cannot give anything because they have nothing to give, those that can only cause fright, and those that have gifts. The one you saw last night was a silent one; it has nothing to give; it is only a shadow. Most of the time, however, another type of being is associated with the silent one, a nasty spirit whose only quality is to cause fear and which always hovers around the abode of a silent one. That is why I decided to get out of there fast. That nasty type follows people right into their homes and makes life impossible for them. I know people who have had to move out of their houses because of them. There are always some people who believe they can get a lot out of that kind of being, but the mere fact that a spirit is around the house does not mean anything. People may try to entice it, or they may follow it around the house under the impression that it can reveal secrets to them. But the only thing people would get is a frightful experience. I know people who took turns watching one of those nasty beings that had followed them into their house. They watched the spirit for months; finally someone else had to step in and drag the people out of the house; they had become weak and were wasting away. So the only wise thing one can do with that nasty type is to forget about it and leave it alone."

I asked him how people enticed a spirit. He said that people took pains to figure out first where the spirit would most likely appear and then they put weapons in its way, in hopes that it might touch the weapons, because spirits were known to like paraphernalia of war. Don Juan said that any kind of gear, or any object, that was touched by a spirit rightfully became a power object. However, the nasty type of being was known never to touch anything, but only to produce the auditory illusion of noise.

I then asked don Juan about the manner in which those spirits caused fear. He said that their most common way of frightening people was to appear as a dark shadow shaped as a man that would roam around the house, creating a frightening clatter or creating the sound of voices, or as a dark shadow that would suddenly lurch out from a dark corner.

Don Juan said that the third type of spirit was a true ally, a giver of secrets; that special type existed in lonely, abandoned places, places which were almost inaccessible. He said that a man who wished to find one of these beings had to travel far and go by himself. At a distant and lonely place the man had to take all the necessary steps alone. He had to sit by his fire and if he saw the shadow he had to leave immediately. He had to remain, however, if he encountered other conditions, such as a strong wind that would kill his fire and would keep him from kindling it again during four attempts; or if a branch broke from a nearby tree. The branch really had to break and the man had to make sure that it was not merely the sound of a branch breaking off.

Other conditions he had to be aware of were rocks that rolled, or pebbles which were thrown at his fire, or any constant noise, and he then had to walk in the direction in which any of these phenomena occurred until the spirit revealed itself.

There were many ways in which such a being put a warrior to the test. It might suddenly leap in front of him, in the most horrendous appearance, or it might grab the man from the back and not turn him loose and keep him pinned down for hours. It might also topple a tree on him. Don Juan said that those were truly dangerous forces, and although they could not kill a man hand to hand, they could cause his death by fright, or by actually letting objects fall on him, or by appearing suddenly and causing him to stumble, lose his footing, and go over a precipice.

He told me that if I ever found one of those beings under inappropriate circumstances I should never attempt to struggle with it because it would kill me. It would rob my soul. So I should throw myself to the ground and bear it until the morning.

"When a man is facing the ally, the giver of secrets, he has to muster up all his courage and grab it before it grabs him, or chase it before it chases him. The chase must be relentless and then comes the struggle. The man must wrestle the spirit to the ground and keep it there until it gives him power."

I asked him if these forces had substance, if one could really touch them. I said that the very idea of a "spirit" connoted something ethereal to me.

"Don't call them spirits," he said. "Call them allies; call them inexplicable forces."

He was silent for a while, then he lay on his back and propped his head on his folded arms. I insisted on knowing if those beings had substance.

"You're damn right they have substance," he said after another moment of silence. "When one struggles with them they are solid, but that feeling lasts only a moment. Those beings rely on a man's fear; therefore if the man struggling with one of them is a warrior, the being loses its tension very quickly while the man becomes more vigorous. One can actually absorb the spirit's tension."

"What kind of tension is that?" I asked.

"Power. When one touches them, they vibrate as if

they were ready to rip one apart. But that is only a show. The tension ends when the man maintains his grip."

"What happens when they lose their tension? Do they become like air?"

"No, they just become flaccid. They still have substance, though. But it is not like anything one has ever touched."

Later on, during the evening, I said to him that perhaps what I had seen the night before could have been only a moth. He laughed and very patiently explained that moths fly back and forth only around light bulbs, because a light bulb cannot burn their wings. A fire, on the other hand, would burn them the first time they came close to it. He also pointed out that the shadow covered the entire fire. When he mentioned that, I remembered that it was really an extremely large shadow and that it actually blocked the view of the fire for an instant. However, it had happened so fast that I had not emphasized it in my earlier recollection.

Then he pointed out that the sparks were very large and flew to my left. I had noticed that myself. I said that the wind was probably blowing in that direction. Don Juan replied that there was no wind whatsoever. That was true. Upon recalling my experience I could remember that the night was still.

Another thing I had completely overlooked was a greenish glow in the flames, which I detected when don Juan signaled me to keep on looking at the fire, after the shadow had first crossed my field of vision. Don Juan reminded me of it. He also objected to my calling it a shadow. He said it was round and more like a bubble.

Two days later, on December 17, 1969, don Juan said in a very casual tone that I knew all the details and necessary techniques in order to go to the hills by myself and obtain a power object, the spirit catcher. He urged me to proceed alone and affirmed that his company would only hinder me.

I was ready to leave when he seemed to change his mind.

"You're not strong enough," he said. "I'll go with you to the bottom of the hills."

When we were at the small valley where I had seen the ally, he examined from a distance the formation in the terrain that I had called a hole in the hills, and said that we had to go still further south into the distant mountains. The abode of the ally was at the furthermost point we could see through the hole.

I looked at the formation and all I could distinguish was the bluish mass of the distant mountains. He guided me, however, in a southeasterly direction and after hours of walking we reached a point he said was "deep enough" into the ally's abode.

It was late afternoon when we stopped. We sat down on some rocks. I was tired and hungry; all I had eaten during the day was some tortillas and water. Don Juan stood up all of a sudden, looked at the sky, and told me in a commanding tone to take off in the direction that was the best for me and to be sure I could remember the spot where we were at the moment, so I could return there whenever I was through. He said in a reassuring tone that he would be waiting for me if it took me forever.

I asked apprehensively if he believed that the affair of getting a spirit catcher was going to take a long time.

"Who knows?" he said, smiling mysteriously.

I walked away toward the southeast, turning around a couple of times to look at don Juan. He was walking very slowly in the opposite direction. I climbed to the top of a large hill and looked at don Juan once again; he was a good two hundred yards away. He did not turn to look at me. I ran downhill into a small bowl-like depression between the hills, and I suddenly found myself alone. I sat down for a moment and began to wonder what I was doing there. I felt ludicrous looking for a spirit catcher. I ran back up to the top of the hill to have a better view of don Juan but I could not see him anywhere. I ran downhill in the direction I had last seen him. I wanted to call off the whole affair and go home. I felt quite stupid and tired.

"Don Juan!" I yelled over and over.

He was nowhere in sight. I again ran to the top of another steep hill; I could not see him from there either. I ran quite a way looking for him but he had disappeared. I retraced my steps and went back to the original place where he had left me. I had the absurd certainty I was going to find him sitting there laughing at my inconsistencies.

"What in the hell have I gotten into?" I said loudly.

I knew then that there was no way to stop whatever I was doing there. I really did not know how to go back to my car. Don Juan had changed directions various times and the general orientation of the four cardinal points was not enough. I was afraid of getting lost in the mountains. I sat down and for the first time in my life I had the strange feeling that there never really was a way to revert back to an original point of departure. Don Juan had said that I always insisted on starting at a point I called the beginning, when in effect the beginning did not exist. And there in the middle of those mountains I felt I understood what he meant. It was as if the point of departure had always been myself; it was as if don Juan had never really been there; and when I looked for him he became what he really was—a fleeting image that vanished over a hill.

I heard the soft rustle of leaves and a strange fragrance enveloped me. I felt the wind as a pressure on my ears, like a shy buzzing. The sun was about to reach some compact clouds over the horizon that looked like a solidly tinted orange band, when it disappeared behind a heavy blanket of lower clouds; it appeared again a moment later, like a crimson ball floating in the mist. It seemed to struggle for a while to get into a patch of blue sky but it was as if the clouds would not give the sun time, and then the orange band and the dark silhouette of the mountains seemed to swallow it up.

I lay down on my back. The world around me was so still, so serene and at the same time so alien, I felt overwhelmed. I did not want to weep but tears rolled down easily.

I remained in that position for hours. I was almost unable to get up. The rocks under me were hard, and right where I had lain down there was scarcely any vegetation, in contrast to the lush green bushes all around. From where I was I could see a fringe of tall trees on the eastern hills.

Finally it got fairly dark. I felt better; in fact I felt almost happy. For me the semidarkness was much more nurturing and protective than the hard daylight.

I stood up, climbed to the top of a small hill, and began repeating the motions don Juan had taught me. I ran toward the east seven times, and then I noticed a change of temperature on my hand. I built a fire and set a careful watch, as don Juan had recommended, observing every detail. Hours went by and I began to feel very tired and cold. I had gathered quite a pile of dry twigs; I fed the fire and moved closer to it. The vigil was so strenuous and so intense that it exhausted me; I began to nod. I fell asleep twice and woke up only when my head bobbed to one side. I was so sleepy that I could not watch the fire any more. I drank some water and even sprinkled some on my face to keep awake. I succeeded in fighting my sleepiness only for brief moments. I had somehow become despondent and irritable; I felt utterly stupid being there and that gave me a sensation of irrational frustration and dejection. I was tired, hungry, sleepy, and absurdly annoyed with myself. I finally gave up the struggle of keeping awake. I added a lot of dry twigs to the fire and lay down to sleep. The pursuit of an ally and a spirit catcher was at that moment a most ludicrous and foreign endeavor. I was so sleepy that I could not even think or talk to myself. I fell asleep.

I was awakened suddenly by a loud crack. It appeared that the noise, whatever it was, had come from just above my left ear, since I was lying on my right side. I sat up fully awake. My left ear buzzed and was deafened by the proximity and force of the sound.

I must have been asleep for only a short while, judging by the amount of dry twigs which were still burning in the fire. I did not hear any other noises but I remained alert and kept on feeding the fire.

The thought crossed my mind that perhaps what woke

me up was a gunshot; perhaps someone was around watching me, taking shots at me. The thought became very anguishing and created an avalanche of rational fears. I was sure that someone owned that land, and if that was so they might take me for a thief and kill me, or they might kill me to rob me, not knowing that I had nothing with me. I experienced a moment of terrible concern for my safety. I felt the tension in my shoulders and my neck. I moved my head up and down; the bones of my neck made a cracking sound. I still kept looking into the fire but I did not see anything unusual in it, nor did I hear any noises.

After a while I relaxed quite a bit and it occurred to me that perhaps don Juan was at the bottom of all this. I rapidly became convinced that it was so. The thought made me laugh. I had another avalanche of rational conclusions, happy conclusions this time. I thought that don Juan must have suspected I was going to change my mind about staying in the mountains, or he must have seen me running after him and taken cover in a concealed cave or behind a bush. Then he had followed me and, noticing I had fallen asleep, waked me up by cracking a branch near my ear. I added more twigs to the fire and began to look around in a casual and covert manner to see if I could spot him, even though I knew that if he was hiding around there I would not be able to discover him.

Everything was quite placid: the crickets, the wind roughing the trees on the slopes of the hills surrounding me, the soft, cracking sound of the twigs catching on fire. Sparks flew around, but they were only ordinary sparks.

Suddenly I heard the loud noise of a branch snapping in two. The sound came from my left. I held my breath as I listened with utmost concentration. An instant later I heard another branch snapping on my right.

Then I heard the faint faraway sound of snapping branches. It was as if someone was stepping on them and making them crack. The sounds were rich and full, they had a lusty quality. They also seemed to be getting closer to where I was. I had a very slow reaction and did not know whether to listen or stand up. I was deliberating what to do when all of a sudden the sound of snapping branches happened all around me. I was engulfed by them so fast that I barely had time to jump to my feet and stomp on the fire.

I began to run downhill in the darkness. The thought crossed my mind as I moved through the shrubs that there was no flat land. I kept on trotting and trying to protect my eyes from the bushes. I was halfway down to the bottom of the hill when I felt something behind me, almost touching me. It was not a branch; it was something which I intuitively felt was overtaking me. This realization made me freeze. I took off my jacket, bundled it on my stomach, crouched over my legs, and covered my eyes with my hands, as don Juan had prescribed. I kept that position for a short while and then I realized that everything around me was dead still. There were no sounds of any kind. I became extraordinarily alarmed. The muscles of my stomach contracted and shivered spasmodically. Then I heard another cracking sound. It seemed to have occurred far away, but it was extremely clear and distinct. It happened once more, closer to me. There was an interval of quietness and then something exploded just above my head. The suddenness of the noise made me jump involuntarily and I nearly rolled over on my side. It was definitely the sound of a branch being snapped in two. The sound had happened so close that I heard the rustling of the branch leaves as it was being cracked.

Next there was a downpour of cracking explosions; branches were being snapped with great force all around me. The incongruous thing, at that point, was my reaction to the whole phenomenon; instead of being terrified, I was laughing. I sincerely thought I had hit upon the cause of all that was happening. I was convinced that don Juan was again tricking me. A series of logical conclusions cemented my confidence; I felt elated. I was sure I could catch that foxy old don Juan in another of his tricks. He was around me cracking branches, and knowing I would not dare to look up, he was safe and free to do anything he wanted to. I figured that he had to be alone in the mountains, since I had been with him constantly for days. He had not had the time or the opportunity to engage any collaborators. If he was hiding, as I thought, he was hiding by himself. and logically he could produce only a limited number of noises. Since he was alone, the noises had to occur in a linear temporal sequence; that is, one at a time, or at most two or three at a time. Besides, the variety of noises also had to be limited to the mechanics of a single individual. I was absolutely certain, as I remained crouched and still, that the whole experience was a game and that the only way to remain on top of it was by emotionally dislodging myself from it. I was positively enjoying it. I caught myself chuckling at the idea that I could anticipate my opponent's next move. I tried to imagine what I would do next if I were don Juan.

The sound of something slurping jolted me out of my mental exercise. I listened attentively; the sound happened again. I could not determine what it was. It sounded like an animal slurping water. It happened again very close by. It was an irritating sound that brought to mind the smacking noise of a big-jawed adolescent girl chewing gum. I was wondering how don Juan could produce such a noise when the sound happened again, coming from the right. There was a single sound first and then I heard a series of slushing, slurping sounds, as if someone were walking in mud. It was an almost sensual, exasperating sound of feet slushing in deep mud. The noises stopped for a moment and started once more toward my left, very close, perhaps only ten feet away. Now they sounded as if a heavy person were trotting with rain boots in mud. I marveled at the richness of the sound. I could not imagine any primitive devices that I myself could use to produce it. I heard another series of trotting, slushing sounds toward my rear and then they happened all at once, on all sides. Someone seemed to be walking, running, trotting on mud all around me.

A logical doubt occurred to me. If don Juan was doing all that, he had to be running in circles at an incredible speed. The rapidity of the sounds made that alternative impossible. I then thought that don Juan must have confederates after all. I wanted to involve myself in speculation as to who his accomplices could be but the intensity of the noises took all my concentration. I really could not think clearly, yet I was not afraid, I was perhaps only dumbfounded by the strange quality of the sounds. The slushings actually vibrated. In fact their peculiar vibrations seemed to be directed at my stomach, or perhaps I perceived their vibrations with the lower part of my abdomen.

That realization brought an instantaneous loss of my sense of objectivity and aloofness. The sounds were attacking my stomach! The question occurred to me, "What if it was not don Juan?" I panicked. I tensed my abdominal muscles and tucked my thighs hard against the bundle of my jacket.

The noises increased in number and speed, as if they knew I had lost my confidence, their vibrations were so intense I wanted to vomit. I fought the feeling of nausea. I took deep breaths and began to sing my peyote songs. I got sick and the slushing noises ceased at once; the sounds of crickets and wind and the distant staccato barking of coyotes became superimposed. The abrupt cessation allowed me a respite and I took stock of myself. Only a short while before I had been in the best of spirits, confident and aloof; obviously I had failed miserably to judge the situation. Even if don Juan had accomplices, it would be mechanically impossible for them to produce sounds that would affect my stomach. To produce sounds of such intensity they would have needed gadgetry beyond their means or their conception. Apparently the phenomenon I was experiencing was not a game and the "another one of don Juan's tricks" theory was only my rude explanation.

I had cramps and an overwhelming desire to roll over and straighten my legs. I decided to move to my right in order to get my face off the place where I had gotten sick. The instant I began to crawl I heard a very soft squeak right above my left ear. I froze on the spot. The squeak was repeated on the other side of my head. It was a single sound. I thought it resembled the squeak of a door. I waited but I heard nothing else, so I decided to move again. No sooner had I started to inch my head to the right when I was nearly forced to jump up. A flood of squeaks engulfed me at once. They were like squeaks of doors at times; at other times they were like the squeaks of rats or guinea pigs. They were not loud or intense but very soft and insidious and produced agonizing spasms of nausea in me. They stopped as they had begun, diminishing gradually until I could hear only one or two of them at a time.

Then I heard something like the wings of a big bird sweeping over the tops of the bushes. It seemed to be flying in circles over my head. The soft squeaks began to increase again, and so did the flapping wings. Above my head there seemed to be something like a flock of gigantic birds beating their soft wings. Both noises merged, creating an enveloping wave around me. I felt that I was floating suspended in an enormous undulating ripple. The squeaks and the flapping were so smooth I could feel them all over my body. The flapping wings of a flock of birds seemed to be pulling me up from above, while the squeaks of an army of rats seemed to be pushing me from underneath and from around my body.

There was no doubt in my mind that through my blundering stupidity I had unleashed something terrible on myself. I clenched my teeth and took deep breaths and sang peyote songs.

The noises lasted a very long time and I opposed them with all my might. When they subsided, there was again an interrupted "silence" as I am accustomed to perceiving silence; that is, I could detect only the natural sounds of the insects and the wind. The time of silence was for me more deleterious than the time of noises. I began to think and to assess my position, and my deliberation threw me into a panic. I knew that I was lost; I did not have the knowledge nor the stamina to fend off whatever was accosting me. I was utterly helpless, crouched over my own vomit. I thought that the end of my life had come and I began to weep. I wanted to think about my life but I did not know where to start. Nothing of what I had done in my life was really worthy of that last ultimate emphasis, so I had nothing to think about. That was an exquisite realization. I had changed since the last time I experienced a similar fright. This time I was more empty. I had less personal feelings to carry along.

I asked myself what a warrior would do in that situation and I arrived at various conclusions. There was something about my umbilical region that was uniquely important; there was something unearthly about the sounds; they were aiming at my stomach; and the idea that don Juan was tricking me was utterly untenable.

The muscles of my stomach were very tight, although I did not have cramps any longer. I kept on singing and breathing deeply and I felt a soothing warmth inundating my entire body. It had become clear to me that if I was going to survive I had to proceed in terms of don Juan's teachings. I repeated his instructions in my mind. I remembered the exact point where the sun had disappeared over the mountains in relation to the hill where I was and to the place where I had crouched. I reoriented myself and when I was convinced that my assessment of the cardinal points was correct I began to change my position, so I would have my head pointing in a new and "better" direction, the southeast. I slowly started moving my feet toward my left, inch by inch, until I had them twisted under my calves. Then I began to align my body with my feet, but no sooner had I begun to creep laterally than I felt a peculiar tap; I had the actual physical sensation of something touching the uncovered area of the back of my neck. It happened so fast that I yelled involuntarily and froze again. I tightened my abdominal muscles and began to breath deeply and sing my peyote songs. A second later I felt once more the same light tap on my neck. I cringed. My neck was uncovered and there was nothing I could do to protect myself. I was tapped again. It was a very soft, almost silky object that touched my neck, like the furry paw of a giant rabbit. It touched me again and then it began to cross my neck back and forth until I was in tears. It was as if a herd of silent, smooth, weightless kangaroos were stepping on my neck. I could hear the soft thump of their paws as they stepped gently over me. It was not a painful sensation at all and yet it was maddening. I knew that if I did not involve myself in doing something I would go mad and stand up and run. So I slowly began again to maneuver my body into a new position. My attempt at moving seemed to increase the tapping on my neck. It finally got to such a frenzy that I jerked my body and at once aligned it in the new direction. I had no idea whatsoever about the outcome of my act. I was just taking action to keep from going stark, raving mad.

As soon as I changed directions the tapping on my neck ceased. After a long, anguished pause I heard a distant snapping of branches. The noises were not close any more. It was as if they had retreated to another position far away from me. The sound of snapping branches merged after a moment with a blasting sound of leaves being rustled, as if a strong wind were beating the entire hill. All the bushes around me seemed to shiver, yet there was no wind. The rustling sound and the cracking of branches gave me the feeling that the whole hill was on fire. My body was as tight as a rock. I was perspiring copiously. I began to feel warmer and warmer. For a moment I was utterly convinced that the hill was burning. I did not jump up and run because I was so numb I was paralyzed; in fact I could not even open my eyes. All that mattered to me at that point was to get up and escape the fire. I had terrible cramps in my stomach which started to cut my intake of air. I became very involved in trying to breathe. After a long struggle I was capable of taking deep breaths again and I was also capable of noticing that the rustling had subsided; there was only an occasional cracking sound. The snapping sound of branches became more and more distant and sporadic until it ceased altogether.

I was able to open my eyes. I looked through my half-closed lids to the ground underneath me. It was already daylight. I waited a while longer without moving and then I started to stretch my body. I rolled on my back. The sun was over the hills in the east.

It took me hours to straighten out my legs and drag myself downhill. I began to walk toward the place where don Juan had left me, which was perhaps only a mile away; by midafternoon I was barely at the edge of some woods, still a good quarter of a mile away.

I could not walk any more, not for any reason. I thought of mountain lions and tried to climb up a tree, but my arms could not support my weight. I leaned against a rock and resigned myself to die there. I was convinced that I would be food for mountain lions or other predators. I did not have the strength even to throw a rock. I was not hungry or thirsty. Around noon I had found a small stream and had drunk a lot of water, but the water did not help to restore my strength. As I sat there in utter helplessness I felt more despondent than afraid. I was so tired I did not care about my fate and I fell asleep.

I woke up when something shook me. Don Juan was leaning over me. He helped me sit up and gave me water and some gruel. He laughed and said that I looked wretched. I tried to tell him what had happened but he hushed me up and said that I had missed my mark, that the place where I was supposed to meet him was about a hundred yards away. Then he half carried me downhill. He said he was taking me to a large stream and was going to wash me there. On the way he plugged my ears with some leaves he had in his pouch and then he blindfolded me, putting one leaf on each eye and securing them both with a piece of cloth. He made me take off my clothes and told me to place my hands over my eyes and ears to make sure I could not see or hear anything.

Don Juan rubbed my entire body with leaves and then dumped me in a river. I felt it was a large river. It was deep. I was standing and I could not touch the bottom. Don Juan was holding me by the right elbow. At first I did not feel the coldness of the water, but little by little I began to feel chilled, and then the cold became intolerable. Don Juan pulled me out and dried me with some leaves that had a peculiar scent. I put on my clothes and he led me away; we walked a good distance before he took the leaves off my ears and my eyes. Don Juan asked me if I felt strong enough to walk back to my car. The weird thing was that I felt very strong. I even ran up the side of a steep hill to prove it.

On the way to my car I stayed very close to don Juan. I stumbled scores of times and he laughed. I noticed that his laughter was especially invigorating and it became the focal point of my replenishing; the more he laughed the better I felt.

The next day I narrated to don Juan the sequence of events from the time he left me. He laughed all the way through my account, especially when I told him that I had thought it was one of his tricks.

"You always think you're being tricked," he said. "You trust yourself too much. You act like you know all the answers. You know nothing, my little friend, nothing."

This was the first time don Juan had called me "my little friend." It took me aback. He noticed it and smiled. There was a great warmth in his voice and that made me very sad. I told him that I had been careless and incompetent because that was the inherent bent of my personality; and that I would never understand his world. I felt deeply moved. He was very encouraging and asserted that I had done fine.

I asked him the meaning of my experience.

"It has no meaning," he replied. "The same thing could happen to anyone, especially someone like you who has his gap already opened. It is very common. Any warrior who's gone in search of allies would tell you about their doings. What they did to you was mild. However, your gap is open and that is why you're so nervous. One cannot turn into a warrior overnight. Now you must go home and don't return until you're healed and your gap is closed."

17

I did not return to Mexico for months; I used the time to work on my field notes and for the first time in ten years, since I started the apprenticeship, don Juan's teachings began to make real sense. I felt that the long periods of time I had to stay away from the apprenticeship had had a very sobering and beneficial effect on me; they had allowed me the opportunity to review my findings and to arrange them in an intellectual order proper of my training and interest. The events that took place on my last visit to the field, however, pointed to a fallacy in my optimism about understanding don Juan's knowledge.

I made the last entry in my field notes on October 16, 1970. The events that took place on that occasion marked a transition. They not only closed a cycle of instruction, but they also opened a new one, which was so very different from what I had done thus far that I feel this is the point where I must end my reportage.

As I approached don Juan's house I saw him sitting in his usual place under his *ramada* in front of the door. I parked in the shade of a tree, took my briefcase and a bag of groceries out of the car and walked toward him, greeting him in a loud voice. I then noticed that he was not alone. There was another man sitting behind a high pile of firewood. Both of them were looking at me. Don Juan waved and so did the other man. Judging from his attire he was not an Indian but a Mexican from the Southwest. He was wearing Levis, a beige shirt, a Texan cowboy hat and cowboy boots.

I talked to don Juan and then looked at the man; he was smiling at me. I stared at him for a moment.

"Here's little Carlos," the man said to don Juan, "and he doesn't speak to me any more. Don't tell me that he's cross with me!"

Before I could say anything they both broke up laughing and only then did I realize that the strange man was don Genaro.

"You didn't recognize me, did you?" he asked, still laughing.

I had to admit that his attire had baffled me.

"What are you doing in this part of the world, don Genaro?" I asked.

"He came to enjoy the hot wind," don Juan said. "Isn't that right?"

"That's right," don Genaro echoed. "You've no idea what the hot wind can do to an old body like mine."

I sat down between them.

"What does it do to your body?" I asked.

"The hot wind tells extraordinarily things to my body," he said.

He turned to don Juan, his eyes glittering.

"Isn't that so?"

Don Juan shook his head affirmatively.

I told them that the time of the hot Santa Ana winds was the worst part of the year for me, and that it was certainly strange that don Genaro would come to seek the hot wind while I was running away from it.

"Carlos can't stand the heat," don Juan said to don Genaro. "When it gets hot he becomes like a child and suffocates."

"Suffo what?"

"Suffo . . . cates."

"My goodness!" don Genaro said, feigning concern, and made a gesture of despair which was indescribably funny.

Don Juan explained to him next that I had been away for months because of an unfortunate incident with the allies.

"So, you've finally encountered an ally!" don Genaro said.

"I think I did," I said cautiously.

They laughed loudly. Don Genaro patted me on the back two or three times. It was a very light tapping which I interpreted as a friendly gesture of concern. He rested his hand on my shoulder as he looked at me, and I had a feeling of placid contentment, which lasted only an instant, for next don Genaro did something inexplicable to me. I suddenly felt that he had put the weight of a boulder on my back. I had the sensation that he had increased the weight of his hand, which was resting on my right shoulder, until it made me sag all the way down and I hit my head on the ground.

"We must help little Carlos," don Genaro said and gave a conspiratorial look to don Juan.

I sat up straight again and turned to don Juan, but he looked away. I had a moment of vacillation and the annoying thought that don Juan was acting as if he were aloof, detached from me. Don Genaro was laughing; he seemed to be waiting for my reaction.

I asked him to put his hand on my shoulder once more, but he did not want to do it. I urged him at least to tell me what he had done to me. He chuckled. I turned to don Juan again and told him that the weight of don Genaro's hand had nearly crushed me.

"I don't know anything about it," don Juan said in a comically factual tone. "He didn't put his hand on my shoulder."

With that both of them broke up laughing.

"What did you do to me, don Genaro?" I asked.

"I just put my hand on your shoulder," he said innocently.

"Do it again," I said.

He refused. Don Juan interceded at that point and asked me to describe to don Genaro what I had perceived in my last experience. I thought he wanted me to give a bona fide description of what had happened to me, but the more serious my description became the more they laughed. I stopped two or three times but they urged me to go on.

"The ally will come to you regardless of your feelings," don Juan said when I had finished my account. "I mean, you don't have to do anything to lure him out. You may be sitting twiddling your thumbs, or thinking about women and then suddenly, a tap on your shoulder, you turn around and the ally is standing by you."

"What can I do if something like that happens?" I asked.

"Hey! Hey! Wait a minute!" don Genaro said. "That's not a good question. You shouldn't ask what can you do, obviously you can't do anything. You should ask what can a warrior do?"

He turned to me, blinking. His head was slightly tilted to the right, and his mouth was puckered.

I looked at don Juan for a cue whether the situation was a joke, but he kept a solemn face.

"All right!" I said. "What can a warrior do?"

Don Genaro blinked and made smacking sounds with his lips, as if he were searching for a right word. He looked at me fixedly, holding his chin.

"A warrior wets his pants," he said with Indian solemnity.

Don Juan covered his face and don Genaro slapped the ground, exploding in a howling laughter.

"Fright is something one can never get over," don Juan said after the laughter had subsided. "When a warrior is caught in such a tight spot he would simply turn his back to the ally without thinking twice. A warrior cannot indulge, thus he cannot die of fright. A warrior allows the ally to come only when he is good and ready. When he is strong enough to grapple with the ally he opens his gap and lurches out, grabs the ally, keeps him pinned down and maintains his stare on him for exactly the time he has to, then he moves his eyes away and releases the ally and lets him go. A warrior, my little friend, is the master at all times."

"What happens if you stare at an ally for too long?" I asked.

Don Genaro looked at me and made a comical gesture of outstaring.

"Who knows?" don Juan said. "Maybe Genaro will tell you what happened to him."

"Maybe," don Genaro said and chuckled.

"Would you please tell me?"

Don Genaro got up, cracked his bones stretching his arms, and opened his eyes until they were round and looked crazy.

"Genaro is going to make the desert tremble," he said and went into the chaparral.

"Genaro is determined to help you," don Juan said in a confidential tone. "He did the same thing to you at his house and you almost *saw*."

I thought he was referring to what had happened at the waterfall, but he was talking about some unearthly rumbling sounds I had heard at don Genaro's house.

"By the way, what was it?" I asked. "We laughed at it, but you never explained to me what it was."

"You have never asked."

"I did."

"No. You have asked me about everything else except that."

Don Juan looked at me accusingly.

"That was Genaro's art," he said. "Only Genaro can do that. You almost *saw* then."

I told him that it had never occurred to me to associate "seeing" with the strange noises I had heard at that time.

"And why not?" he asked flatly.

"*Seeing* means the eyes to me," I said.

He scrutinized me for a moment as if there were something wrong with me.

"I never said that *seeing* is a matter of the eyes alone," he said and shook his head in disbelief.

"How does he do it?" I insisted.

"He has already told you how he does it," don Juan said sharply.

At that very moment I heard an extraordinary rumble.

I jumped up and don Juan began to laugh. The rumble was like a thunderous avalanche. Listening to it, I had the funny realization that my inventory of experiences in sound comes definitely from the movies. The deep thunder I heard resembled the sound track of a movie when the whole side of a mountain falls into a valley.

Don Juan held his sides as if they hurt from laughing. The thunderous rumble shook the ground where I stood. I distinctly heard the thump of what seemed to be a monumental boulder that was rolling on its sides. I heard a series of crushing thumps that gave me the impression that the boulder was rolling inexorably toward me. I experienced a moment of supreme confusion. My muscles were tense; my whole body was ready for fleeing.

I looked at don Juan. He was staring at me. I then heard the most frightening thump I had ever heard in my life. It was as if a monumental boulder had landed right behind the house. Everything shook, and at that moment I had a most peculiar perception. For an instant I actually "saw" a boulder the size of a mountain right behind the house. It was not as if an image had been superimposed on the scenery of the house I was looking at. It was not the view of a real boulder either. It was rather as if the noise was creating the image of a boulder rolling on its monumental sides. I was actually "seeing" the noise. The inexplicable character of my perception threw me into the depths of despair and confusion. Never in my life would I have conceived that my senses were capable of perceiving in such a manner. I had an attack of rational fright and decided to flee for my life. Don Juan held me by the arm and ordered me imperatively not to run away and not to turn around either, but face the direction in which don Genaro had gone.

I heard next a series of booming noises, which resembled the sound of rocks falling and piling on top of each other, and then everything was quiet again. A few minutes later don Genaro came back and sat down. He asked me if I had "seen." I did not know what to say. I turned to don Juan for a cue. He was staring at me.

"I think he did," he said and chuckled.

I wanted to say that I did not know what they were

talking about. I felt terribly frustrated. I had a physical sensation of wrath, of utter discomfort.

"I think we should leave him *here* to sit alone," don Juan said.

They got up and walked by me.

"Carlos is indulging in his confusion," don Juan said very loudly.

I stayed alone for hours and had time to write my notes and to ponder on the absurdity of my experience. Upon thinking about it, it became obvious to me that from the very moment I saw don Genaro sitting under the *ramada* the situation had acquired a farcical mood. The more I deliberated about it the more convinced I became that don Juan had relinquished the control over to don Genaro and that thought filled me with apprehension.

Don Juan and don Genaro returned at dusk. They sat down next to me, flanking me. Don Genaro drew closer and almost leaned on me. His thin and frail shoulder touched me lightly and I experienced the same feeling I had had when he tapped me. A crushing weight toppled me over and I tumbled onto don Juan's lap. He helped me to sit up straight and asked in a joking tone if I was trying to sleep on his lap.

Don Genaro seemed to be delighted; his eyes shone. I wanted to weep. I had the feeling I was like an animal that had been corraled.

"Am I frightening you, little Carlos?" don Genaro asked and seemed really concerned. "You look like a wild horse."

"Tell him a story," don Juan said. "That's the only thing that calms him."

They moved away and sat in front of me. Both of them examined me with curiosity. In the semidarkness their eyes seemed glassy, like enormous dark pools of water. Their eyes were awesome. They were not the eyes of men. We stared at each other for a moment and then I moved my eyes away. I noticed that I was not afraid of them, and yet their eyes had frightened me to the point that I was shivering. I felt a most uncomfortable confusion.

After a moment of silence don Juan urged don Genaro to tell me what had happened to him at the time he had tried to outstare his ally. Don Genaro was sitting a few feet away, facing me; he did not say anything. I looked at him; his eyes seemed to be four or five times the size of ordinary human eyes; they were shining and had a compelling attraction. What seemed to be the light of his eyes dominated everything around them. Don Genaro's body seemed to have shriveled and looked more like the body of a feline. I noticed a movement of his cat-like body and became frightened. In a completely automatic way, as if I had been doing it all my life, I adopted a "fighting form" and began beating rhythmically on my calf. When I became aware of my acts I got embarrassed and looked at don Juan. He was peering at me as he does ordinarily; his eyes were kind and soothing. He laughed loudly. Don Genaro made a purring sound and stood up and went inside the house.

Don Juan explained to me that don Genaro was very forceful and did not like to piddle around and that he had been just teasing me with his eyes. He said that, as usual, I knew more than I myself expected. He made a comment that everyone who was involved with sorcery was terribly dangerous during the hours of twilight and that sorcerers like don Genaro could perform marvels at that time.

We were quiet for a few minutes. I felt better. Talking to don Juan relaxed me and restored my confidence. Then he said that he was going to eat something and that we were going for a walk so that don Genaro could show me a technique for hiding.

I asked him to explain what he meant by a technique for hiding. He said he was through with explaining things to me because explaining only forced me to indulge.

We went inside the house. Don Genaro had lit the kerosene lantern and was chewing a mouthful of food.

After eating, the three of us walked into the thick desert chaparral. Don Juan walked almost next to me. Don Genaro was in front, a few yards ahead of us.

It was a clear night, there were heavy clouds, but enough moonlight to render the surroundings quite visible.

At one moment don Juan stopped and told me to go ahead and follow don Genaro. I vacillated; he pushed me gently and assured me it was all right. He said I should always be ready and should always trust my own strength.

I followed don Genaro and for the next two hours I tried to catch up with him, but no matter how hard I struggled I could not overtake him. Don Genaro's silhouette was always ahead of me. Sometimes he disappeared as if he had jumped to the side of the trail only to appear again ahead of me. As far as I was concerned, this seemed to be a strange and meaningless walk in the dark. I followed because I did not know how to return to the house. I could not understand what don Genaro was doing. I thought he was leading me to some recondite place in the chaparral to show me the technique don Juan had talked about. At a certain point, however, I had the peculiar sensation that don Genaro was behind me. I turned around and caught a glimpse of a person some distance behind me. The effect was startling. I strained to see in the darkness and I believed I could make out the silhouette of a man standing perhaps fifteen yards away. The figure was almost merged with the bushes; it was as if he wanted to conceal himself. I stared fixedly for a moment and I could actually keep the silhouette of the man within my field of perception even though he was trying to hide behind the dark shapes of the bushes. Then a logical thought came to my mind. It occurred to me that the man had to be don Juan, who must have been following us all the time. The instant I became convinced that that was so, I also realized I could no longer isolate his silhouette; all I had in front of me was the undifferentiated dark mass of the desert chaparral.

I walked toward the place I had seen the man, but I could not find anybody. Don Genaro was nowhere in sight either, and since I did not know my way I sat down to wait. A half hour later, don Juan and don Genaro came by. They called my name out loud. I stood up and joined them.

We walked to the house in complete silence. I welcomed that quiet interlude, for I felt completely disoriented. In fact, I felt unknown to myself. Don Genaro was doing something to me, something which kept me from formulating my thoughts the way I am accustomed to doing. This became evident to me when I sat down on the trail. I had automatically checked the time when I sat down and then I had remained quiet as if my mind had been turned off. Yet I sat in a state of alertness I have never experienced before. It was a state of thoughtlessness, perhaps comparable to not caring about anything. The world seemed to be, during that time, in a strange balance; there was nothing I could add to it and nothing I could subtract from it.

When we arrived at the house don Genaro rolled out a straw mat and went to sleep. I felt compelled to render my experiences of the day to don Juan. He did not let me talk.

October 18, 1970

"I think I understand what don Genaro was trying to do the other night," I said to don Juan.

I said that in order to draw him out. His continual refusal to talk was unnerving me.

Don Juan smiled and shook his head slowly as if agreeing with what I had said. I would have taken his gesture as an affirmation except for the strange glint in his eyes. It was as if his eyes were laughing at me.

"You don't think I understand, do you?" I asked compulsively.

"I suppose you do . . . you do, in fact. You do understand that Genaro was behind you all the time. However, understanding is not the real point."

His statement that don Genaro had been behind me all the time was shocking to me. I begged him to explain it.

"Your mind is set to seek only one side of this," he said.

He took a dry twig and moved it in the air. He was not drawing in the air or making a figure; what he did resembled the movements he makes with his fingers when he cleans the debris from a pile of seeds. His movements were like a soft prodding or scratching the air with the twig.

He turned and looked at me and I shrugged my shoulders automatically in a gesture of bafflement. He drew closer and repeated his movements, making eight points on the ground. He circled the first point.

"You are here," he said. "We are all here; this is feeling, and we move from here to here."

He circled the second, which he had drawn right above number one. He then moved his twig back and forth between the two points to portray a heavy traffic.

"There are, however, six more points a man is capable of handling," he said. "Most men know nothing about them."

He placed his twig between points one and two and pecked on the ground with it.

"To move between these two points you call understanding. You've been doing that all your life. If you say you understand my knowledge, you have done nothing new."

He then joined some of the eight points to the others with lines; the result was a long trapezoid figure that had eight centers of uneven radiation.

"Each of these six remaining points is a world, just like feeling and understanding are two worlds for you," he said.

"Why eight points? Why not an infinite number, as in a circle?" I asked.

I drew a circle on the ground. Don Juan smiled.

"As far as I know there are only eight points a man is capable of handling. Perhaps men cannot go beyond that. And I said handling, not understanding, did you get that?"

His tone was so funny I laughed. He was imitating or rather mocking my insistence on the exact usage of words.

"Your problem is that you want to understand everything, and that is not possible. If you insist on understanding you're not considering your entire lot as a human being. Your stumbling block is intact. Therefore, you have done almost nothing in all these years. You have been shaken out of your total slumber, true, but that could have been accomplished anyway by other circumstances."

After a pause don Juan told me to get up because we were going to the water canyon. As we were getting into my car don Genaro came out from behind the house and joined us. I drove part of the way and then we walked into a deep ravine. Don Juan picked a place to rest in the shade of a large tree.

"You mentioned once," don Juan began, "that a friend of yours had said, when the two of you saw a leaf falling from the very top of a sycamore, that that same leaf will not fall again from that same sycamore ever in a whole eternity, remember?"

I remembered having told him about that incident.

"We are at the foot of a large tree," he continued, "and now if we look at that other tree in front of us we may see a leaf falling from the very top."

He signaled me to look. There was a large tree on the other side of the gully; its leaves were yellowish and dry. He urged me with a movement of his head to keep on looking at the tree. After a few minutes' wait, a leaf cracked loose from the top and began falling to the ground; it hit other leaves and branches three times before it landed in the tall underbrush.

"Did you see it?"

"Yes."

"You would say that the same leaf will never again fall from that same tree, true?"

"True."

"To the best of your understanding that is true. But that is only to the best of your understanding. Look again."

I automatically looked and saw a leaf falling. It actually hit the same leaves and branches as the previous one. It was as if I were looking at an instant television replay. I followed the wavy falling of the leaf until it landed on the ground. I stood up to find out if there were two leaves, but the tall underbrush around the tree prevented me from seeing where the leaf had actually landed.

Don Juan laughed and told me to sit down.

"Look," he said, pointing with his head to the top of the tree. "There goes the same leaf again."

I once more saw a leaf falling in exactly the same pattern as the previous two.

When it had landed I knew don Juan was about to signal me again to look at the top of the tree, but before he did I looked up. The leaf was again falling. I realized then that I had only seen the first leaf cracking loose, or, rather, the first time the leaf fell I saw it from the instant it became detached from the branch; the other three times the leaf was already falling when I lifted my head to look.

I told that to don Juan and I urged him to explain what he was doing.

"I don't understand how you're making me see a repetition of what I had seen before. What did you do to me, don Juan?"

He laughed but did not answer and I insisted that he should tell me how I could see that leaf falling over and over. I said that according to my reason that was impossible.

Don Juan said that his reason told him the same, yet I had witnessed the leaf falling over and over. He then turned to don Genaro.

"Isn't that so?" he asked.

Don Genaro did not answer. His eyes were fixed on me.

"It is impossible!" I said.

"You're chained!" don Juan exclaimed. "You're chained to your reason."

He explained that the leaf had fallen over and over from that same tree so I would stop trying to understand. In a confidential tone he told me that I had the whole thing pat and yet my mania always blinded me at the end.

"There's nothing to understand. Understanding is only a very small affair, so very small," he said.

At that point don Genaro stood up. He gave a quick glance to don Juan; their eyes met and don Juan looked at the ground in front of him. Don Genaro stood in front of me and began swinging his arms at his sides, back and forth in unison.

"Look, little Carlos," he said. "Look! Look!"

He made an extraordinarily sharp, swishing sound. It was the sound of something ripping. At the precise instant the sound happened, I felt a sensation of vacuity in my lower abdomen. It was the terribly anguishing sensation of falling, not painful, but rather unpleasant and consuming. It lasted a few seconds and then it subsided, leaving a strange itch in my knees. But while the sensation had lasted I experienced another unbelievable phenomenon. I saw don Genaro on top of some mountains that were perhaps ten miles away. The perception lasted only a few seconds and it happened so unexpectedly that I did not have time really to examine it. I cannot recall whether I saw a man-size figure standing on top of the mountains, or a reduced image of don Genaro. I cannot even recall whether or not it was don Genaro. Yet at that moment I was certain beyond any doubt that I was seeing him standing on top of the mountains. However, the moment I thought that I could not possibly see a man ten miles away the perception vanished.

I turned around to look for don Genaro, but he was not there.

The bafflement I experienced was as unique as everything else that was happening to me. My mind buckled under the strain. I felt utterly disoriented.

Don Juan stood up and made me cover the lower part of my abdomen with my hands and press my legs tightly against my body in a squat position. We sat in silence for a while and then he said that he was truly going to refrain from explaining anything to me, because only by acting can one become a sorcerer. He recommended that I leave immediately, otherwise don Genaro would probably kill me in his effort to help me.

"You are going to change directions," he said, "and you'll break your chains."

He said that there was nothing to understand about his or about don Genaro's actions, and that sorcerers were quite capable of performing extraordinary feats.

"Genaro and I are acting from here," he said and pointed to one of the centers of radiation in his diagram.

"And it is not the center of understanding, yet you know what it is."

I wanted to say that I did not really know what he was talking about, but he did not give me time and stood up and signaled me to follow him. He began to walk fast and in no time at all I was puffing and sweating trying to keep up with him.

When we were getting inside the car I looked around for don Genaro.

"Where is he?" I asked.

"You know where he is," don Juan snapped at me.

Before I left I sat down with him, as I always do. I had an overwhelming urge to ask for explanations. As don Juan says, explanations are truly my indulgence.

"Where's don Genaro?" I asked cautiously.

"You know where," he said. "Yet you fail every time because of your insistence on understanding. For example, you knew the other night that Genaro was behind you all the time; you even turned around and saw him."

"No," I protested. "No, I didn't know that."

I was truthful at that. My mind refused to intake that sort of stimuli as being "real," and yet, after ten years of apprenticeship with don Juan my mind could no longer uphold my old ordinary criteria of what is real. However, all the speculations I had thus far engendered about the nature of reality had been mere intellectual manipulations; the proof was that under the pressure of don Juan and don Genaro's acts my mind had entered into an impasse.

Don Juan looked at me and there was such sadness in his eyes that I began to weep. Tears fell freely. For the first time in my life I felt the encumbering weight of my reason. An indescribable anguish overtook me. I wailed involuntarily and embraced him. He gave me a quick blow with his knuckles on the top of my head. I felt it like a ripple down my spine. It had a sobering effect.

"You indulge too much," he said softly.

Epilogue

Don Juan slowly walked around me. He seemed to be deliberating whether or not to say something to me. Twice he stopped and seemed to change his mind.

"Whether or not you return is thoroughly unimportant," he finally said. "However, you now have the need to live like a warrior. You have always known that, now you're simply in the position of having to make use of something you disregarded before. But you had to struggle for this knowledge; it wasn't just given to you; it wasn't just handed down to you. You had to beat it out of yourself. Yet you're still a luminous being. You're still going to die like everyone else. I once told you that there's nothing to change in a luminous egg."

He was quiet for a moment. I knew he was looking at me, but I avoided his eyes.

"Nothing has really changed in you," he said.